FEEDING ANOREXIA

BODY, COMMODITY, TEXT

Studies of Objectifying Practice

A series edited by Arjun Appadurai,

Jean Comaroff, and Judith Farquhar

FEEDING ANOREXIA

Gender and Power at a Treatment Center

Helen Gremillion

DUKE UNIVERSITY PRESS

Durham & London 2003

© 2003 Duke University Press

All rights reserved

Printed in the United States of America on
acid-free paper ∞ Designed by Amy Ruth
Buchanan. Typeset in Scala by Keystone Type-
setting, Inc. Library of Congress Cataloging-
in-Publication Data appear on the last printed
page of this book. Substantial portions of
chapter 1 as well as portions of the Introduction originally appeared in *Signs: Journal of
Women in Culture and Society* 27, no. 2, ©
2001 University of Chicago Press.

IN MEMORY

OF PAM,

WHO LEFT US

AT TOO YOUNG

AN AGE.

CONTENTS

ACKNOWLEDGMENTS

This book is the product of many years of study, unfolding relationships, and interdisciplinary affiliations that cut across both my professional and personal life. It has been nurtured by more people than I can count, and it would be impossible to thank them all individually. Foremost are the patients and parents who took part in this project. Their powerful stories and struggles are the most important motivation for this book. I also thank the clinicians and staff who shared with me many aspects of their work and lives, as well as their own struggles. I am grateful to all participants in the treatment program I studied for their active interest in this project, as well as their productive points of disagreement. I hope they find in these pages a depiction of hospital life that resonates with their experiences, and that they recognize something new in my descriptions as well.

Donald Pollock introduced me to the field of medical anthropology in a way that allowed for interdisciplinary articulations, and he encouraged this project at an early stage. At the University of Chicago, Jean Comaroff and Sharon Stephens provided intellectual and practical support, kind words, patient advice, and enthusiasm. At Stanford, I benefited immeasurably from the guidance and support of Jane Collier, George Collier, Carol Delaney, Akhil Gupta, Purnima Mankekar, and Sylvia Yanagisako. This book would not have been possible without their mentorship and ongoing collegiality, and their careful review of grant proposals and of this text at various stages. The same is true of my relationship with Lorna Rhodes, who has helped me maintain a vision about this study that sustained me during challenging periods. I am also grateful for lively and insightful conversations with Amy Borovoy, Piya Chatterjee, Katherine Hayles, Stefan Helmreich, Aida Hernandez, Tom Lyons, Bill Maurer, Heather Paxson, and Nicholi Ssorin-Chaikov, as well as the graduate fellows at the Institute for Research on Women and Gender at Stanford with whom I had the pleasure and privilege of working.

My colleagues and friends at Indiana University have supported this project in a number of important ways. Faculty in the Department of Gender Studies in particular have gone out of their way to help me generate the intellectual and creative space needed to further develop my ideas and my writing "voice." Their interdisciplinary vision for gender studies scholarship, their academic rigor, and their friendship have taken me a long way. I owe an enormous debt of gratitude to Dale and Norman Leff, whose vision and generosity have been instrumental in providing an institutional platform for my work. Dale has also been very warm and encouraging, and I thank her more than I can say.

Fieldwork for this book was funded by a grant from the National Science Foundation (1993–1994) and a research assistantship from the Stanford University Anthropology Department (1993–1994). An Andrew W. Mellon Fellowship, administered through Stanford's Department of Anthropology, funded data analysis (1994–1995). Writing time was funded by a fellowship from the Institute for Research on Women and Gender at Stanford (1994–1995), an American Fellowship from the American Association of University Women (1995–1996), and a Summer Faculty Fellowship from the Research and University Graduate School at Indiana University (2001).

Parts of this manuscript benefited from public discussion while I was in the process of developing and working through my ideas; I mention some of these contexts here. Portions of chapter 1 were presented at an invited talk during the 2001 annual Narrative Therapy and Community Work conference in Adelaide, Australia, titled "Therapy as Cultural Practice: Anorexia Nervosa, Psychiatric Power, and Discourses of Resistance"; at the Inaugural Lecture for the Peg Zeglin Brand Chair in Gender Studies at Indiana University in Bloomington in 1999, titled "Gendered Bodies and Psychiatric Power: Anorexia Nervosa in Cultural Context"; and at a 1995 panel titled "Studying UP/Studying US: Discourses of American Institutions" at the American Anthropological Association Meetings in Washington, D.C. Early formulations of points in chapter 1 were part of an invited talk at Stanford University's Medical School in 1993, titled "The Treatment of Eating Disorders: An Anthropological Perspective." At these forums, comments and questions from Judith Allen, John Bancroft, Gene Combs, Prue Delamater, Rudolf Gaudio, and Stephanie Kane were particularly helpful to me. An early version of ideas developed in the introduction was written up during 2000 for a panel I co-organized titled "Theorizing the 'Post' in Postmodern Constructions of Identity" at the American Ethnological Society Meetings in Tampa, Florida. I am grateful for discussions that ensued with Carol Greenhouse and Mei Zhan. Excerpts from chapter 2 appeared in a 1997 panel I organized titled "Risk as Lived Experience: The Production and Management of Medical Risk" at the American Anthropological Association Meetings in Washington, D.C. I am appreciative of conversations with David Hess and Ann Russ there. Donald Pollock provided insights for the selections from chapter 4 I presented at a 1996 panel titled "Psychiatry and Psychiatric Practice" at the Society for Medical Anthropology Annual Meetings in Seattle, Washington. Sections of the epilogue were developed for an invited talk during the 2002 annual Narrative Therapy and Community Work conference in Atlanta, Georgia, titled "Narrative Therapy as Poststructuralist Practice"; for a 2002 panel I organized titled "Shifting Narratives of Gender Identity in Therapeutic Conversations" at the Lewis and Clark Gender Studies Symposium in Portland, Oregon; and for a 2000 panel I co-organized titled "Feminist Theories of Knowledge in Research and Practice" at the National Women's Studies Association Meetings in Boston, Massachusetts. Portions of the epilogue were also presented at (ongoing) Indiana University faculty seminars: a 2001 meeting of an interdisciplinary group on life writing, and a 2000 colloquium offered through the Department of Anthropology. For thoughtful comments after these presentations, I am indebted to Elsa Almaas, Mary Ellen Brown, Gracia Clark, Gene Combs, Della Cook, Vicki Dickerson, John Eakin, Johnathan Elmer, Jane Goodman, Rachel Hare-Mustin, Stephanie Kane, Stephen Madigan, Rick Maisel, Anna Martinson, Radhika

Parameswaran, Nigel Pizzini, Ann Pyburn, Rick Wilk, and John Woodcock, among others. I also wish to acknowledge here the graduate students who took part in my spring 2002 seminar at Indiana University, "Feminist Knowledge and Scientific Practice." They offered insightful points and asked provocative questions about this book that inspired some clarifying last-minute revisions.

Special thanks are in order to my editor at Duke University Press, Ken Wissoker, for his enthusiasm, patience, and practical advice. Thanks also to the incredibly helpful and encouraging reviewers at Duke Press. Jamie Allen, Sarah Dodd, and Christina Dulude assisted with library work at crucial times in the production of the book.

I have been blessed with wonderful friends and loved ones throughout the process of working on this project. Important revisions of the manuscript took place during a writing retreat for which Jane and George Collier provided a warm and supportive space. Susan Kelly has reminded me constantly of the multiple meanings and larger purposes of this work, bringing me comfort and compassion while also amazing me with her incisive editorial eye. Radhika Parameswaran shared with me many a conversation, meal, and hearty laugh in the process of research and writing; our friendship and our overlapping academic and political interests have sustained me during several critical moments. I am also very grateful to her for feedback on earlier versions of parts of this book that sharpened my arguments considerably. Susan and Radhika, along with Anna Martinson, Julie Thomas, and JoNelle Toriseva, have helped nurture my writing process. Tom Schutz was a loving companion during an important period. He facilitated my initial contact with the hospital unit discussed in this book and patiently supported long nights of reviewing fieldnotes and transcribing interviews. Beatrice Aranow has offered her love, smarts, and wonderfully irreverent humor through many phases of this book's production. Stephe McMahon has long provided invaluable perspective and encouragement, as well as full-body laughs just when they are needed. Heartfelt thanks to Hannah and Graham, as well.

This book owes much to David Epston, who introduced me to narrative therapy and whose passion and vision in working with the problem of anorexia is truly inspirational. David's excitement about my work and his efforts to connect me with like-minded people have taken this project to places it would not otherwise have gone. He and his wife Ann, and their friend Bella, took me into their home during a long research trip that further developed my knowledge and understanding of narrative work. I will never forget their hospitality and generosity. I have benefited more than I can say from my friendships and working relationships with Lisa Berndt, Johnella Bird, Aileen Cheshire, David Denborough, Vicki Dickerson, Dorothea Lewis, John Neal, Bev McKenzie, Wally McKenzie, Jim Sparks, Cheryl White, and Michael White.

I give very special thanks to Rudolph Gaudio. Rudi's compassion, intellectual acumen, political commitments, and joyful friendship have meant the world to me. Many thanks to Rudi also for his careful reading of the manuscript at a number of points in its unfolding. My parents, Ginny and Mike, have given me love and unending support of many kinds. They have always believed in me and have made sure that I know this. And finally, I thank my partner Nigel Pizzini for his love, numerous helpful conversations, hugs, thorough work to help finalize the manuscript, provision of a heavenly living and writing space, and many delicious dinners. With his integrity and his warm, playful sense of humor, Nigel helped me usher this book to completion.

This book is an ethnographic study of a psychiatric program in North America that specializes in the treatment of anorexia nervosa (or anorexia) among adolescent girls. Anorexia is a phenomenon of self-starvation, often coupled with rigorous exercise, occurring primarily among girls and young women. It is notoriously difficult to cure. This difficulty is ordinarily attributed to patients' "pathology" and tenacity, but in this study, I shift the focus of concern to problems with therapeutic practices. In addressing the question of why treatments for anorexia are so fraught with conflict and struggle, I argue that mainstream therapies participate unwittingly in historically specific, dominant cultural discourses of gender, individualism, physical fitness, and family life that help constitute anorexia's conditions of possibility.

The site for this study is a small inpatient unit called Walsh (a pseudonym, as are all names used for participants in the treatment program), located in a major teaching and research hospital in the western part of the United States. I spent time in the outpatient clinic associated with the unit as well, but the inpatient unit is the site for the fullest elaboration of treatment protocols and is the focus of my analysis. In many ways, Walsh is ideal for this book project. Many medical and mental-health professionals agree that the program at Walsh is cutting edge in the field; conducting research there has allowed me to situate state-of-the-art treatments for anorexia in their social context. In addition, I have been able to analyze both biomedical and psychological approaches to anorexia, because Walsh combines talk therapies (including individual, family, group, and "milieu" therapies) with medical and behaviorist interventions. At the same time, however, my choice of an inpatient unit presented some constraints and dilemmas that I would not have faced had I conducted research in a residential treatment center, or in an outpatient clinic alone. I begin here with a discussion of these institutional constraints. Whereas much of this book explores the effects, and broad contexts, of certain treatment practices on program participants (especially patients and their parents), this prologue locates Walsh as a particular kind of treatment program and also provides a window onto my own position as a social scientist working in a psychiatric setting.

A few months before my fieldwork began, I met with Mark Blevins, the head psychiatrist at Walsh, to discuss my role as a participant-observer on the unit. Mark had authorized my project some time before this meeting, assuring me of his belief that my status as an "outside" researcher—someone who is not a clinician or a clinician in training—would not be a hindrance or even felt as anomalous to the people who worked and lived (temporarily) at Walsh. He had explained that I would be one of a number of adults on the unit (not only clinicians and staff but also researchers) who might come and go, record observations and thoughts, and occasionally sit quietly during a meal, a group therapy session, or a recreational activity. However, I still wanted to talk through in some detail my options for, and the potential effects of, different levels of participation and observation for the range of therapies, activities, meetings, and interventions that go on at Walsh. I knew that I would be spending considerably more time on the unit than most researchers. I also knew that as an anthropologist and a feminist activist, I had some concerns and questions about the impacts of my presence that would not be part and parcel of a research strategy for, say, a psychologist investigating links between anorexia and depression, or for a medical resident comparing the physical symptoms of pre- and postpubescent anorexic patients.

While I felt sure from my conversations with Mark and others that my project would not disrupt the everyday work practices of clinicians and staff, my remaining, and primary, concern was to avoid increasing or intensifying patients' inevitable experiences of surveillance on the unit (as much as possible)—whether that might result from my note taking, my silence at times when speaking would be out of place, or the mere fact of my presence as an adult at Walsh who would be there consistently but also had the freedom to leave when she wished. By the end of our talk that day, Mark and I both felt reasonably confident that once I explained the overall purposes of my project to participants and obtained consent for interviews and for sitting in on therapy sessions, my presence would not be problematic with regard to exacerbating patients' experiences of being watched. Mark and I did agree that because I was not a medical student, it would not be appropriate for me to be present for patients' routine physical exams or for any invasive medical procedures that might occur while I was there (e.g., the rare tube feeding). I was aware that although medical interventions make up only a small part of proceedings at Walsh, they carry significant meaning, representing a "bottom line" of patient care. One of the constraints of conducting my research on an inpatient unit was that direct observation of this important set of treatment practices could not be a part of my analysis (although I did hear reports about these practices in doctors' rounds). This book focuses on the various "talk therapies," the milieu and group therapies, and the behavior modification program surrounding food intake and weight gain at Walsh. I do not discuss physiological problems and concerns involved in weight restoration. (For discussions of the medical—and, occasionally, biochemical—"management" of anorexia and some complications for therapy and weight gain, see Andersen, Bowers, and Evans 1997; Mehler and Andersen 1999.)

Another constraint was my identity as a "soft" scientist in a context that is legitimized largely through appeals to "hard" science. There were, at times, benefits to my positioning as a somewhat "naive observer"; for example, I could comfortably ask mental-health professionals, patients, and parents alike to describe and explain unit practices in their own words. However, because I am a disciplinary "outsider," many clinicians and staff in particular saw me as a scholar whose views and methods are inherently less significant than those of psychiatry and biomedicine for understanding and addressing anorexia. This positioning is, of course, tied to institutional and financial arrangements that extend well beyond the beliefs and careers of individual practitioners at Walsh. The unit has developed a prestigious reputation through networking and publications in biomedical and psychiatric venues, and insurance companies constantly reinforce these connections, requiring for reimbursement an account of patients' progress in biomedical terms. While many clinicians and staff were quite interested in my work, no one seriously considered the idea that my study might contribute to changes in treatment approaches. In my meeting with Mark about my participant-observation on the unit, I mentioned the influence of feminist therapies and theories on my project. Mark smiled and said, "We'll show you what anorexia is *really* about."

Mark also commented that day, laughing and ribbing me verbally a bit, that it seemed to him I would be examining the "culture" of the unit, as constituted by the people who work there, as if it were "an exotic tribe." I was to hear this idea a number of times from clinicians and staff during my fieldwork. Here Mark and others were speaking to my "insider" status as an anthropologist who would render strange some of the taken-for-granted beliefs and practices of her own society. But they were also speaking to disciplinary relations of power: because anthropologists have traditionally studied less-powerful "others" (and sometimes represented these "other cultures" as bounded and exotic entities), it was amusing to imagine that I could turn an anthropological gaze onto a powerful group of people—amusing, in part, because of my status as a "soft" scientist in this context.

But if the head psychiatrist could find my position as a social scientist at Walsh amusing, the medical director of the unit—a younger psychiatrist named Bob Peters, who was new to the unit and under Mark's supervision—was quite openly unsettled by my unique role in the treatment program (unlike most researchers there, whose work was attached to a larger project under the direction of a psychiatrist, pediatrician, or psychologist, I was operating independently). I met with Bob before my fieldwork was to begin, and he let me know that Mark had agreed to give him the authority to make decisions about the parameters of my research activities. Bob's tone was clear when he added that there could well be a significant delay in my getting started: I was to respect unit hierarchy, which, in my case, now stopped with him. For about four weeks, my fieldwork consisted of a one-hour lunch once a week with Bob, who tried to discourage the project and emphasized his role as (in his words) "captain" of the "ship" that is Walsh. Bob's discomfort was not about the content of my work; rather, it spoke to differentials of power on the unit—between a junior and senior psychiatrist, for whom my presence at Walsh had different implications, and among a range of clinicians and staff in relation to Bob. The dilemmas I was to face in negotiating my place within the hierarchical structure of an inpatient environment thus began with access to the unit and continued throughout my fieldwork.

Of course, these dilemmas and positionings were constitutive of my research topics and methods. How are unit boundaries and hierarchies constructed and maintained? How could I, a feminist anthropologist interested in supporting particular changes in treatment practices, best represent the psychiatric status quo—along with the points of conflict, innovations, and resistances in its midst—when my (inter)disciplinary affiliations render me "soft" for many of the people with the institutional power to help effect change? What was I to do with the fact that, during the course of my fieldwork, I found myself aligned with, and supported by, some patients, parents, clinicians, and staff more than others? How could I keep from writing about participants in the program, in ways that inscribe another version of power relations that exist on the unit—for example, would some readers be left with the idea that patients are "cases" for, or "objects" of, social scientific analysis in addition to biomedical and psychiatric analyses?

I wrestled with these questions during my entire research project and also in the process of writing. I never fully resolved them. They remained active for me when I interacted with and observed program participants, when their dilemmas and knowledges shaped and shifted my own, and while I considered the possible effects of my representations in this book for a number of different audiences. In her study of the social impact of amniocentesis, Rayna Rapp (1999) states that the ethics of her work included "a constant assessment of the limited benefits and possible harm" her research might afford or do (22). I too have found that these assessments have been constant and ongoing, informing a range of considerations: smaller ones such as my decision to get to know patients before eating meals with them (and to refrain from taking notes during mealtimes—the forms of surveillance and note taking that already exist in this context are particularly fraught for patients), as well as larger considerations, such as formulating descriptions of medical power that capture both its contradictions and its seemingly totalizing effects.

On the latter topic, I received feedback via e-mail (in March 2002) from a clinician at Walsh indicating that my critical accounts of clinicians' beliefs and actions seem viable and also sufficiently complex to her. This person was the only program participant to provide me with feedback (for this purpose, an earlier version of my manuscript was made available at Walsh in 1996, as well as to interested patients who had been discharged); I am sure that others on the unit would disagree with her opinion. But I am pleased that many of my arguments seem reasonable to a relatively powerful person there.

The treatment modalities described in this book are similar to those found in most hospital-based programs, and in many outpatient and residential programs as well, in the United States (and perhaps elsewhere) today. A multidimensional treatment approach has become de rigueur for eating disorders during the past fifteen years or so and almost always combines some form of behavior modification (surrounding the goal of weight gain) with milieu and group therapies, individual therapy, and family therapy. However, there is some variation across the country in the specific content of, and the interrelationships among, these therapies. In addition, quite "alternative" treatments are available as well, mostly outside of inpatient treatment settings. Although they are not the focus of this book, some of these alternatives have emerged through a critical questioning of dominant treatment paradigms that resonates with aspects of my own analysis. I discuss one such alternative—"narrative therapy"—in the epilogue. I mention a few more here as a way to frame my own project.

Although developing and sustaining an alternative practice is of course never easy, individual and family therapists probably have the most room to vary their approaches from the norm, even on inpatient units. For some time now, a number of feminist psychotherapists and family therapists have challenged powerful cultural assumptions that predominate at Walsh and elsewhere: namely, that people who are healthy have "separated and individuated" from their families of origin (particularly from their mothers), and that autonomous individualism is the linchpin of psychological maturity (Gilligan 1982; Miller 1976;

Walters et al. 1988). What is more, many feminist therapists who work with "eating-disordered" clients believe that these assumptions are constitutive of the problems facing young women and girls who are in extreme conflict negotiating independence along with competing demands: for example, demands for self-sacrifice and nurturing others, along with pressures to shape their bodies in ways that reflect not only self-control but also self-denial (Boskind-Lodhal 1976; Lawrence 1984; Orbach 1985, 1986; Steiner-Adair 1986; Wooley 1980). Some of these ideas have made their way into inpatient (as well as outpatient and residential) treatment programs through the work of individual therapists, and sometimes in a more structured fashion. A number of programs today (but not the one at Walsh) acknowledge a sociocultural context for eating disorders and incorporate discussions of women's and girls' socialization and their struggles with body image (Levendusky and Dooley 1985; Roth 1986).

The work of feminist therapists has influenced many of the ideas in this book. At the same time, my study unpacks certain culturally dominant assumptions that are left intact in much of this work: views about the creation of gender differences, about processes of "socialization," and about operations of power on the body. In contrast to poststructuralist feminist scholarship in the therapy world (Brown 1994; Hare-Mustin and Marecek 1990), many feminist therapists work with models of female development that codify distinctively feminine selves, and they sometimes slip into essentializing or totalizing understandings of male and female identity formation. Or, as feminist sociologist Morag MacSween (1993) puts it, they assume that "an individualized self exists a priori and in ungendered form, and that the social structure prevents women from fully developing this self. . . . What results is the *addition* of a feminist view to underlying bourgeois patriarchal models of self and the body, rather than a feminist *critique* of those concepts" (52–53). In this book, I attempt such a critique by examining the production of normalized and gendered subjectivities, bodies, and families in the clinic. I can therefore pose questions about the construction of health and illness that are not readily available as interesting or important questions in the absence of a "close-up" critical analysis of standard psychiatric practices.

This kind of critical analysis is particularly important, I believe, for larger institutional and economic reasons as well, given recent and rapid changes in the provision of health care. The past decade has seen what many consider to be ill-informed decisions regarding program closures and shifts in the content, availability, and duration of treatments for eating disorders. With the rise of managed care and an effort on the part of some insurance companies to severely limit, or exclude altogether, coverage for eating disorders, many inpatient units have shut down, and those that remain open are focusing on medical stabilization and weight gain. There are serious concerns here about who has access to affordable and effective treatment, especially the kind of comprehensive (multidimensional) treatment that many would argue eating disorders require. On the other hand, there may be opportunities now to develop new therapies that are more effective than the current mainstream models. Indeed, a range of programs, including outpatient and day treatment centers, have recently emerged to provide alternatives to (or continuations of) more traditional inpatient care. While many of these programs offer some of the same treatments I analyze here, some incorporate practices such as yoga, biofeedback, 12-Step programs, music therapy, and meditation (Lemberg and Cohn 1999; see also http://www.edreferral.com). But without a thoroughgoing examination of dominant medical and psychological models—one that contextualizes and questions the very terms of health and illness at work within these models—both the effectiveness and the institutional power of alternatives may well be compromised.

This book attempts such an examination of mainstream psychiatric therapies. By situating a luxurious form of care by today's standards—Walsh is a costly unit with considerable resources—in its particular postindustrial cultural context, it is my aim to interrogate the disciplinary boundaries of psychiatry in one of its more prestigious, and therefore powerful, forms. In addition, by studying the everyday activities and meanings that constitute "normal medicine" in the treatment of anorexia, and investigating their potential to re-create the problem, I hope to generate an effective call for change.

In Fitness and in Health

A number of feminist scholars and therapists have argued that anorexia is an important "case study" for examining problems
with the embodiment of feminine identity
in the contemporary United States. Works
such as "Anorexia Nervosa: Psychopathology
as the Crystallization of Culture" (Bordo
1993a) and *Hunger Strike: The Anorectic's
Struggle as a Metaphor for Our Age* (Orbach
1986) emphasize that although anorexia is
considered to be a psychiatric illness, it must
be situated within new cultural expectations
about ideal femininity. Anorexia's incidence
increased more than 50 percent in the 1970s
and 1980s,[1] at the same time that there was
an increasing focus within mainstream U.S.
society on women achieving autonomy, self-
control, and bodily fitness through dieting
and exercise. Pressures for women and girls
to diet and "keep fit" contain contradictions
about females' capacities for self-control:
self-control (through control over the body)
is thought to be both a necessary and a difficult achievement. The "battle of the bulge"
is culturally coded as an unending struggle
for women, and many scholars suggest that
anorexia embodies this call to perpetual effort in a dramatic way. This struggle is linked
to discourses of class, race, and ethnicity, as

well as gender. Most patients are middle-class and white, and the diet and fitness industries target this population and those who are "up-wardly mobile" (note, however, that a number of scholars have recently raised important questions about this "typical" patient profile).[2] To the extent that fatness is associated with laziness, passivity, lack of produc-tivity, and lower-class status—often conflated with nonwhite status—women and girls who live with anorexia can be seen to be engaged in a battle against "downward mobility."[3]

Anorexia has been singled out as a significant case study within a very different body of literature as well: that of mainstream psychiatrists and other mental health professionals who are interested in a critical history of various theories and paradigms within their disciplines.[4] Be-cause anorexia has been quite difficult to treat, the history of ap-proaches to it "recapitulates the megalithic history of psychiatry" in many ways (Sours 1980, 8). Anorexia has been assimilated to reigning psychiatric and medical theories and practices since it was first identi-fied as a "disorder" in 1873.[5] It was considered to be a type of hysteria in the late 1800s, when diagnoses were few and far between and at a time when a range of "female complaints" were corralled under the rubric of hysteria.[6] Beginning in 1914, anorexia was widely considered a mani-festation of pituitary dysfunction because of the identification of an endocrine disease (Simmonds' disease) whose symptoms were super-ficially similar to those of anorexia. Anorexia was treated accordingly until the 1930s, when this theory of causation was thrown out and the concept of Simmonds' disease itself came under question (see Sours 1980. These treatments persisted until the 1930s in spite of strong evidence before that time against their efficacy; see Selvini-Palazzoli 1974). From the 1930s through the 1950s, Freudian depth psychology enjoyed wide popularity, and psychoanalytic theories about anorexia took center stage. These theories circulated around fantasies and fears of oral impregnation, and the aim of therapy was to instantiate desires for a properly maternal form of femininity.[7] But in the 1960s, a number of therapists began to mount challenges against Freudian ideas and to develop new forms of psychotherapy. In this context, and owing to efforts to find rapidly effective treatments that would curb anorexia's chronicity, behaviorist approaches became the new focus for the treat-ment of anorexia.[8] Here, simple (forced) "refeeding" protocols were translated into programs that included "positive reinforcement" for weight gain (e.g., increased social contact) and "negative reinforce-ment" for weight loss (e.g., bed rest).

However, beginning in the 1970s, most therapists agreed that be-haviorist approaches alone are not helpful in the long term. As a result, and at a time when the incidence of anorexia was rising dramatically, many treatment programs began following the multidimensional treat-ment paradigms that are still popular today. These paradigms combine strategies for weight gain, which usually involve some behaviorist prin-ciples, with individual therapy, family therapy, group therapies, and biomedical interventions (e.g., antidepressant medications) when they are deemed necessary.[9] Most therapies no longer assume the strictly differentiated gender roles that were part of Freudian theory, and they emphasize patients' (supposed) needs for individual autonomy.[10] But even with this multipronged treatment approach, anorexia—widely un-derstood since the 1960s to be a syndrome of complex ("multifac-torial") or unknown etiology—remains extremely difficult to treat. It has the highest mortality rate of any psychiatric illness (approximately 10 percent),[11] and according to a number of studies, most patients continue to struggle with significant anorexic symptoms many years after treatment. Follow-up studies conducted six years or more after treatment indicate that, of patients who live, about 10 percent meet full criteria for anorexia, and as many as 50 percent experience severe eating problems (Herzog, Schellberg, and Deter 1997; Sullivan et al. 1998).[12] For these reasons, anorexia has engendered almost as much critical reflection about psychiatric theory and practice during the past few decades as it has about contemporary ideals of female bodies and identities.

This book provides a bridge between psychiatric and "culturalist" accounts of anorexia as an important case study by investigating diffi-culties in treatment as themselves social and cultural problems. Pa-tients diagnosed with anorexia are notorious for their often concerted resistance to therapeutic processes. Their noncompliance to treatment is usually explained as a consequence, or even a confirmation, of their illness.[13] Although there is little question that patients often delay and resist treatment because of ideals of autonomy and self-sufficiency that are amplified and folded into many people's experiences of anorexia, I will show that therapies directly re-create conflicts that patients and their families have been experiencing in their lives, conflicts that cannot be reduced to epiphenomena of medicalized "disorder."[14] For example, I argue that power struggles in treatment participate in the cultural production of patients' experience that they cannot control themselves (and that they should be able to). More generally, I will demonstrate that therapies for anorexia unwittingly engage cultural practices and ideologies that are constitutive of this syndrome.

By focusing on patients' resistance to treatment—as well as disagreements among parents, doctors, therapists, and nursing staff—I show that participants in the program at Walsh actively struggle to negotiate agency and bodily control in the treatment process. My analysis brings together research in medical anthropology, feminist cultural studies, and critical studies of science. In addition to interrogating the disciplinary boundaries of psychiatry, I show how ethnographic analysis can extend social constructionist theories of science and the body, which can sometimes slip into totalizing, or monodiscursive, representations of corporeal experience and of human agency. Much of this book explores the multiple, and often contradictory, discourses that constitute the "anorexic body," as well as the so-called anorexic psyche and family.

Throughout the book, I examine ways in which psychiatric treatments for anorexia participate in a core contradiction entailed in the making of "ideal" persons within contemporary capitalist culture, through the simultaneous construction of (1) a self-possessed individualism—in the shape of self-control, "boundaries" around the self, willpower, autonomy, and productivity—and (2) domains such as the body and the family that appear as "natural" constraints in people's efforts to achieve autonomous individualism. I address the question of how dominant ideas about the fit body and about the consumption of food inform purportedly gender-equalizing notions of mental "fitness" today, as well as the question of how a focus on individual productivity articulates with powerful cultural and therapeutic representations of familial nurturance. I situate these questions historically by exploring changing ideals and practices surrounding femininity, women's roles in the family, and women's individual autonomy from the 1950s to the present. I also relate these changes to major shifts in psychiatric paradigms during this period—for example, the development of family systems approaches and new kinds of (individualizing) therapies. My aim is to locate popular and psychiatric discourses about the female body and psyche, and about the "naturalness" of the family, within a particular sociocultural formation that enables anorexia—that nurtures its conditions of possibility.

I analyze these discourses as they are expressed and lived for many people in the United States. I should note that North America is not the only place where these discourses—or anorexia—can be found. Anorexia is most common in the United States, Canada, parts of Europe, Australia, New Zealand, and South Africa (American Psychiatric Association 2000). Although cases of anorexia have been reported elsewhere, the numbers are small, except in places where, apparently, a surge of capitalist development has accompanied a rapid increase in the incidence of eating disorders.[15] There is a strong argument to be made that the phenomenon we diagnose today as "anorexia" is largely unique to contemporary industrialized and industrializing social contexts.[16] However, there is some debate in the literature regarding anorexia's historical (and contextual) specificity. For example, Rudolf Bell (1985) argues that fasting (female) medieval saints were "anorexic," but Caroline Bynum (1987) offers convincing evidence that while these medieval saints and women diagnosed with anorexia may seem similar on the surface, the meanings of food and body shape in these two cases are quite different. Joan Brumberg (1989) notes that although the diagnosis "anorexia" was coined in the late 1800s, the experience of anorexia today—which includes calculated self-control and, often, exercise regimes—differs markedly from "the sentimental and doleful Victorian phenomenon of 'wasting' " (99).[17] This book foregrounds the particular social arrangements and cultural meanings that are salient for an experience of anorexia in the United States today, and that also inform certain psychiatric theories and practices at work in this same context.

In addition, by focusing on moments of conflict and struggle in the treatment process, I argue that while ideas expressed in therapy about the self and about feminine "nature" are culturally dominant, they are also unstable. Following Probyn (1987), I show that even as these ideas powerfully position people, their sometimes uneasy articulations also create spaces for negotiation. Power differentials in the treatment program reveal the different meanings and contradictions embedded in the discourses that constitute anorexia, which are inflected by gender, ethnicity, class, age, and professional status. This book explores how the normalizing experiences of psychiatric treatment both produce and unsettle dominant constructions of gender, individualism, the body, and the family in late-twentieth-century U.S. society.

Research Site and Ethnographic Data

Walsh is a small, unlocked, psychosomatic inpatient unit located in an urban area in the western part of the United States. To protect the privacy of participants in the program, its exact location will remain confidential, and I provide only very general information here about my research site. Walsh accepts adolescents and children with combined medical and psychological diagnoses.[18] At any given time, about one-half of the patients are adolescent girls diagnosed with anorexia; accordingly, there is a separate treatment program and set of protocols for so-called "anorexic patients,"[19] including outpatient follow-up. I was a participant-observer in both the inpatient and outpatient contexts of this program during a fourteen-month period, from July 1993 to September 1994. I followed a total of fifty-two patients and participated in the program as much as I could. I attended therapeutic groups, doctors' and therapists' meetings about patients' progress, individual therapy sessions, family therapy meetings, and staff meetings. I also ate meals with patients, took part in outings and recreational activities, and spent time at the nursing station and in the charting room (where clinicians and nursing/counseling staff record notes in patients' medical charts and consult with one another informally). In addition, I conducted 146 interviews with patients, their parents, and the professionals and trainees who worked at Walsh.

One important feature of the program to note at the outset is a marked power differential between patients and caretakers. The average age of patients diagnosed with anorexia at Walsh is sixteen, so hospital admission and discharge for most require parental consent.[20] More often than not, patients say they do not want to be hospitalized, but parents usually insist. Parents are under considerable pressure to agree with medical recommendations. Their daughters are dangerously, perhaps fatally, ill. Also, if parents go against medical advice (a rarity), this decision is recorded in patients' charts, creating the potential for adverse effects on insurance coverage (e.g., for future care). Patients are subordinate players in these negotiations.

The ratio of females to males diagnosed with anorexia is greater than ten to one (American Psychiatric Association 1987, 1994, 2000). Hospital admissions during my fieldwork at Walsh reflected a ratio of approximately twenty to one. In this book, I discuss female patients only.[21]

Professionals and trainees at Walsh include psychiatrists, pediatricians, psychologists, nurses, "milieu counselors" (who manage the therapeutic milieu along with nurses), a nutritionist, recreation therapists, physical therapists, interns in psychology and psychiatry, and medical students. Nurses and milieu counselors perform almost all of the day-to-day work required to run the program at Walsh—I use the term "staff" to refer to this group. The term "clinicians" refers to all the other professionals and trainees listed. Note that the treatment environment includes more professional adults, and adults in training for similar positions, than patients: the staff/clinician-to-patient ratio in the program is about three to one. Clinicians consult among each other (and with staff) about patients and about their work almost as much as they interact with patients.[22]

In addition, an intake coordinator manages patient admissions, a social worker helps to organize outpatient services and living arrangements on request, and one person from the hospital's department of utilization management—a "case manager"—is assigned to Walsh to authorize and process insurance coverage and convey information about any pending or potential discontinuation of coverage. The unit also employs recreation therapists and physical therapists. The phrase "the treatment team" is a gloss for everyone who works at Walsh.

During the time I was conducting my fieldwork, clinicians and staff operated with a definition of anorexia provided by *The Diagnostic and Statistical Manual of Mental Disorders, Third Edition Revised* (American Psychiatric Association 1987, 67). The *DSM*, which is revised periodically to reflect new psychiatric judgments or findings, is an encyclopedic volume that lists every psychiatric illness along with the typical features and expected course of each. The diagnostic criteria for anorexia in the third edition revised are as follows:

> A. Refusal to maintain body weight over a minimal normal weight for age and height, e.g., weight loss leading to a maintenance of body weight 15% below that expected; or failure to make expected weight gain during period of growth, leading to a body weight 15% below that expected.
>
> B. Intense fear of gaining weight or becoming fat, even though underweight.

C. Disturbance in the way in which one's body weight, size, or shape is experienced, e.g., the person claims to "feel fat" even when emaciated, believes that one area of the body is "too fat" even when obviously underweight.

D. In females, absence of at least three consecutive menstrual cycles when otherwise expected to occur (primary or secondary amenorrhea). (A woman is considered to have amenorrhea if her periods occur only following hormone, e.g., estrogen, administration).

In addition to fulfilling these criteria, some of the patients I met also engaged in occasional food binges, and/or one or more forms of "purging," such as self-induced vomiting, the abuse of laxatives or diuretics, and vigorous "compensatory" exercise. Bingeing and purging are symptoms of bulimia nervosa.[23] Some patients' bulimic symptoms were so significant that they were diagnosed with both anorexia and bulimia. Note that for the fourth edition of the *DSM*, published in 1994 at the end of my fieldwork, the diagnostic criteria for both anorexia and bulimia were altered so that it is no longer possible to be diagnosed with both syndromes at once, although "restricting" versus "binge-eating/purging" "types" of anorexia are now specified. These changes reflect ongoing discussions and debates about the similarities, as well as the differences, between anorexia and bulimia.[24] Patients diagnosed with bulimia only were also admitted to Walsh, but most did not stay very long (these patients are usually not dangerously underweight and can therefore be removed from immediate medical danger very quickly). Bulimia was much more common in the outpatient clinic.

When patients diagnosed with anorexia are first admitted to the inpatient unit, they are extremely vulnerable: their physical health is acutely compromised. Criteria for admission are a body weight that is below 75 percent of a person's "ideal body weight," which is calculated by a nutritionist using a standard formula (taking into account a person's age, sex, and height), and/or medical instability, often referred to as "vital sign instability" (e.g., a low pulse, usually caused by low weight and malnutrition, and/or overexercise—and sometimes by vomiting or laxative abuse). From the beginning of any given patient's hospital stay, medical analyses and manipulations of the body take center stage. During hospitalization, which spans an average of about three weeks, patients' lives are heavily structured by eating—which involves a closely monitored, 100 percent liquid diet in the beginning, followed by calorie counting, agonizing choices from menus, and sometimes the threat of tube feeding if daily calorie quotas are not met. Meanwhile, for each patient, weight limits and goals are defined and become pivot points for negotiating many aspects of their hospital experience, ranging from calorie requirements to a discharge date. Monitoring calorie intake and weight, and linking both to specific "consequences," constitute the treatment program's behavior modification component. A "discharge weight" is established and is often identical to a patient's "exercise weight," a weight at which exercise is considered medically safe (thus exercise is not allowed for most patients during a hospital stay). Also, an "admission weight" is determined, in the highly likely event that the patient begins to lose weight after she is discharged and will be readmitted to the hospital in the future. Patients are strongly advised to gain more weight after they are discharged from the hospital, and they are monitored for this goal on an outpatient basis.[25]

In short, the major focus of the program is on food, calories, and body weights.[26] Many would argue that such a focus is inevitable, given the obstacles that treatment must overcome: "A person who is significantly underweight will have a hard time eating enough to gain weight without a great deal of structure around food intake. Because of metabolic abnormalities [due to starvation], such individuals usually require a huge number of calories to restore the metabolism to normal before they even begin to gain weight. For a person with a terror of food, this can be a seemingly impossible task" (Ellis-Ordway 1999, 189). However, as noted earlier, multidimensional treatment programs like the one at Walsh—which proliferated in the 1980s—aim to move beyond purely behaviorist solutions, and for good reason. Therapies that were prevalent in the 1970s focused entirely on weight gain and were not effective; in fact, many argued that they worsened patients' symptoms by precipitating battles between patients and clinicians over bodily control (Bemis 1978; Bruch 1974, 1982; Lawrence 1979). Hilde Bruch (1974), a pioneering psychotherapist in her work with anorexic patients, writes that many patients experience strict behavior modification programs as "brutal coercion" and "unmitigated misery" (1421, 1422). Patients would often simply "eat their way out of the hospital" (1421) and then experience relapse or become suicidal or bulimic (see also Bruch 1978; Bemis 1978). Today's programs are designed to circumvent these problems. For example, patients hospitalized at Walsh—both willingly and unwillingly—are captive audiences for therapies that are designed to uncover the intra- and interpersonal meanings of weight loss. Caretakers consider the therapeutic milieu quite important for promoting a "holistic" approach to therapy and change. However, the medical justification for hospitalization, presented to patients and insurance companies alike, is the need for weight gain, and behavior modification techniques still loom large in most hospital programs.[27]

There is little evidence that inpatient treatment programs have improved their success rates since the days when hospitalization was more of a last resort and forced feeding was commonplace. Arguably, behavior modification—regardless of a given program's additional components—exacerbates patients' problems by ensuring a constant surveillance and manipulation of the body on a very intimate scale. In addition to calorie counting at mealtimes, patients at Walsh are ritually weighed to one-tenth of a kilogram every morning, and their precise weights assume enormous significance in the program on a daily basis, affecting not only calorie requirements and length of stay in the hospital but also allowable physical activity and visitation. Ironically, when patients enter the hospital program, counting their calories and weighing and measuring their bodies often already intensely preoccupy them. Unfortunately, some learn how to engage in these activities with greater precision *during* a hospital stay.

In addition, feminist psychotherapist Robin Sesan (1994) notes that gendered hierarchies within professional treatment teams, and mystified notions of "expert knowledge" that often accompany these hierarchical power structures, are prominent features of most specialized and multidimensional programs, and Sesan argues that these features can also work to reinforce anorexia.[28] In fact, she suggests that the detrimental effects of hospitalization have become *more* widespread with the growth of specialized programs and the increased opportunity to hospitalize patients on a long-term basis. Multiple admissions to Walsh—often four or five for a given patient—are not unusual and can span the course of four years or more.

I should note here that since the mid-1990s, long-term inpatient hospitalization is slowly becoming more of a rarity once again. With the growth of managed care, a typical course of treatment now entails more outpatient and partial hospitalization services, and inpatient treatments are increasingly geared toward acute medical care only. Evidence of these changes was apparent during my fieldwork—a number of staff talked to me about shortened hospital stays at Walsh (compared to longer stays during the 1980s). I discuss these topics in greater detail elsewhere in this book. But whereas Walsh in the mid-1990s resembles fewer programs today, my analysis here is directly relevant to the shape of the field today and to decision making about its future direction. Many practitioners today idealize programs like the one I studied and strive (or wish) to emulate its practices and principles as much as possible. Also, the centerpiece of most "pared-down" hospital programs remains, not surprisingly, weight gain through behavior modification. In fact, some hospital programs are now *narrowing* to this focus.

There is evidence that the "revolving-door" phenomenon in the treatment of anorexia—that is, multiple repeat admissions—has recently increased (Kaye, Kaplan, and Zucker 1996). Medical anthropologist Lorna Rhodes (1991) has documented this phenomenon on an emergency psychiatric unit, as well. In both cases, return visits are clearly linked to the shortsighted goal of limiting the length—and cost— of care in the first instance. However, unlike the emergency room practitioners who were part of Rhodes's study, who (for complex reasons) accepted the imperative to (as Rhodes puts it) "empty beds" on their unit, most specialists who treat anorexia fight to keep patients hospitalized as long as possible and decry the economically motivated "revolving door" of late. It seems likely that the privileged social status of many patients diagnosed with anorexia leads to a higher level of visibility and advocacy when it comes to problems with illness chronicity. At the same time, however, when I was conducting research at Walsh in the early 1990s, multiple admissions to the unit and illness chronicity (like resistance to treatment) were cited as status quo and as unsurprising effects of anorexia itself. Again, for many, the program at Walsh at that time was, and is still today, considered ideal (although most staff members who had worked there ten years or more preferred the much longer admissions of the 1980s.[29] However, few considered a return to those days to be a realistic option). No one I spoke to believed that the system itself could play into illness chronicity.

Furthermore, clinicians and staff, while acknowledging the central role of behavior modification at Walsh, self-consciously guarded against a "top-down" (and chronicity-promoting) implementation of this form of medical power by merging it with therapist/patient/parent interactions that actively engaged patients in the therapeutic process on multiple fronts.[30] For most mental health practitioners, patients' difficulties in such a well-designed multidimensional treatment program can be attributed largely to patients' (and parents') "pathologies." For this reason, it is important to analyze conflict and chronicity at Walsh in ways that unpack not only the effects of behavior modification protocols but also assumptions and practices surrounding family relationships, practitioner/patient relations, patients' subjectivities, and the overall treatment milieu.

A Day on the Unit

To begin describing unit practices and the eating disorder treatment program at Walsh, let me walk readers through part of a "typical" day of fieldwork.[31] For my purposes here, I will render a composite portrait from events and from conversations with various people that actually occurred on different days. I will save descriptions of individual and family therapy sessions, and patient rounds, for future chapters. As I present and analyze these various scenarios, I will pause to reflect on my own experiences and my position as an ethnographer on the unit, and to provide some background information about clinicians' and staff's roles.

One weekday morning, I arrived on the unit at about 7:00 A.M. As I opened the heavy double doors near the nursing station, I felt my usual stomachache coming on. The stomachache was partly an ethnographer's "performance anxiety," I knew; but it was unique to my experiences on the inpatient unit, and it lingered too long to be attributable only to that. I was about to witness elaborate, meticulous, and emotionally intense investments in eating, food, calories, and body weights. I was also about to witness, and participate in, a very high degree of surveillance over patients I had come to know well. As someone who grew up believing that dieting for several weeks was important preparation for special occasions, I always greeted my days on the unit with a bit of an upset stomach. That particular morning, the feeling was not too strong, because I was looking forward to accompanying Lorna, who had been a nurse on the unit for many years, through her shift.

As I walked onto the unit, the nursing station was buzzing with activity. I had arrived during a shift change, and while staff from the night shift were signing off on patients' medical charts, nurses and counselors on the day shift were waking patients up, preparing medications, and trying to listen to tape-recorded nursing reports on each patient from the previous evening's shift. Over time, I had learned to slip in quietly and position myself unobtrusively. I would chat with people if they approached me, but usually I would keep busy myself by writing field notes, even when there was nothing of particular interest to write down. Waiting for Lorna, I thought about several ironies here. Patients are often said to avoid informal interpersonal interactions through "busywork" (e.g., calorie counting and perfectionistic approaches to homework). In addition, staff's (crucial) acceptance of my daily presence on the unit had been, I was told, due to my respectful, "low-key," and "unbiased" approach to my work—while anorexic patients on the unit were routinely characterized as overly quiet, deferential, and unopinionated. Finally, I reflected that my field notes were probably as detailed as patients' medical charts (if not more so). In fact, I recalled that one day, when patients were complaining in group therapy about staff watching them and recording their behaviors and words in "the red books" (their medical charts), Sally, a psychologist, said to me privately: "It's interesting that they don't complain about *your* observations and note taking; you notice and record more details about the treatment program than any of us do."

The difference, of course, was my lack of power over patients' fates in the treatment program. Clinicians and staff could write something in patients' charts that would prolong their stay in the hospital, or increase their calorie requirements (which were determined by a nutritionist and reassessed on a daily basis, depending on weight gain or loss). But Sally's comment also spoke to some clinicians' uneasiness about my role on the unit, especially near the beginning of my research. Generally speaking, the higher up in the power hierarchy a given person who worked on the unit, the more unsettled he or she was about my location within the treatment program's complex layers of mutual watching.[32]

When Lorna arrived for work that morning, we talked briefly at the nursing station. Lorna was excited about our arrangement for the day. She had let me know, as had several other female staff and clinicians, that she enjoyed the way I attended to her experiences and listened to her ideas,[33] especially given the pronounced gendered hierarchy within the unit's treatment team. Pediatricians and psychiatrists are at the top of the hierarchy, and most are men. Psychologists and staff are next in the hierarchy, and almost all are women. One nurse told me that she often had trouble with her "voice" on the unit,[34] "and that's what eating disorders are all about. We are all in it—the way women are treated."

While Lorna stored her purse and jacket in the charting room, I waited for her for a few minutes just outside the nursing station, reflecting on the unit's layout. The nursing station is centrally located in a wide, single hallway, with all of the patients' rooms, as well as a large community room, located on the opposite side.[35] Many patients' rooms are visible from the nursing station, and all rooms had internal glass panels and large windows to the outside to convey a sense of continuous visibility.[36] Foucault (1980b) discusses this arrangement of physical space as an important aspect of much of hospital medicine, modeled after Jeremy Bentham's panopticon, an eighteenth-century proposal for the architectural design of prisons (and also applicable to hospitals and schools; see Foucault 1979). Foucault writes that panoptical spatial arrangements ensure "a surveillance which [is] both global and individualising while at the same time carefully separating [of] the individuals under observation" (1980b, 146).

When Lorna was ready, we began to pick up urine "hats" (plastic containers) from anorexic patients' bathrooms, in order to measure patients' urine output from the night. We did not address any of the patients, many of whom were having their vital signs taken by another staff member. One patient's "orthostatic vitals"—a measure of the difference in pulse rate from lying down to standing—was found to be unsafe. She would be in a wheelchair all day, a conservative measure to guard against fainting, and to mark the seriousness of the patient's medical condition. Another patient was requesting that her vitals be taken *after* she was weighed. Usually patients' vitals are taken before their ritual weigh-in every morning (sometime between 7:30 and 8:30). This patient explained that she was so upset about the prospect of having gained a lot of weight, she was afraid her pulse would be artificially high.

Lorna measured and recorded patients' urine volume and density. She said that for the fourth morning in a row, Rebecca, who was on her second inpatient admission, had a urine density that was markedly low. This meant that Rebecca might be drinking extra water on the sly ("waterloading") to engineer the appearance of a higher body weight. Over the years, staff and clinicians had learned these patient "tricks" (which were then passed on from patient to patient). In fact, testing urine densities is a practice that was developed in response to patients' waterloading. It is meant as a deterrent but of course underlines waterloading as a possibility for patients by institutionalizing a response to it. Struggles around bodily surveillance and control can take on a life of their own in the hospital. Lorna said that she would recommend a "random weight" for Rebecca, meaning that at some unspecified time during the day she would be weighed again, once any excess water weight had passed through her body. Random weights are also used if a patient is suspected of hiding weights—for example, batteries—in their hair or their underwear (patients are weighed in underwear and a medical gown only). Lorna said they avoid random weights as much as possible, because they are intrusive (staff are supposed to watch patients undress and put on their gowns for random weights).[37]

Next, Lorna and I went to Carla's room, and Lorna told her it was time for her to be weighed. Without a word, Carla walked with us to the scale, which was in a room a few doors down from the nursing station. Carla was eighteen years old and an "old-timer": this was her fourth admission over a span of three years (not at all unusual). Carla stepped up on the scale. Lorna asked, "Do you want to do it?" Carla said no and watched nervously as Lorna determined her weight. "Up by .2," Lorna said, writing it down. Two-tenths of a kilogram is just under one-quarter of a pound and is the least amount of weight a patient can gain to avoid having her calorie minimum raised for the day. At this point, Carla's weight registered just under ninety pounds. Expressionless, Carla stepped off the scale and left the room. Lorna whispered,

> Gaining is really hard for them. Even though it's healthy, you never say "good job," or anything like that. Carla's happy that her calories won't go up, but she's upset about the gain. I had a patient once who insisted her gain was too much; she was worried her weight would go down the next day. About a half an hour after she was weighed, she came up to me, really flustered, and said she'd had a really big bowel movement, that's what it was, and could we weigh her again? I explained that we could, and that we could even write the new weight in her chart, but that the *official* weight would be the one that was already recorded. We've learned over the years, just never compromise with these patients, they'll start splitting hairs until it drives you crazy.

After weighing two more patients, it was time to get ready for breakfast, which began promptly at 8:30 in the community room. Patients picked up their trays from a cart in the hallway, which had been brought up by the hospital's kitchen staff. Lorna and I sat with our own food at a table of patients who were "on observed," meaning that a staff member was to record each item of food these patients ate and the number of calories (and amount of liquid) they consumed. Patients who were "on unobserved" were nearing the end of their stay in the hospital and were responsible for monitoring their own caloric intake and keeping their own records. They sat at a table of their own that morning, along with a few non-eating-disordered patients. Susan, a milieu counselor, was also helping to observe that morning and was the only adult sitting at a third table of patients. (Milieu counselors do not have nursing degrees and cannot perform certain medical procedures but are otherwise identical to nurses in their roles on the unit. In general, milieu counselors are considered to be better skilled at group process than nursing staff.) A few minutes into the meal, Susan started up a casual conversation with Lorna about a recreational outing the previous afternoon (to a nearby mall), inviting patients to share their experiences, but not pressuring them to do so. Some patients chimed in with a few words, but most of them were concentrating on their food.

Patients are under considerable pressure to consume a specified number of calories each day, and several patients that morning were deciding what items to save for lunch or a snack as they slowly nibbled at their breakfasts. A few patients had brought calculators to breakfast to parcel out their required calories for the day's three meals and two snacks in various permutations. Sylvia, a new patient, had no choice about what to eat: she was on a strict diet of 100 percent liquid nutrition, or Ensure, and was expected to drink one can that morning. Ensure is easier to digest than solid food, an important factor for some patients when they first arrive and are severely malnourished.[38] Lorna explained to her: "I need to see you open the can, just to make sure we're starting with a whole can." Meanwhile, Pam, a patient who was on her ninth admission in four years, was squeezing two small boxes of Shredded Wheat cereal and one box of Bran Flakes. After pouring the crushed cereal into a bowl, she added water while looking over at Susan, the milieu counselor sitting at her table: "Susan?" Susan said, "Six ounces?" and Pam nodded. While Susan recorded Pam's liquid intake for the morning, Pam walked over to the microwave and "cooked" her cereal for a bit. Returning to the table, she added cottage cheese and began eating very slowly.[39]

Valerie, a patient who was on her second admission, was still calculating different permutations of her menu for the day after fifteen minutes and had not started eating. It was not unusual for patients to spend a good deal of time at meals calculating and recalculating their calories for the day, and therefore to delay eating (my analyses in chapter 1 suggest one way to understand this practice: it appropriates a mode of surveillance in the hospital—the requirement for precise calorie counting, with results that go on record—to "anorexic" ends). Looking over at Valerie, Lorna announced that it was 8:45, which meant that breakfast ended in twenty minutes. By this time, all the non-eating-disordered patients were finished with breakfast and had gone to their rooms. Valerie nervously wrapped up a bagel in cellophane, then got up to fetch a package of graham crackers from the kitchen's communal food bins. Lorna gently reminded her that this was her second time up from the table, and that she would have to stay seated for the rest of the meal. Meanwhile, Susan spoke quietly with Lisa, a new patient who had just started on solid food the previous day. Susan was explaining that if Lisa did not finish her banana, she would have to count it at half its caloric value. Upset, Lisa asked, "But what if I eat three-fourths of it?" Susan told her that it was a rule, that they had to draw the line somewhere. Later that day, Susan, who was clearly flustered by Lisa's challenge, told me that the eating disorder program has so many rules as it is, no one can remember them all.

The end of the meal was, as usual, a tense time. Valerie had begun eating only in the final five minutes, after Lorna reminded her that she had had a difficult time the day before at evening snack trying to make up for eating so little earlier in the day. Valerie had a doctor's order for an "NG backup," meaning that if she did not finish her calories for the day and was unable to complete them with Ensure after evening snack (within a designated period of time), staff were to force-feed her with a nasal/gastric (NG) tube. In practice, NG tubes were very rarely used: the threat of a tube was usually effective in convincing patients to finish their calories on their own. As the meal drew to a close and several patients struggled with the remaining food on their plates, one patient pointed to her calculator and to Lorna's clipboard at the same time and said with a wry smile, "You're five calories off!" Lorna added up her figures again and smiled, too, pulling out an eraser. "I've never been good at math," she said, "but I can always rely on these folks to correct me."

Pam and Sylvia finished their breakfasts on time, along with the unobserved patients, and they all returned to their rooms to fill out their menus for the next day (a rather time-consuming process for patients diagnosed with anorexia, who consider food choices extremely carefully). Valerie and Lisa had to be ushered out at 9:05, with plenty of food still on their plates. On our way back to the nursing station, Lorna said, "We're worried that Lisa might be hiding food in her shirtsleeves. I'll make a note of it in her medical chart."

At this point in the day, Walsh was bustling with activity. The head pediatrician and several medical students had completed their rounds (a meeting among themselves where they discuss patients' medical progress and treatment protocols) and were trying to examine a few patients before school began at 9:30. The psychologists and psychiatrists who worked on the unit had also completed their morning rounds, and several were trying to arrange their schedules to see their patients that day for an hour's worth of individual therapy each. Bob, the medical director, was writing a note in a patient's chart. José in utilization management emerged from the charting room and came over to say hello. In his usual agitated state, he said, "I was just on the phone trying to authorize insurance coverage for Sylvia, the new eating-disordered patient." José explained that Sylvia's insurance company was planning to deny their claim (a common occurrence). José said that he would probably be successful in authorizing coverage, but in the meantime Sylvia's parents would get the bill, "and at over $1,500 a day, they're gonna flip."[40] Lorna interrupted to say that she and I should go pay Sylvia a visit.

Lorna had been assigned to Sylvia as her staff advocate, and because Sylvia was new, Lorna made the time to have a "one-to-one" with her. After introducing me, Lorna asked Sylvia if she had any questions. They talked for a while about Sylvia's vital signs from that morning, how often vitals are taken, and so on. As Lorna spoke, Sylvia was so nervous and distracted that she was barely listening. After Lorna finished talking, Sylvia blurted, "Ann [the nutritionist] said I need five cans of Ensure today. Can I have them only at meals? One, two, and two? I don't like snacks." Lorna asked which snack she did not like, and Sylvia said, "Neither one." Lorna replied, "You know, let's check with Ann and your doctor. I'll bet they'll want you to spread them out until your vital signs are more stable. When they are, you'll be more on your own with that. But now, I'll bet they'll want you to spread it out. But we can ask." After talking for a few more minutes, Lorna and I left Sylvia's room and talked briefly in the hallway. Lorna remarked (and I paraphrase):

> Especially at this early stage, education is really important. She's pretty overwhelmed, and I just explain what we do and why as clearly

as I can, and try to show how it's linked up with the state her body is in. And I try to empower patients, let them know they can ask for things, even if they won't get what they want all the time. After patients get a handle on the routine here, I'll talk with them about experiences other kids have had on the unit, and even share some of my own life experiences with them sometimes, in a way that's supportive of them. And sometimes I'll tell them girls are taught to keep things inside, so it's hard to say how you feel all the time, or express your anger.

Lorna said that in general, she saw her role with patients (particularly in one-to-ones) as supportive and educational—not "therapy" but "therapeutic."

Let me skip ahead now to a brief description of "community meeting," which takes place after lunchtime. Community meeting is one of the daily activities on the unit and counts as "milieu therapy." It is considered more of a business meeting than "group therapy," and a chance for all patients who are living at Walsh (including those who are not in the eating disorders program) to interact among themselves in a structured way. Normally, the meeting is held in the community room, but that week it was being held in Marlo's room, because Marlo was on "strict medical bed rest." When a patient's anorexia is extreme, she may have a very low body temperature and chronic vital sign instability. Under these circumstances, patients are usually confined to their beds with a bed warmer and placed on a cardiac monitor. Marlo lay quietly, surrounded by machinery, as Lorna, several patients, and I brought chairs into her room. Once everyone had arrived, Lorna asked, "Who's the chairperson?" It was Pam that week. Pam was eligible for the role— that of (figurehead) facilitator of the meeting—because she had reached "level 2" of the behavioral level system on the unit, meaning she had attended groups regularly and was making progress toward her therapeutic goals. Before Pam could begin the meeting, Joey, a sixteen-year-old patient with asthma and "behavioral problems," said he had an announcement. Pam said, "We have to do introductions first" (for Sylvia, the new patient). With tremendous sarcasm, Valerie said, "Oh, Joey, what a faux pas!" Valerie, her eyes heavy and narrow with depression and stress, was known for her bitter wit, and for delighting in critical remarks about unit procedure. Lisa, who was a poised and precise meeting secretary, included the crack in her notes.

After introductions and Joey's announcement that he was leaving the hospital that afternoon, Pam asked if anyone had any issues to raise. Instead of the familiar complaints about the length of community meeting, the group was quiet. Lorna wondered out loud about the silence, and Marlo asked, "Do we always have to analyze everything?" Pam decided to move on to Joey's "good-bye questions." Someone asked what he had learned while he was here (how better to control his anxiety); another patient asked what he would do when he got home (watch TV whenever he wanted). Then Lisa asked Joey what he would tell his friends if they asked where he had been. Joey looked upset and confused. Lorna spoke up: "Sometimes we ask patients what they would say if someone asked them a question about their stay here that makes them uncomfortable." Joey visibly relaxed and said, "I'll tell them it's none of their business." After a few more questions, Pam noticed the time and wrapped up the meeting.

On my own for a short time at this point in the day, I reflected on the fact that interactive "social time" at Walsh is almost always carefully scripted. Some friendships are formed, often between roommates, but in general there is not much room for spontaneous socializing. Patients in the eating disorders program spend most of their free time by themselves—planning menus, counting calories, thinking about therapy sessions, perfecting homework assignments, and strategizing ways to prevent gaining weight and/or return home quickly. Also, according to some staff members and to several patients I got to know well, patients often compare themselves with one another in jealous ways. For example, they may ask themselves: Who here is thinner than I am? Are staff easier on her than they are on me? I wondered whether the (frequently reported) anorexic experiences of isolation and competitiveness are amplified in this treatment setting.

Shortly after community meeting, Lorna and I attended afternoon rounds, which included clinicians from both child psychiatry and adolescent medicine. (I will describe rounds in some detail later.) After rounds, Lorna was nearing the end of her shift. She picked up the medical charts of her assigned patients, and we went to the small charting room just next to the nursing station, where Lorna would write up her nursing reports. At this time of day, the charting room was crowded. Several interns and medical students were also "charting on their patients." An intern in psychiatry was debriefing a therapy session with the medical director. Karen, a psychology intern, was on the phone with a patient's parent, arranging a family therapy meeting, which, ideally, took place once a week. At one point in the conversation, Karen said, "Yes, I know she's a minor, but there's certain information that should really come from her. We've found over the years that patients should be the ones to tell their parents about their weight and that sort of thing, if they choose to." As I began thinking to myself about therapeutic accounts of healthy individualism in families,[41] Lorna came over to tell me she was finished charting and was ready to go. I saw her out, and we said we'd see each other the following day. I left soon thereafter myself, to head home and write up my field notes for the day.

Interviews

The foregoing account is an example of my participant-observation at Walsh. I also conducted semistructured interviews with forty-five patients, thirty parents, seventeen staff, ten clinicians, and several other people affiliated with the unit (e.g., the intake coordinator). Many of these people were interviewed two or three times. Most interviews took place on site at the hospital, either in a private room (ordinarily used for therapy) or in the hospital cafeteria. In addition to these more formal interviews, I had many casual conversations with people over lunch, over coffee, in hallways, in patients' rooms, in waiting rooms, and at social functions.

I began most interviews with an exploration of peoples' personal and professional histories with the treatment program. I then asked a variety of open-ended questions related to everyday experiences on the unit or in the clinic; patients' resistance to treatment; explanations of, and ideas about, anorexia and its relationship to gender, race, and class; notions of femininity and ideas about gender roles in the family; dynamics of gender and power within the treatment team; and parents' roles in the treatment process. Here is a sample of the questions I asked: What are the strengths and limitations of the treatment program as you see it? What are the pros and cons of such "detail-oriented" treatment protocols for a detail-oriented problem like anorexia? Why do you think so many patients resist treatment? Why do you think that more than 90 percent of anorexic patients are girls and women? Do you think patients' mothers and fathers are treated in a similar way, or differently, at Walsh? Many people have worked here for a long time— what do you think is compelling about this place? How could Walsh's "team approach" to treatment be improved, in your opinion?

Data Collection and Confidentiality

During participant-observation, I hand-recorded details of events and others' descriptions of events "live," whenever possible. There were times when it was inappropriate or would have been disrespectful for me to take notes about events while they were occurring—for example, I decided not to put pen to paper during mealtimes with patients. In these situations, I would take a break from participant-observation as soon as was practicable and find a quiet place in the hospital (e.g., an available therapy room on the unit or a small table in the hospital cafeteria) to take notes from memory. At the end of each of my days or evenings at Walsh, I would review and flesh out my notes at home and record questions or lines of inquiry I might want to pursue as my research progressed. Interviews were tape-recorded whenever possible (some interviewees preferred that I take notes by hand), and transcribed along with several therapy sessions I was able to tape-record. Once I had collected all data, I read through my notes many times and began organizing them into broad themes, a process that initiated the organization of this book.

To protect patients' privacy, I have disguised certain identifying data about the treatment program. It has also been necessary to disguise certain personal data about patients so that, for example, a parent who took part in the treatment program will not have access to confidential information about another person's child. Also, I sometimes protect the identities of clinicians and staff within the unit's "community." To these ends, I occasionally create composite characters, slightly alter quotations, and attribute some people's words to others.

Critically Applied Medical Anthropology

My stance toward unit practices in this book is a critical one. I argue that Walsh's elaborate methods of surveillance; its meticulous accounting of patients' "progress" in terms of body weight, calories consumed, et cetera; its professional sexual politics of caretaking; and even its attention to patients' psychological "development," family lives, and interpersonal skills all participate in contemporary cultural discourses that help constitute what I am calling anorexia's conditions of possibility. At the same time, however, there is no doubt that in many important ways, the treatment program "works." Lives are certainly saved, and many patients improve over time. Clinicians and staff at Walsh claim, and the unit has a reputation for, successful treatment—although "success" is open to a range of interpretations in this area of specialization (Lemberg and Cohn 1999).[42] However, it is not my purpose to evaluate the effectiveness of this treatment program in psychiatric or biomedical terms, strictly defined. Rather, my focus is as follows: What do patients, parents, staff, and clinicians *mean* when they say that the treatment program works or does not work well? What are the politics of personhood that support these views? To borrow terms from cultural anthropologist Gananath Obeyesekere (1985), how can we characterize the "work of culture" that renders conceptualizations of health and illness on the unit powerful and persuasive?

In addressing these questions, I employ a critically applied medical anthropology. Critically applied work in this field can be distinguished from work that is clinically applied (Scheper-Hughes 1990). While these two approaches need not be mutually exclusive, the latter usually signals an allegiance to biomedical definitions and categories of illness, health, and personhood; often, the goal is to improve biomedical practice through a "cultural sensitivity" that helps assimilate or more effectively translate patients' explanatory models of illness into physicians' models (see Armstrong 1987; Scheper-Hughes 1990). In contrast, a critically applied medical anthropologist "works at the margins and sometimes (but not necessarily) from the outside, pulling at loose threads, deconstructing key concepts, looking at the world from a topsy-turvy position in order to reveal the contradictions, inconsistencies, and breaks in the fabric of the moral order without necessarily offering to 'resolve' them . . . [challenging the] economic and power relations that inform . . . every medical encounter" (Scheper-Hughes 1990, 191). My aim in this book is to situate psychiatric approaches to anorexia within certain powerful, problematic, and contradictory discourses that surround feminine identity and family life in the United States today. I want to emphasize that such a stance does not imply a disgruntled acceptance of the psychiatric status quo, or "mere criticism." Critical work in the field can include an advocacy role (see M. Lock 1993). Such a role may be directed toward unmet patient/family demands, shifts in the practice or "culture" of medicine, and economic inequalities in the provision of medical services. It is my hope that this book could provide a groundwork for advocacy on a number of fronts.

Accordingly, when I write about patients' resistance to treatment, I do not depict mere "rituals of resistance" (see Gluckman 1963) that serve only to reinscribe, even to strengthen, (apparently) totalizing forms of cultural and medical power.[43] While I borrow from Obeyesekere, my stance differs from his in one crucial respect: the "work of culture" on the unit that "fuses into a conception" (Obeyesekere 1985, 136) called "anorexia"—and also a conception of fitness and health—is not uniform and all-determining; rather, it is fractured and contested. My analysis takes its cue from Good and Good's work on the creation of medical knowledge (Good and Good 1993; Good 1994), and from Lorna Rhodes's 1991 research on cultural contradictions within psychiatry, in challenging the assumption that biomedical discourse is seamless and therefore constitutes bodies and identities in a top-down fashion.[44] My goal is to make explicit the potentially transformative tensions and contradictions that already exist on the unit. Like cultural anthropologist Nancy Scheper-Hughes (1992, 29), but in a very different context (Scheper-Hughes writes about hunger and child malnutrition among shantytown dwellers in Northeast Brazil), I think of my role as an ethnographer at Walsh as, in part, that of a "clerk" or "'keeper' of the records." I have recorded and interpreted a version of events that are not told as such in official records at Walsh, and that indeed challenge these records in many ways—even as they crosscut and participate in the narratives and practices that constitute status quo medicine.[45]

While recognizing contradictions at Walsh, I also recognize that many clinicians and staff lay claim to noncontradictory and authoritative accounts of illness and health, and that real forms of power accompany these claims. Throughout this book, I am clear about my political and intellectual stance against such claims, and against the hierarchies of gender, class, ethnicity, age, and professional status that support them. However, precisely because these authoritative accounts are produced within social fields of inequality, they sometimes falter on their own terms. These are the moments I seek to highlight. In other words, my critical analyses of unit practices emerge out of "practical" criticisms that are already unfolding. Believing that the potential effectiveness of "alternative" discourses lies in their potential to reconfigure dominant social forms persuasively, I focus on modes of resistance that patients, parents, staff, and clinicians express in situ (and that sometimes have conservative effects). Of course, when I ground my critique of unit practices in terms that are already available in the treatment program, I am never "neutral" about the *particular* terms that I notice and then make explicit. Hence, my analysis does point in specific directions regarding treatment improvement (addressed in the epilogue).

This book is, of course, a partial account of cultural discourses at work in the treatment of anorexia. Much of my analysis circulates around the trope of "fitness" and unpacks a particular set of ideas and practices that intersect with it, focusing on hegemonic constructions of health, illness, and (hetero)normative family lives. There are a number of important debates in the field that I do not address—for instance, the role of childhood sexual abuse in the creation and experience of anorexia.[46] Also, I should note that with the exception of chapter 3, this book highlights experiences and clinical representations of patients and parents at Walsh. Although I include detailed ethnographic analyses of clinicians' and staff members' negotiations with patients and parents and with one another in the process of treatment, the primary subjects of this study are those who seek help at Walsh and (often) appear there as clinical "objects." This choice on my part reflects my desire to challenge the pervasive privileging of powerful "expert" accounts of anorexia. The risk here is that clinicians and staff may at times appear merely to ventriloquize such accounts, when it is one of my central aims to show how these accounts are actively, if not fully consciously, produced.[47] I hope that I succeed in describing enough of the differences among, and uncertainties of, clinicians and staff to convey the complexities of their own positions as psychiatric professionals.[48]

I anticipate that some people at Walsh will disagree with my interpretations. My analysis of the treatment program should be read in light of the fact that several patients and parents I interviewed supported the unit's therapeutic practices (sometimes only in retrospect), in spite of their often bitter criticisms. In addition, most staff and clinicians found their jobs highly rewarding, especially compared to their previous experiences working in other psychiatric facilities. However, I do not believe that these points weaken my critical analyses. I am concerned not only with ruptures in, and resistances against, dominant ideas about feminine fitness and familial "health" but also with the creation of these ideas as normative, "natural," and beneficial. Of course, the analyses presented here are my own. But they are informed by the mutual interests and ideas of many people I met during the course of my fieldwork.

Naturalizing Power: Thinking Through Intersections of Feminist Theory, Cultural Studies, and Medical Anthropology

Theorizing Anorexia as a Cultural and Psychiatric Phenomenon

Debate about the relative importance of "sociocultural factors" in anorexia's etiology is ongoing. Few disagree that anorexia is culturally and historically situated, and that so-called sociocultural factors play a part in its development and maintenance, as well as its prevalence among young women and girls. Also, recent social changes have facilitated the emergence of many cases of anorexia—it is difficult to explain its increase in incidence in the 1970s and 1980s in any other terms (Bordo 1993d; R. Gordon 2000). Indeed, a number of cultural theorists and also some clinicians refer to anorexia as a "culture-bound syndrome."[49] However, a vast body of clinical research on anorexia and much of the literature about its treatment include only passing mention of these issues, if they are mentioned at all. A majority of psychologists and psychiatrists follow a medical model in considering psychological, physiological, and familial "factors" to be entirely separable from cultural factors, and to be the only ones of real etiological significance.[50] In contrast, some feminist scholars assert that anorexia differs only (or primarily) in degree from "normal" dieting, which is chronic or problematic for many women and girls.[51] In many of these latter accounts, biomedical and psychological categories fall by the wayside or are seen to misrepresent social problems as individual and familial "dysfunctions." Sometimes, these categories sit uneasily beside a feminist cultural analysis.[52]

Feminist historian Joan Brumberg (1989) claims to formulate a compromise between a medical model and what I will gloss as "the feminist cultural model" in her influential book on anorexia's social history; but in fact, she too separates biology/psychology and culture in her analysis of anorexia's etiology. Brumberg argues that psychological, biological, and cultural factors converge to cause anorexia, but that the psychological and biological variables involved are themselves culturally neutral, are not shared by "normal" dieters, and call for "objective" psychiatric treatment. Most clinicians who hold that sociocultural factors are significant in anorexia's etiology share Brumberg's view (including Dare and Eisler [1997] and Richard Gordon [2000], who count anorexia as a culture-bound syndrome). Gordon, for example, points to "developmental vulnerabilities" to explain the difference between a person who lives with anorexia and "normal" dieters. Other (indeed, most) clinicians, using similar logic, have for some time now claimed to debunk or minimize the feminist cultural model through the argument that only a biomedical and/or psychological problem (or "vulnerability") can account for the fact that only some, and relatively few, people develop anorexia (see Bordo 1993d; Way 1995). Proponents of the feminist cultural model reply that there are at least two different theories of illness causality at work in the debate between mental health professionals and cultural theorists on this subject: whereas clinicians are dedicated to identifying and repairing "internal" causes (internal to individuals and families), cultural theorists often conceptualize anorexia as an *internalization* of sociocultural norms that expresses an extreme form of "normal" behavior (Polivy and Herman 1987), or a "crystallization" of various gendered cultural streams revolving around bodily control (Bordo 1993c). Not everyone, of course, inhabits or lives with these discourses in the same way (which is another way to explain why only some people develop anorexia).

This debate often invokes reified concepts of psyche, soma, and culture. Psychiatric "nature" and cultural "context" remain conceptually distinct for many scholars and practitioners on both sides. For example, clinicians' familiar charge that the feminist cultural model ignores the real suffering of those diagnosed with anorexia relies on the notion that suffering is, in this case, a psychiatric problem by definition. It also calls up the stereotype of vanity and privilege (as opposed to "true suffering") that is sometimes associated with simplified, "cultural" explanations of eating disorders in the popular press.[53] Meanwhile, claims since the 1980s that an "epidemic" of eating disorders is upon us rely on a generic notion of cultural influence and simultaneously medicalize and pathologize all chronic dieting. A number of researchers imply that a majority of American girls are "at risk" of developing an eating disorder, and inflated statistics about the prevalence of anorexia and bulimia circulate in some quarters.[54] The latter can be understood as an overzealous application of the feminist cultural model, whose proponents are fighting an uphill battle on an institutionally uneven playing field in their efforts to challenge a medical model that draws a clean line between normal and abnormal, a line that encourages apathy about the cultural production of anorexia and also of chronic dieting. However, as cultural theorists Julie Hepworth and Christine Griffin point out (Hepworth 1999; Hepworth and Griffin 1995), many versions of the feminist cultural model tend to leave intact a reified concept of "anorexia" and to search for its "causes" (in an extrapsychiatric domain). When the illness category itself is not questioned and a familiar narrative of "finding causes" remains on the table, the door is open for understanding this model in terms of "culture" writ large producing "pathology" and its precursors. Lester (1997) and Malson and Ussher (1996) note a corollary of this problem: a poorly theorized account of internalization within many socioculturally oriented analyses of anorexia. These analyses often do not question the liberal humanist assumption that pregiven "individuals" absorb or react to cultural "overlays" and to processes of socialization (see MacSween 1993), and they often emphasize "dieting and the idealization of thinness to the exclusion of other aspects of anorexia or female subjectivity, without theorizing the sociocultural aspects of (gendered) embodiment and without exploring the wider cultural and political significances of female slenderness" (Malson and Ussher 1996, 268).

In this book, I follow suggestions from Bordo (1993c), Malson and Ussher (1996), and Probyn (1987) to locate anorexia within a complex sociocultural field, and at the intersection of multiple, and sometimes contradictory, discourses of feminine identity.[55] My aim is to avoid a reified concept of "culture" and thus also allow for a more nuanced account of subjectivity (a topic I address later in this introduction). I also take up the call from Hepworth (1999), Hepworth and Griffin (1995), and Malson (1991) to question anorexia's status as a "pre-given medico-psychological entity" (Malson 1991, 31). In these ways, this book challenges the persistent drawing of contrasts between "nature" and "culture" in debates about "sociocultural factors" in anorexia's etiology.

Embodied Forms of Power and Resistance

My ethnographic analysis of cultural discourses operating in the treatment of anorexia—a context that privileges biomedical and psychological explanations of bodily states—allows me to move beyond the argument that psychiatric accounts of anorexia *misrepresent* social problems as individual (and familial) dysfunctions. This dichotomy of individual / social is somewhat useful as a description of psychiatric ideology, but it is not useful for understanding the production or the power of beliefs in the clinic. Accounting for the day-to-day creation of identities and bodies at Walsh requires an analytic shift that can contextualize this dichotomy. In this section, I focus on scholarship informing my analysis that unpacks presumed splits between individual bodies and "culture," as well as attending dichotomies that cordon off biology and psychiatry from culture. Central to my discussion are theories that problematize any clear-cut distinction between medical power and individual agency/resistance.

In her review of "epistemologies of bodily practice and knowledge" within anthropology, Margaret Lock (1993) writes that research since the early 1980s "decentering the physical body of the basic sciences and questioning the epistemological assumptions entailed in the production of natural facts has radicalized and relativized our perspective on several recalcitrant dichotomies, in particular nature/culture, self/other, mind/body" (134). My own approach draws on such research in medical anthropology.[56] There are two particularly compelling reasons to question the commonsense notion that "the body" (or "the psyche") is separable from "culture" in the case of anorexia: first, a struggle with anorexia *actively crafts* a certain kind of body; and second, no clinical study to date has been able to determine an etiology for anorexia that can be framed in terms of an "objective" psychological or biological cause (every physiological disturbance associated with anorexia can be shown to be secondary to extreme weight loss). I suggest that one of the challenges anorexia presents to the discipline of psychiatry is a living "cultural critique" of the assumption that the body is an acultural entity. At the same time, then, I take issue with some feminist arguments about anorexia's etiology that appear to bracket out "the body" as less important than "culture."

Increasingly, scholars in a range of disciplines are analyzing the body as a socially and culturally constituted entity. Much of this research is concerned with the naturalization of power through the body and draws on the work of Foucault (1975, 1978, 1979, 1980a)—and, for some, Bourdieu (1977, 1984, 1990)—who argue that normative perceptions of the body, both lay and "official" (e.g., psychiatric), are rooted in everyday cultural practices that work to socialize the body. Individuals literally shape their bodies in expected ways, and in this process, social expectations are made to seem "natural." Foucault's work along these lines is particularly relevant for my discussion here, and is well known in critical accounts of medicine and psychiatry: he shows how medicalized ideas about bodily health and fitness are culturally produced, so that seemingly "objective" (acultural) psychiatric mandates to control the body actually encode powerful social norms (see especially Foucault 1975). This insight is important for understanding why anorexia is difficult to treat. Because the discipline of psychiatry helps to naturalize and even to create dominant Euro-American symbolic formulations and practices of bodily ordering, and because anorexia embodies contemporary ideals of femininity, it is no surprise that therapies often recreate anorexic symptomatology. For example, as I show in my previous work (Gremillion 1992), psychoanalytic therapies coupled with behaviorist treatments represent health as an "objective" control over an internal weakness or deficit; but ironically, patients themselves work to control a perceived "internal weakness" as part of their illness experience.

However, while Bourdieu's and Foucault's theories help to explain how therapies for anorexia participate in the problem, they can go only so far in helping us to understand patients' resistance to treatment. Both authors tend to unify operations of power in their writings, even though they analyze the sociocultural constitution of different forms of subjectivity. Although Foucault (1978) has famously claimed that "where there is power, there is resistance" (95), he tends to write about both power and resistance in generalized ways.[57] To adequately explore the phenomenon of anorexic patients' resistance, it is important to consider the specific and disruptive effects of gender. Here I draw on the work of a number of feminist scholars who have developed Foucault's work by examining contradictory or contested constructions of gendered bodies, particularizing his overly abstract remarks about subjects' resistance to power.[58]

In her influential work *The Woman in the Body: A Cultural Analysis of Reproduction*, anthropologist Emily Martin (1987) shows that in a clinical setting, female patients are likely to be cast as "victims" of their own bodies, even when, as in the case of anorexia, they conform to values that are culturally sanctioned. She analyzes the cultural construction of childbirth in this light and shows that many women are compelled to resist medical practices surrounding labor and delivery. Martin argues that the dramatic increase in the number of cesarean sections performed in the decades before the publication of her book was due primarily not to medical emergencies but to a cultural notion that women are passive during childbirth. Several of Martin's informants who had received C-sections in the past, and were advised against future vaginal deliveries, asserted their own wishes to deliver a child vaginally by refusing to appear at the hospital to deliver their next child until it was too late to perform a C-section. Martin's work shows how medical constructions of feminine "nature" can highlight *social* relationships and cultural ideals that inhibit women and often engender struggle and resistance.

My own analysis draws on Martin's work and related scholarship about gender and the body, and it also emphasizes the complexities of resistance and its relationship to the status quo. A number of cultural anthropologists and cultural studies scholars have challenged the notion that resistance to sociocultural ideals and relations of power necessarily implies a fully *oppositional* stance. For example, in an early account of this kind addressing youth subcultures in postwar Britain, Dick Hebdige (1988) shows how rockers, skinheads, and punks often express rebellion through the appropriation and reconfiguration of dominant symbols and values. This theoretical approach allows for an analysis of cultural struggle and change as it occurs gradually, in practice, at a level that is not always self-consciously "activist."[59] There have been few applications of this approach to ethnographic studies of illness and medicine in American or European contexts, even though the medical anthropological literature widely recognizes that illness can often express a subtle and ambiguous form of social "protest" (Comaroff 1981; Good 1977; I. Lewis 1971; Scheper-Hughes and Lock 1991). One notable exception is feminist anthropologist Rayna Rapp's 1999 study of a range of women's responses to amniocentesis. Rapp shows that refusing amniocentesis, or interpreting its meanings in ways that clinicians might not predict or support, is not the same as refusing the medicalization of pregnancy. The two can coexist, and Rapp's research also suggests that ethnographic attention to difference and dissent in this area could reconfigure received understandings of motherhood and, to some extent, conceptualizations of viable personhood. Another exception is medical anthropologist Mark Nichter's 1998 essay "The Mission within the Madness," which describes a hospital patient's so-called "borderline personality disorder, hypochondriasis, and chronic pain of psychogenic origin" as "self-initiated medicalization," which afforded this patient agency and control in a system that could not control or "manage" her to clinicians' satisfaction (330). Nichter analyses self-initiated medicalization as a complex form of resistance against medical authority on its own terms.

Anorexia provides an ideal case study for this type of analysis. Unlike the women Martin interviewed—who *rejected* the imposed idea that they should play a passive role during childbirth—patients diagnosed with anorexia challenge medical and social power by *exaggerating* medicalized norms of self-control and bodily "fitness." Patients' resistance to treatment points to culturally constituted instabilities and fractures within medical discourse itself. In fact, chapter 1 shows that clinicians and staff at Walsh are compelled to accommodate, and even encourage, patients' resistances, in part because of changing cultural definitions of anorexia. These resistances have been constitutive of the rapidly shifting set of clinical practices designed to treat anorexia.

Note that hospital settings are not the only sites where the embodied forms of power I analyze in this book are both naturalized and contested. But it is particularly important to examine critically the cultural production of medical discourse about anorexia. Following Taussig, I argue that when clinicians and patients objectify patients' problems, they *"invigorate* cultural axioms" (Taussig 1980, 3; italics mine). Psychiatric treatments for anorexia invigorate contradictory cultural axioms about, for example, feminine fitness and individualism, not only re-creating but also intensifying patients' historically particular sociocultural conflicts. Because of this intensification, a clinical setting is ripe for exploring anorexia's cultural constitution. In other words, claims to psychiatric "objectivity"—claims that sometimes incite the charge of medical "alienation" from cultural meaning[60]—in fact do more than paper over the cultural conditions of their production. Hospital settings are important sites of struggle because these claims to objectivity render explicit what are normally implicit, everyday assumptions about the "nature" of bodies and subjectivities (for related arguments, see Comaroff 1982; Comaroff and Maguire 1981). I will show that in the treatment of anorexia, when psychiatric discourse mystifies the social shaping of bodies and persons through medical objectification, it also crystallizes certain ideas and practices that are designed to create fit and healthy bodies (and that, ironically, patients can use to support their anorexia).

My analysis is indebted to recent feminist readings of technoscientific discourse and practice.[61] Charis Cussins's (1998a) account of medical objectification in an infertility clinic is a good example. Unlike many feminist critics of science, Cussins shows that objectification does not necessarily lead to a loss of agency for women patients, and that, in fact, some important forms of agency in the clinic require it.

What is more, medical discourse allows patients "new access" to bodily processes and parts related to pregnancy: "it renders the parts visible and manipulable" (180).[62] Of course, infertility patients are different from most patients at Walsh, in that they actively seek treatment and are therefore self-consciously motivated to achieve embodied agency in medicalized terms. Nevertheless, Cussins's ideas are helpful for my own analysis because at Walsh, as in the infertility clinic, moments of overt rebellion are by no means the only moments that afford opportunities for critical analysis and for the renegotiation of medical meanings: "there is every reason to believe that [the clinics'] *normal* workings can yield clues as to its construction" (171; italics mine). For this reason, it is important to "work with a reconceptualization of agency that decouples any unproblematic linking between agency and the good"—as in, good for "escaping" medical objectification (193).[63] At Walsh, patients' resistance to treatment sometimes takes the form of deploying "objective" psychiatric discourse in surprising ways, underlining the power of "objectivity," but also disrupting psychiatric claims to seamless and authoritative accounts of illness and health.

Theorizing the Body

Because a person who struggles with anorexia alters and shapes her body in conjunction with historically and culturally specific discourses, one might say that anorexic bodies are "constructed": they are thoroughly embedded in culturally normalized, gendered ideals surrounding dieting, fitness, the micromanagement of food and of body shape, and efforts to subordinate the flesh to willpower. But a difficult question arises when analyzing anorexia and its treatment in this way, and it is a question that can be posed about constructionist analyses of the body more generally: What is the status of the real material stakes involved? How can one speak about the "construction" of anorexia—and the "anorexic body" in particular—and also communicate serious concern about the physical dangers of the problem, and the real suffering involved? Does a constructionist approach risk ignoring actual anorexic bodies? These questions echo clinicians' criticisms of the feminist cultural model cited earlier but are more focused on theorizing the body than they are with defining disciplinary "turf."

Constructionism does not preclude attention to bodily "reality." I take seriously the lived, material realities of both anorexia and biomedical practice, and I argue that these realities cannot be explained adequately in biomedical terms (as they are currently conceived). At the same time, I suggest that certain of these biomedical terms remain unproblematized by, and can even be reproduced within, constructionist theory.

Some constructionist scholarship does appear to ignore the "reality" of the body. As cultural theorist R. W. Connell (1995) remarks about these constructionists, "with so much emphasis on the signifier, the signified tends to vanish"; their discussions seem oddly disembodied (50–51). In their analysis of "postmodern bodies," Arthur Kroker and Marilouise Kroker (1987) assert explicitly that the body is no more, claiming that a general obsession with the body in the United States today gives the matter away: "Why the concern over the body today if not to emphasize the fact that the (natural) body in the postmodern condition has *already* disappeared, and what we experience as the body is only a fantastic simulacra of body rhetorics?" (21–22).[64]

However, in spite of claims to remove the body from the realm of "nature," much of this research actually (implicitly) posits a prediscursive corporeality in an effort to articulate social and cultural determinations of the body. This prediscursive body appears to be, necessarily, devoid of meaningful content (in this sense, it differs from the "natural body" posited in biomedicine, a body that is subject to "natural law"). But the assumed body in these constructionist theories does, in fact, carry a specific meaning: it is imagined as a kind of blank slate for imprinting dominant social scripts and is therefore—like the biomedical body—a relatively passive object available for human intervention (Grosz 1994; Haraway 1991b, 1991d; Price and Shildrick 1999). So I suggest that when constructionist accounts do not adequately theorize the lived materiality of bodily experience, the problem is not so much that they ignore the body; rather, they define constructionism as a (rather totalizing) process that operates on and through a material plane that is taken for granted. For example, in her analysis of anorexia as a "crystallization" of "cultural pathology," Susan Bordo (1993a) asserts that gendered forms of social control are "etched" on the anorexic body (164), even as she argues that "there is no 'natural' body," because the body "is constantly 'in the grip,' as Foucault puts it, of cultural practices" (142). As Elizabeth Grosz (1994) points out about Bordo's position on this topic, the "very status of the body as [cultural] product . . . remains at stake here" (143).[65]

The status of the body as a cultural product is very much at stake within biomedicine, as well. The cultural production of bodies remains almost entirely untheorized within biomedicine, but as I have stressed throughout this introduction, it is important not to assume an absence of cultural discourses in the medical treatment of bodies. This book shows how medical and psychiatric practitioners actively craft the particular kinds of bodies that they claim merely to describe, diagnose, and normalize (according to seemingly "universal" standards)—producing very real, and socially located, embodied effects by acting as if these bodies preexist both socialization and medicalization. Further, I show that the female body is not simply given as raw material for the cultural and medical work that goes on in the clinic; rather, it is created in and through this work. More specifically, and more to the point regarding a critical analysis of social constructionist theory, I argue that treatments for anorexia invoke and produce an understanding and a lived experience of the body as stubbornly "natural"—an understanding and experience that is culturally and historically specific (although it is *represented* as objective, biomedical truth). I suggest that these are the ethnographic and analytic terrains to explore in order to adequately understand the undeniable corporeality of anorexic bodies. My approach follows Judith Butler (1993) and Donna Haraway (1991c, 1997b) in their understanding of normalized bodies as the *material effects,* the corporeal instantiations (over time), of particular sociocultural practices and discourses. I bring this kind of analysis to bear on certain institutional practices and lived experiences of "health" in the making. My analysis is mindful of Haraway's claim that many arguments "against 'biological determinism' and for 'social constructionism' . . . have [not] been] powerful in deconstructing how bodies . . . appear as objects of knowledge and sites of intervention in 'biology' " (1991b, 134).

While I agree with the intent of "radical" constructionist approaches to deontologize representations of the body as natural, I believe that they overlook a crucial question: namely, how is it that people *experience* their bodies as natural? In other words, "deconstructing" the body does not allow for a consideration of the social and cultural practices that render the body a seemingly natural object. In failing to consider this question, some constructionists fall short on their own terms by reinscribing the body as an acultural "thing."[66] In these accounts, the body tends to be cordoned off as a mere resource for the activity of social construction itself.[67]

But the metaphor of corporeality as "resource" can be unpacked—

this kind of body is an imagined natural object of a particular kind. I will show that to understand anorexia and its treatment, it is imperative that we not reproduce this metaphor uncritically, because it is the very subject at hand: patients and clinicians alike view the body and biomedical criteria of health as resources for the construction of identities. In addition, I show that the female body is read and experienced as *both* a resource *and* a "natural limit"—that is, as an uncooperative resource— in this task. If the crafting of feminine identity is experienced in these ways, and not merely as abstract social forces but in and through lived, embodied practices and through struggles over bodies "on the ground," we can consider the problematic status of "material stakes" and "physical limits" in social constructionist theories to be part and parcel of the (gendered) cultural field in question.

One could argue that an anthropologically informed phenomenological account of anorexic embodiment would offer an alternative to a radical constructionist approach without falling into biological determinism. While some of my descriptions in this book might be characterized as phenomenological, I am less concerned with the kind of questions that usually inform such an analysis (for example, questions about the relationship between the body and consciousness) than I am with unraveling lived articulations of historically specific North American discourses of identity that are manifest in anorexic bodies.[68] For example, I ask: What particular cultural practices lead anorexic patients, and the clinicians who work with them, to construe the female body as an uncooperative resource? More generally, why is the body such a productive effect of power in the United States today, such an important site for identity construction (and such a popular topic of analysis in the social sciences)?

Hegemonic Constructions of Identity

Throughout this book, I situate the body as one discourse among many within a particular social formation—postindustrial U.S. society—in which "fitness" is figured as a cultural dominant. I borrow this approach from cultural theorist Stuart Hall (1986, 1988), who maintains that hegemony is achieved when a *multiplicity* of ideas, practices, and institutions are aligned in a system of rule, which therefore always contains "a plurality of discourses—[e.g.,] about the family, the economy, national identity, morality, crime, law, women, human nature" (Hall 1988, 53). Furthermore, these discourses do not at every moment converge into a neatly unified construct. By unpacking the naturaliza-tion of fit bodies and subjectivities within psychiatric categories, I show that these categories are continually created and negotiated through contested social processes. If patients and clinicians struggle over the terms of fitness even when they are explicitly naturalized (as part of an "objective" discourse), then the fit body must be seen as an unstable entity within a wider cultural nexus of identity formation.

In two different chapters, I focus on hegemonic constructions of family life. A vast body of clinical literature on "anorexic families" and family therapy normalizes and authorizes particular ideals of person-hood that warrant scrutiny. Mother blaming is widespread and arguably contributes to anorexia's conditions of possibility. Attending to repre-sentations of maternal caretaking in both family therapy discourse and clinical practice, I suggest that mothers, like female bodies, are figured as problematic "resources" for the creation of their daughters' identi-ties. A critical analysis of these representations within psychiatry and psychology is important not only for pointing up their unstable and contested character but also as an intervention against their naturaliza-tion. The prominent sociologist of the body Bryan Turner cites "facts" in the psychological literature on anorexia to support the claim that a "principal dynamic in the social aetiology of this disease is the conflict between the daughter and the over-protective mother" (1992, 224), who is "overpowering," "dominant," preoccupied with her own career, and known to "raise [her] children to satisfy [her] own interests" (1984, 192). When a sociologist can cite as truth such deeply problematic sociocultural constructions of identity because they have been natu-ralized in psychological discourse—especially when we consider that much of Turner's work challenges psychiatric discourse—these repre-sentations require careful unpacking.[69]

I also explore articulations of race, class, and gender in psychiatric accounts of "human nature" by considering how psychiatric practices help to create a higher number of (recognized) cases of eating disorders among relatively privileged young women. Patients who are perceived as ideal candidates for treatment tend to be middle-class and white, and clinicians often argue that certain patients, patients who are both non-white and working-class, cannot participate fully in the treatment pro-gram because of a "personality disorder" or a "chaotic family." I show that disagreements among hospital staff about how to care for these "difficult" patients can highlight, disturb, and sometimes begin to transform culturally dominant ideas about "good" patients and families in the clinic.

My analysis of identity construction as a hegemonic process extends a perspective that is often adopted in cross-cultural research within the fields of medical and psychological anthropology. In their efforts to show how the notion of bounded, rational, autonomous individualism—assumed in Western medical constructions of illness and health—is a "cultural" rather than (or in addition to) a "natural" phenomenon, some scholars in these fields write about a singular "Western self," as a way to provide a foil for examining selfhood in (a) "non-Western" context(s) (see especially Kleinman 1986; Scheper-Hughes and Lock 1987; Schweder 1991). For example, Anne Becker (1995) argues that attention to feeding and nurturing bodies in Fiji is not about cultivating the individual body but about congealing specific kinds of social relationships and collective concerns within bodily practices. The key to her analysis is a contrast between American and Fijian ideas about personhood. Becker argues that in Fiji, one is focused on the bodily experiences of *others* because of a relational understanding of personhood, while in the United States, autonomous individualism leads to a focus on one's own bodily experiences. But I would argue that collective concerns and multiple narratives are at work in the United States in the production and naturalization of *individual* bodies and selves, as well. Certain of these discourses—those that predominate in the treatment of anorexia—are the subject of this book. I now provide an overview of these topics by chapter.

Chapter Summaries

In chapter 1, I argue that the fit body is an icon for contemporary American imperatives to achieve individual productivity and self-control by successfully managing new incitements to consume, incitements to indulge the body with food and other forms of leisure. Fitness practices are both predicated on, and productive of, bodies that are imagined as personal resources for work on the "self," work that signals an ability to consume in a productive and efficient way. But because fitness as a cultural dominant contains multiple meanings, it also contains contradictions, and anorexia reveals that feminine fitness in particular is a contradictory construct. I show that in the second half of the twentieth century, uneven changes in dominant discourses about women's "consumption work" have rendered the female body a more problematic resource for fitness than the male body. Many women and girls today experience repeated temptations to eat and serve food, even as they are enjoined to diet and exercise, so that crafting a fit female body seems to require heroic efforts. Anorexia, and chronic dieting more generally, are dramatic enactments of the contradictions entailed in feminine fitness: the harder one works to create a fit body and identity, the more the body's desires and appetites seem to be obstacles in this task, until finally the body itself is at risk of being consumed.

Psychiatric treatments for anorexia participate in the contradictions of feminine fitness. While treatment practices are meant to create fit and healthy bodies, young women struggling with anorexia take them up for their own purposes. Patients are consistently able to deploy seemingly "objective" and gender-neutral psychiatric assessments of the body and psyche in the service of anorexia, pointing to the gendered contradictions implicit in these assessments.

Chapter 2 provides a concrete ethnographic example of gradual change in American ideals of the family. Most patients are engaged in family therapy as part of their treatment, and in keeping with the perceived need for "flexible" family structures in an advanced capitalist system, which Judith Stacey (1990) describes in her work, therapists attempt to loosen family ties—mother-daughter "enmeshment," in particular—in order to support "individuation" in the family. But patients' mothers are still expected to assume nurturing familial roles, putting others' needs before their own as a matter of choice. This chapter shows that rhetorics of individual freedom and choice reconfigure, but do not revolutionize, "traditional" ideas about maternal caretaking. For instance, patients' mothers are encouraged to give up the role of caretaking to the treatment program, but a "minimal" degree of natural mothering is still required. Further, assumptions about what I call "minimal motherhood" help to justify keeping from mothers information about their daughters' progress in treatment, an exclusion that, paradoxically, produces a level of maternal investment in the treatment process that is seen as a central part of patients' problems.

Chapter 3 continues the analysis begun in chapter 2 by exploring the hierarchical production of sexual difference, and the naturalization of "minimal" motherhood, within the so-called "therapeutic family." Clinicians and staff think of the treatment team as a substitute family that models gender equality, but when a female clinician voices a controversial opinion, her assertion of difference is often seen as a sign that the supposed unity of the therapeutic family—ordinarily expressed as such by a powerful male figure on the treatment team—needs to be reestablished. So even as contemporary psychiatric discourse actively challenges prescribed gender roles in the family, ideas about familial health continue to create and conceal familiar gendered inequalities. At the same time, the imagined effects of personal family histories on the professional work of female staff highlight contradictions in the cultural and therapeutic construction of minimal motherhood. As a result, the gendered logic of therapeutic family "unity" is sometimes disrupted.

Chapter 4 analyzes the race and class politics of "healthy" families and subjectivities at Walsh. White, middle-class patients are the only patients imagined to be always already "fit" for effective treatment, and certain nonwhite, working-class patients are excluded from full participation in the treatment program. At the same time, these "difficult" patients seem to embody, to an excessive degree, important qualities of personhood that relatively privileged patients and their families appear to lack. In this way, notions of health on the unit are written in and through the exclusion of identities that seem to deviate from white, middle-class ideals of personhood. This chapter also traces a history of these ideals in the development of structural family therapy, an influential model for conceptualizing therapeutic "family" relations at Walsh (relations among clinicians, staff, and patients).

In the epilogue, I discuss "narrative therapy" both as an alternative approach to the treatment of anorexia and as a clinical application of many of the theories of identity formation, medical power, and resistance that are explored in this book. Drawing on a Foucauldian critique of scientific epistemology and practice to reformulate concepts and experiences of identity that dominate the mental-health professions, narrative therapists treat illness as a "problem story" that is supported by powerful cultural specifications for identity, and they create alternative stories with clients by focusing on life experiences that these norms fail to capture. As a result, the active, collaborative, and ongoing work involved in both the construction of, and resistance against, "problem identities" is rendered more visible. In many ways, a narrative approach to anorexia is a radical departure from current practice at

Walsh, but I suggest that its conditions of possibility are present there (in fact, as I discuss in chapter 2, there is at least one clinician at Walsh who engages in narrative work with patients one-on-one). The full incorporation of such an approach would render more explicit, and would begin to transform, important tensions and contradictions that already exist in the treatment program.

ONE

Crafting Resourceful Bodies
and Achieving Identities

This chapter explores the ways in which patients diagnosed with anorexia and the clinicians and staff who work with them construe bodies as resources for fitness and health. I situate this corporeal imaginary within advanced capitalist consumer culture in the United States, in which the fit body is an icon for achieving individualism, productivity, and "self-actualization." The crafting of bodies in the treatment process participates in the cultural conditions of possibility for imagining the fit body in these ways and also for the flourishing of eating disorders. Clinicians and staff at Walsh often represent health as an "objective" category, but the ever-negotiated meanings of health on the unit—and the problematic effects of objectivism itself on patients—belie claims that definitions of health are simply the product of a unified "expert opinion" (which is, ideally, to be incorporated cleanly into patients' identities).

I begin with a discussion of how patients' resistance to treatment, which clinicians actually encourage, participates in cultural constructions of feminine fitness that have permeated many treatment programs in the past twenty years. Next I provide a broad social and economic context for understanding the contradictions and difficulties involved in the pursuit of fitness for women and girls in particular. Finally, a case study of one patient's struggles in treatment illustrates the contingent and contested character of bodies and selves in the treatment of anorexia.

"Resourcing" Resistance to Treatment

Patients at Walsh are caught up in discourses of health and fitness in complex ways. They are not only medically stabilized through weight gain and engaged in therapeutic discussions about the psychological meanings of anorexia but are also directly enlisted in the reshaping of their bodies according to parameters that are not of their own choosing. Their active participation in this process, and their resistances against it, are analyzed as part and parcel of their therapy. Thus patients' desires and protests, the micromanagement of patients' bodies, patients' lived bodily experiences, and cultural definitions of ideal and pathological bodies are inextricably intertwined.

I first met Sarah in the outpatient clinic, when she was seventeen years old. She had been admitted to the hospital twice in the past, and like many outpatients who are "old-timers," Sarah had learned to hover just above her admission weight, a weight that would medically justify readmission to the inpatient unit. Several clinicians wanted to find another justification for readmitting Sarah to the inpatient ward so that she would comply with a weight gain program. But her psychiatrist, Mark, decided to devise an outpatient plan for her instead, because she was showing a resistance to her caretakers that he considered to be "healthy." Mark pointed out that Sarah was furious, not passive or helpless, about their insistence that she gain weight. According to Mark, Sarah's anger betrayed an investment in the clinicians' designs for her health but also showed that she was not complying by rote. In other words, Sarah was showing a promising balance between compliance and independence, and Mark thought this meant that she was beginning to develop the healthy "sense of self" that she needed to overcome her anorexia. His theory was that as long as Sarah cared enough about her independence to maintain a weight that would keep her out of the hospital, her resistance was a sign that she was capable of developing the desire to gain more weight on her own. Mark's strategy with Sarah was consistent with most clinicians' belief that resistance to treatment can be seen as a form of psychological "work" that locates responsibility with individual patients. On subsequent visits to the outpatient clinic, when Sarah had not gained enough weight for that day (as determined by her new plan), a common refrain was that "she has work to do," and the frequency of her clinic visits would increase (Sarah hated coming to the clinic, so this move was "incentive" for her to gain weight).[1] When Sarah gained the required weight, she was allowed to come to the clinic less often, and as one clinician put it, "She's working hard; this is *hard* for her. She's doing this, and her whole being is telling her not to." Sarah did gain weight as an outpatient, but it was slow going, and she remained incredibly frustrating to those who believed that she should be admitted to the hospital again.

Most patients diagnosed with anorexia resist gaining weight, and Mark's ideas about Sarah's treatment illustrate how some contemporary approaches to treatment have drawn on psychological theory to respond to this problem. Programs like the one where I conducted my research include various psychotherapies designed to facilitate patients' autonomy. For these programs, the ultimate goal of treatment is not just weight gain but also "self-development" and "self-actualization."[2] Generally speaking, contemporary psychological theory about anorexia suggests that the problem results from an inadequate sense of self and that it functions as a kind of substitute identity that is an overrigid, highly controlled "pseudoautonomy" (Crisp 1996; Garner and Garfinkel 1997). As discussed in the introduction, imposed weight gain only seems to heighten patients' experiences that they are not in control of their own identities. Thus treatment focuses increasingly on *creating the desire for health*. With this approach, resistance to treatment is often seen as a sign of healthy independence and is even encouraged. Clinicians often draw on patients' resistance as a way to create a desire for health by tapping into patients' extreme devotion to a work ethic.[3] Clinicians use resistance to treatment as leverage for transforming an "anorexic" work ethic into a "healthy" one, converting a relentless striving for weight loss into effort toward weight gain.[4]

This focus on patients' independence and self-determination, and even on their resistance to medical authority, appears to allow patients more freedom than treatment approaches that focus solely on weight gain. However, "cutting-edge" psychiatric treatments for anorexia have medicalized and invigorated cultural ideals of feminine fitness, ideals that have informed anorexia's recent increase in incidence. Anorexia exaggerates specifications for feminine fitness, and representations of health as an object of patients' resistance—requiring hard work, bodily transformation, and self-development—also adopt the terms of these cultural ideals.

Before I analyze discourses of fitness within psychiatric practice, let me provide some theoretical context for understanding anorexia in terms of fitness ideals. A number of feminist scholars argue that anorexia crystallizes contradictions that many young women experience in striving for individual achievement through physical fitness.[5] While a slender and fit body signifies autonomy and success for women, it also implies dependence on others' approval. In addition, controlling bodily needs through dieting and exercise paradoxically calls attention to these needs. Anorexia highlights this contradiction; food refusal and compulsive exercising are forms of self-control that continually create the very desires that seem to require control. Of course, dominant cultural representations of fitness obscure this contradiction: fitness naturalizes the values of willpower and self-control by construing the body as a kind of personal natural resource for creating a powerful, fit, and achieving self. At the same time, however, it seems that special efforts are required to create a fit *female* body. Fitness gendered female is culturally coded as an unending struggle; as I will discuss, women and girls experience a profound contradiction between the injunction to diet in order to create a fit body, on the one hand, and incitements to consume and to serve food, on the other.

Those who live with anorexia experience this problem acutely; every day, they confront a body that appears as an enemy of willpower. Even after patients reach drastically low body weights, they feel compelled to maintain or even intensify their dieting and exercise regimes. Anorexia challenges the idea that achievement comes "naturally" through practices of fitness by revealing that the female body is imagined not only as a resource but also as an obstacle in the pursuit of fitness, an intractable other to an achieving identity. The anorexic's experience of a control paradox reveals this problem with particular clarity: with every "success" in one's efforts to control the body through dieting and exercise, the body threatens a loss of control (Bordo 1993a; Bruch 1978; Lawrence 1979, 1984). Dieting and exercise then take on a life of their own and become overwhelming preoccupations.[6]

Contemporary psychiatric treatments for anorexia participate in the contradictions of feminine fitness by representing patients' bodies and psyches as simultaneously opposed to one another and dynamically interrelated. Clinicians determine biomedical criteria of health, such as specific weights to be reached in a given time period; but at the same time, the ultimate goal of treatment is for patients to work willingly toward these markers of health. In treatment, patients' bodies are managed through a calculated balance of caloric intake and exercise, which is not up to individual patients' determination. But the body is also seen as personalized raw material (a personal "resource") that patients shape and develop in enacting a "will to health." A person who lives with anorexia is already familiar with this contradiction, "willfully"[7] engaging in forms of bodily regulation and control that, paradoxically, highlight and create hungers and needs that threaten this control precisely because they appear to lie outside of it (as "resources" for continued body work).

The psychiatric representation of "the anorexic"—in particular, the anorexic body—as a pathologized object of therapeutic knowledge and practice re-creates the culturally dominant idea that the female body is an obstacle in the making of fitness/health, and it also reinforces patients' perceived dependence on others even as they seek self-control. And just as patients exaggerate the terms of feminine fitness, they often exaggerate the terms of treatment when they are asked to incorporate biomedical criteria of health into their identities. Sarah, for example, understood her admission weight quite literally: she saw it as a cutoff point for how little she could weigh and still stay out of the hospital, where she would be required to gain more than this. Sarah was thereby subverting her treatment plan—using it to support her anorexia—even as she highlighted one literal meaning of her admission weight, reading it as (just below) an acceptable maximum, rather than minimum, weight. This situation raises the question, How do we understand a form of subversion that exaggerates the very criteria that are being subverted? More generally, how do we make sense of the fact that anorexia disturbs discourses of fitness and health without escaping them?

Cultural anthropologist Lila Abu-Lughod (1990) has suggested that resistance is best understood as "a *diagnostic* of power" (42).[8] This means that resistance is neither located "outside" of power nor merely a predetermined effect of power.[9] This latter idea is compelling in an analysis of anorexia, since resistance through anorexia is clearly self-defeating and because clinicians explicitly condone resistance to treatment as a way ultimately to convince patients to accept health as the treatment program defines it. In my earlier work (Gremillion 1992), I adopted the idea that anorexia is difficult to treat because psychiatric practices reproduce wholesale the specifications of personhood that lead to anorexia and impose these specifications in a top-down fashion. But as I discuss in the introduction, this approach cannot explain patients' resistance to treatment, and it also assumes that these specifications of personhood are totalizing and are fully formed prior to their articulation in practice. My more recent research for this book shows that patients and clinicians help create, and continually negotiate, culturally dominant understandings of subjectivity, embodiment, and health. In both adopting and disrupting treatment practices and protocols, women and girls who struggle with anorexia reveal that discourses of feminine fitness are not pregiven but achieved; even in their dominance, they are unstable.[10]

We can interpret clinicians' encouragement of patients' resistance in this light. Given the lengths to which many anorexic patients will go to resist treatment and their frequent appropriation of treatment protocols to this end, clinicians work with these forms of resistance and even interpret them positively. For example, because patients' weight and calorie intake are monitored so closely, it is no surprise to clinicians that patients will try to take back control over these intimate details of their lives that they have worked so hard to master. Although most clinicians argue that patients cannot simply be left to their own devices in these matters (because they may continue to lose weight and even risk death), patients cannot be expected to give up control over their bodies completely, or they will never learn to care for themselves outside the program. So clinicians consider resistance that incorporates the terms of treatment progress, as the following case study illustrates.

One sixteen-year-old inpatient I knew well, who asked to be called Maude Evans, agreed that she should gain weight but had difficulty doing so, and she thought that her weight criterion for discharge from the hospital was set too high (by less than half a pound). She told me that she planned to lose this much weight once she got home so that she could regain it her "own way." A member of the nursing staff remarked during rounds one day that Maude's attitude was a good sign, because she had entered the so-called legalistic phase of treatment. This phase extends over most of any given patient's history with the treatment program. A psychiatrist in the program explained treatment phases to me: "At first, patients are mousy and compliant. Then they become very legalistic, arguing the fine points of their programs and resisting you tooth and nail.[11] Finally, they start getting better, because they decide that it's not worth their time to hang out in the hospital and talk to us." In this view, nurturing patients' resistance to treatment protocols is the bread and butter of therapy.

I first began to understand that patients' resistance is not a matter of rebellion or "manipulation," as some treatment programs today (and most programs prior to about 1980) would represent it, after getting to know Maude over the course of several hospital admissions and through a series of interviews. But neither was Maude's resistance simply a self-conscious assertion of willpower, a sign of progress toward a healthy self. Maude showed me that patients' resistance to treatment was less a sign of therapeutic "progress" than it was an indication of contradictions within psychiatry that can be used to support anorexia, contradictions that shed light on the psychiatric production of bodies as resources for self-transformation.

I met Maude on the day of her first admission to the hospital, when she was at such a low weight that she was at risk of dying. Like many patients who are medically unstable when they are admitted to the hospital, Maude was immediately confined to her hospital bed with a bed warmer and placed on a heart monitor. Maude said she was scared, that things had gotten out of hand. But she also said she felt fine, that she had been eating healthy foods (in small amounts), and that just a week ago she had been going to high school, making straight As, and keeping up with all her extracurricular activities. It was a relief to Maude to be in the hospital, but it was also very strange, because she had been so independent in her life. After Maude was in the hospital for a while, however, she began to feel that the treatment program was robbing her of her independence, with all of its rules (e.g., strict scheduling for mealtimes, activities, and visiting hours) and assumptions about her behaviors and motives (e.g., that she thought she was fat even though she was underweight). For a while, she even rejected the label "anorexia," because she did not like the fact that the label carried with it such "preconceived ideas."

Several months after her first admission to the hospital, Maude talked to me about the link between weight loss and her creation of a unique and independent identity, which she equated with her ability to achieve (in school and in other activities, as well). For Maude, losing weight was no effort at all. But the effort it took to keep up with all her activities at increasingly lower weights balanced out the ease of losing weight. In this way, weight loss and achievement in other areas of her life were indirectly proportional. Maude implied that she kept losing weight so that she could continually test her ability to achieve. But at the same time, she said that this balancing act was "no big deal." It was important to Maude that her achievements felt natural to her identity, not like a test. Maude did not experience achievement as a self-conscious striving or an act of will; rather, weight loss literally fueled achievement, and Maude imagined weight loss to be an inexhaustible resource. She told me she had heard the theory that you cannot give up an eating disorder until you "hit bottom" and said this idea made no sense to her: "You never hit bottom. You can *always* go lower" (i.e., lose more weight). Maude explained that she did not think she was too fat (much of the literature on anorexia emphasizes this "body image distortion"); rather, she kept losing weight because she could not imagine stopping this form of body work that was a display of achievement.[12]

Caught up in this body work, Maude pushed her body to limits that created extremes of self-control and dependency at once. She controlled her body to an extraordinary degree, but she also became dependent on hospitalization. Not surprisingly, as she gained weight in the hospital and began preparing to go home, she ran into conflict with the treatment program over her independence and autonomy and over how to label her experience. But Maude was not asserting her independence within the treatment program in a purely oppositional way. Rather, to return to the example I mentioned earlier, her plan to lose some of the weight she gained in the hospital in order to gain it again on her own allowed her to convert her dependence on the treatment program—and on its "objective" criteria for her health—into a form of individual achievement that was consistent with the view that one should, ultimately, resource one's own body. Maude took her discharge weight seriously, as an important goal to achieve, but as with other forms of achievement in her life, she was paradoxically compelled to "own" it through weight loss (to be regained on her own time). Of course, Maude ran the risk of never gaining the weight again on her own, just as Sarah had consistently interpreted her admission weight as falling just below her maximum allowable weight. But again, the point I want to emphasize is that patients do not deliberately set out to use treatment protocols for the purpose of crafting anorexic bodies, no more than they display signs of new, healthy bodies and selves through such an appropriation. In the following section, I show that imperatives to accept representations of the female body as a body that will necessarily put on weight (asserted very strongly in the treatment program)—*and* imperatives to resist weight gain (*also* underscored in the treatment process)—are both part and parcel of the cultural practices of feminine fitness that anorexia highlights.

To provide a broader context for analyzing conflicts in treatment, I now briefly examine the ways in which cultural discourses of fitness represent the female body as a quintessentially consuming body and therefore as an obstacle in the pursuit of fitness. Although fitness is a form of bodily control that, ideologically, includes both men and women, the female body is not perceived as a "productive" resource for crafting a fit body. Rather, it is perceived as both a resource and a natural limit in this task. Feminine fitness is construed and experienced as a constant battle to control consumption, in part because, in spite of the fact that fitness is imagined as a gender-equalizing form of body work, "ideal" womanhood today is also tied to seemingly less productive forms of consumption work that are entailed in domestic caretaking.

The Cultural Constitution of Feminine Fitness

Since the mid-1970s in the United States, fitness has become a dominant icon of bodily health and individual productivity. Eating well and working out are now seen as markers of success, and health is a do-it-yourself endeavor, encoding a work ethic. As Robert Crawford (1985) writes, "The ethic of health must be like the ethic of work. The Protestant world view extends to the body; it invades the domain of leisure" (67). But Crawford notes that fitness is not only imagined as an expression of self-control; it also encodes "release." Exercise in particular revitalizes, reduces stress; working out "works out" tension. In turn, exercise is said to energize work.[13]

So fitness is "work" on the self that signifies the ability and energy to perform productive work. "Working out" is a revealing phrase: it indicates a form of work that is extroverted and expressive, a "productive" release of energy. In this way, the construct of the fit body merges the capitalist dualities of control and release, work and play, constraint and freedom. More specifically, fitness expresses personal competence in managing the dynamic and so-called flexible relationship between production and consumption that characterizes advanced capitalism.[14] Exercise allows for a seemingly productive management of consumption;

late capitalist "overconsumptionism" (M. Davis 1984) requires that we put consumption to good use, that we render consumption productive so that we may consume again. Many of us now feel the urge to "work off" the food that we eat. Fitness practices are both predicated on, and productive of, bodies that are imagined as personal resources for work on the self, work that signals an ability to consume in a productive and efficient way.

In allowing one to "work off" the signs of consumption and leisure / relaxation that appear on the body, fitness confers a racialized and classed "distinction" (see Bourdieu 1984). Discourses of fitness target white middle-class groups and the "upwardly mobile" (Bordo 1993b; Nichter and Nichter 1991; H. Schwartz 1986). Crawford notes that the contradictory construct of "health" he examines was expressed primarily by the middle-class professionals he interviewed. "Blue collar workers also spoke of health in terms of the virtues of discipline although there was not the same idea of pursuing health as an active goal" (Crawford 1985, 71). For these interviewees, health as "release" was more often coded as a refusal of discipline than a doctoring of "stress."

But is fitness really coded as white? The visibility and hype of dieting and fitness regimes for nonwhite media celebrities such as Oprah Winfrey might seem to challenge a hegemony of whiteness in this area. Certainly the racial and ethnic "profile" of the fit body may be shifting. But to identify the racialized and classed coding of bodily norms is not to claim that these norms map directly onto particular population groups. Also, arguably, a white middle-class standard is being applied to nonwhite bodies—a standard that is itself written though representations of female bodies of color as quintessentially fleshy and unproductive. In particular, the lingering image of the corpulent "black mammy" haunts U.S. constructions of fit and beautiful female bodies in its position as an other to these constructions (B. Thompson 1994b; Modleski 1997). This image, which has served historically to set white women apart from "deviant" black femininities (Bogle 1973; Collins 2000), today informs representations of poor black welfare mothers as simultaneously lazy, fat, and insufficiently or improperly feminine.[15] It may also contribute to representations of African American women's and girls' body ideals as healthier and less tightly controlled than those of middle- and upper-class white women and girls (but we should be wary of romanticizing generalizations about the black female body, a move that also marks these bodies as other, albeit in a positively valued sense).[16]

Intersections of class, race, and gender here are thoroughgoing. Based on her interviews with African American girls struggling with eating problems, sociologist Becky Thompson (1994b) writes about discourses of slimming within black families as narratives of whitening, feminizing, and moving up the social ladder. She addresses similar themes within Latino and Jewish families, as well. Thompson points out that these discourses do not by any means capture all the meanings of eating difficulties; they can, however, render invisible alternative readings of these difficulties (e.g., readings that consider the effects of racism, poverty, and sexual abuse).

The contemporary ideal of slender and fit femininity appears to cut across racial, class-based, and ethnic lines to the extent that it codes for heteronormativity, a point that Thompson emphasizes in her 1994 book *A Hunger So Wide and So Deep* in a section entitled "Grooming Girls to be Heterosexual." According to Thompson, for the vast majority of girls and young women in the United States, to be thin and "in shape" is to be sexy and therefore pleasing to men and, hence, appropriately feminine. The interlocking set of cultural discourses supporting these notions—from the media, from parents and peers, and from school systems—fixates on the production of sexual difference (later I briefly discuss differences in discourses of masculine and feminine fitness that shed some light on this point). However, feminine fitness is also more complex than this picture alone allows. In contrast to a strong focus for women of color on becoming more feminine by slimming down, fitness for white career women *also* signifies in the popular imagination a purportedly gender-equalizing work ethic that emerged in the 1970s. For these women and girls, fitness is a form of achievement that promises to counterbalance gender difference; in fact, this promise may be part and parcel of the racialized and classed distinctions that fitness confers for this group. White career women, and white women and girls who are upwardly mobile, are seen to be more "like men" when they work toward fitness (in keeping with the tenets of liberal feminism that have gone mainstream).

I focus in this section on problems with, and contradictions within, this gender-equalizing ideology, for two reasons. First, this ideology, when left unquestioned, could mute a critical analysis of feminine body ideals that focuses only on the overt production of a relatively docile (to men) heteronormative femininity. I will argue that sexual difference is produced through gender-equalizing ideals of fitness as well, but in more complicated and covert ways.[17] Second, many feminist analyses of anorexia suggest that it actually entails a *rejection* of heteronormative femininity (even as it exaggerates certain feminine body ideals). In a rereading of Freudian takes on anorexia as a fear of femininity, some see symbolic political protest in the erasure of "womanly" curves, the cessation of menstruation, the crafting of a "boyish" physique, and the reported lack of interest in sexual expression in general.[18] This picture of anorexia's relationship to femininity problematizes the idea that culturally ideal female bodies can be reduced to docile and subordinate players in heteronormative representations of sexual difference. Note, however, that it also paints anorexia as a refusal of the feminine. I believe that a more complex account of anorexia requires a more complex analysis of ideal femininity. Apart from, or rather in addition to, an obvious commitment to thinness, what distinctive representations of female personhood do women and girls struggling with anorexia *embrace* (and at times reconfigure or challenge)?

Let us return, then, to the political economy of fitness as a seemingly gender-equalizing form of body "work." I have mentioned that since the 1970s, fitness ideals have signaled a more dynamic relationship between production and consumption, as well as a new form of social and economic power for women. In contrast, the dichotomy of production/consumption in the 1950s rested on a strong ideological, gendered bifurcation between the workplace and the home space (and between the mind and body). But with the accelerated and "flexible" modes of market production that were consolidated in the 1970s, the gendered spheres of productive work and consumption/leisure have appeared to interpenetrate. As Donna Haraway (1991a) writes, with the extreme mobility of capital and the systematic de-skilling, or "feminization," of work, the "factory, home, and market are integrated on a new scale" (166). The paid workforce includes more and more well-to-do women, and in addition, new imperatives to indulge mean that consumption has gradually moved out of the privatized domestic domain. In this context, fitness becomes a powerful icon for a highly individualistic consumer society in which work and its rewards—that is, consumption and leisure—are thought to combine within successful individuals, male and female, and are thought to "work themselves out" through the body.

However, while relatively privileged women are seen to be just as capable of creating fit, achieving identities as are men, most jobs open to these women are relatively low-paying and unstable jobs in the service sector, and women are still considered to be the sole or primary domestic caretakers. So most women are still socially positioned as less-productive workers than men, and women remain the icons and agents of a seemingly less productive form of consumer management in the home (Ewen 1988; Haraway 1991a). In short, contemporary ideologies of individual productivity exist alongside older discourses of production and consumption that are linked to "women's work" and appear to undermine fitness as an equal-opportunity form of achievement.

Indeed, feminine fitness is coded as a particularly difficult achievement. This difficulty is naturalized through the cultural production of the female body as an inefficient, or uncooperative, resource for fitness. Dominant discourses of feminine fitness represent the female body as a consuming body, a body that is limited in its productivity because it cannot "work off" consumption easily. Eating is seen as a particularly enticing indulgence for women that must be controlled not only through exercise but also through dieting. Roughly 75 percent of women in the United States consider themselves to be "too fat" (Bordo 1993a; Boskind-White 2000), and approximately 50 percent of women in the United States are on a diet at any given time (Boskind-White 2000). However, almost all diets fail, creating desires to eat that disrupt the efficient equation between eating and exercise that supposedly renders consumption productive.[19] Joan Brumberg (1989) notes that more than 95 percent of dieters regain the weight they lose and that they diet again and again. Nevertheless dieting is coded as a necessary component of feminine fitness. A woman's ability to achieve productive individualism depends on her ability to diet successfully, even though most people experience dieting as an endless cycle.

Most patients I interviewed felt compelled to do constant battle with the temptation to eat and with fat on their bodies. I heard many times that any amount of fat in the food one eats will immediately appear as body fat; several people remarked that the body can convert any kind of food into fat. For women and girls who struggle with anorexia, a refusal to show these signs of consumption on their bodies indicates individual achievement.[20] For them, the "solution" to the seemingly unresolvable cultural tension between productivity and consumption is anticonsumption.[21] Many patients described a feeling that as long as one eats at all and carries some body fat, one must "work off" food and fat. As Maude put it, "you never hit bottom": one can always lose more weight. Of course, many young women who do not struggle with an eating disorder feel that fattening foods will "apply directly to their thighs," as the expression goes. As many of us aspire to do, people who live with anorexia eat as little fat as possible (indeed, eat as little as possible). On the whole, this practice feels healthy, even energizing; if it does not, patients wonder about an internal weakness, about their ability to achieve. And as a result, they try harder.

Exercise is a central component of "productive" weight loss for many patients; it is one way to "try harder." One patient I interviewed remarked: "I forget my body needs calories apart from needing them to exercise. It feels like I gain weight *while* I eat, and I feel indulgent if I don't work it off." Another patient suggested to me that managing her weight through exercise created an endless need to continue achieving in this way. She felt a compulsion to exercise and told me that exercise was an anxiety-producing, even frightening test of her ability to control her weight and to create an achieving identity. She said that about a year before our interview, when her anorexia was more acute, "I felt my weight would just shoot up in a day if I didn't exercise. And once I would start I couldn't stop, or else none of it would count. But these days, if I've started exercising and the fan isn't blowing in my direction, it's okay to get up and move it. But before, exercising was scary; it ranked right up there with weighing myself. . . . That sort of paranoid feeling. Am I going to be a worthy person, or unworthy today? Can I do it or not, will I be able to do it?"

Even without directly referencing the need to diet, media images of exercise for women represent the female body as a consuming body, implying that feminine fitness requires a special effort. While it is not my purpose here to compare popular ideals of masculine and feminine fitness in a systematic way, the contrast is illuminating, so I will touch on it briefly. Ideals of fitness for women focus on creating a body that manages the effects of consumption well, a body that is streamlined and controls for "jiggle" (Bordo 1993b). Masculine fitness is coded differently: weight control and fat reduction are certainly concerns, but there is greater emphasis on enhancing the self through body work. Masculine fitness is a more optimistic project—not only because of a focus on building up the body (as opposed to slimming it down) but also because the male body is seen as relatively fit to begin with. Men are said to "keep" fit; women, to achieve fitness. In May 1989, *Psychology Today* advertised an exercise video for men entitled "Fitness: Getting It All Back" ("It's Never Too Late," the ad suggests, to bring forth what has always already been there). The April issue of the same year advertises the "Bellyshapers" video for women, which promises to help one create a new and attractive torso. It is significant that the promised body shape would be "new": for women, a fit body must be *forged*, in spite of difficult odds.

Of course, this is not to say that masculine fitness is viewed or experienced as easy to achieve or as unproblematic.[22] Also, some men may well experience difficulties with fitness that are similar to women's, since the contemporary goal of managing consumption at the level of the individual body applies to men and women alike. However, I suggest that women's struggles with fitness are uniquely overdetermined by economic, social, and symbolic prescriptions and constraints that lead toward a singularly powerful concern about the potentially disruptive corporeal effects of consumption.

An ad for an exercise machine by Marcy shows that feminine fitness is a constant struggle that is written against a subtext of consumer desire.[23] The ad depicts a woman straining under a "Bodybar," and the caption, written in huge boldface type, reads "the joy of cooking." The metaphor here is one of exercise converting—or "cooking"—consumed food into firm flesh. The message conveyed is that the fit female body is first and foremost a consuming body; however, with hard work, this body can overcome its own "natural" propensities. This ad also points to women's changing relationship to food and consumption work more generally over the past several decades. I have pointed out that ideologically, women's primary mode of consumption work has recently shifted from the management of (others') consumption in the home to the regulation of their own consumption. Women may still perform the majority of domestic labor in the United States, but "the joy of cooking" has moved from the kitchen to the exercise room (and has supposedly liberated women in the process). Sociologist Bryan Turner (1984) argues that this shift marks changes in "modes of regulation" over the female body. But the female body is not simply given as the ground for these modes of regulation; rather, it has been constituted as an object of control through historically specific links to changing modes of consumer desire and expressions of leisure. A brief history of these changes will show how the female body has become a problematic resource for creating fit identities.

In the 1950s and 1960s, expert advice offered to women about how to comport themselves and achieve an ideal state of femininity was contained not in diet books but in cookbooks. In this era of the "happy homemaker," food preparation (and the management of consumption for the family more generally) was coded as quintessentially feminine activity during a time of vast consumer output. Of course, the glorification of domesticity for women during the postwar period was part of an effort to reinscribe women's work as housework, given that millions of middle-class women had participated in paid work outside the home for the first time during the war. But it is important not to reduce the dichotomies of work/home, and production/consumption, in the postwar period to a gender-differentiating "function." While women's skills in homemaking were often posited in opposition to a masculine work ethic, they were also aligned with, and *constitutive of,* changing ideas about productive work and its relationship to consumption and leisure. Postwar optimism about (masculine) productive individualism within a booming economy was tempered by fears about the dulling and homogenizing effects of a bureaucratized work world (Ehrenreich 1983), and women were enlisted to nurture and revitalize their husbands by making the home a space for leisure, relaxation, and domestic bliss. Increasingly, leisure as a reward for work—specifically, consumption in the home—was construed as necessary refreshment for the work ethic. Conversely, women were now encouraged to apply a work ethic to homemaking—to "labor" at leisure.[24]

The 1950s and 1960s consolidated ideas about women's agency in consumption that had begun to develop in the 1920s (Breazeale 1994). Compared to the Victorian period, when well-to-do women were, ideally, relatively passive and dependent conduits for the display of their husbands' "market value" (Veblen [1899] 1934), well-to-do women in the early and mid-twentieth century were to manage consumption actively. In the postwar era, this new energy was said to free women from the tedium of homemaking. Cookbooks, advice columns, and advertisements stressed that housework should not feel task oriented or burdensome; rather, it should be infused with loving warmth and energy. Women were to keep their families, and themselves, happy with the glow of "natural" feminine charms applied in the home (Ogden 1986).

Food preparation was a primary arena for this new expression of feminine agency and vitality, and the female body—no longer seen merely as a passive vehicle for the expression of consumer value—was refigured as dynamic resource for nurturing consumer desire. The very popular *Betty Crocker's New Picture Cookbook* of 1965 is a good example. "Refresh your spirits" before starting your day, it counsels in the preface, and it goes on to say, "every morning before breakfast, comb hair, apply makeup and a dash of cologne. Does wonders for your morale and your family's too. Think pleasant thoughts while working and a chore will become a 'labor of love.'" These feminine labors were to culminate at mealtimes: "Make mealtime a special time in your home by serving appetizing food in a relaxed, happy atmosphere. The buoyant health and feeling of well-being that results will be reward enough for the care and loving thought you give to your family's meals."

More active in facilitating consumer desire, the postwar female body was also represented as a body in need of dietary management, a body that would give up its own consumption for the sake of others'. In the early 1960s, both Overeaters Anonymous and Weight Watchers were founded. Slimming through dieting—as opposed to the corset, or the "science" of food management popular in the 1920s—is a "dynamic" mode of managing consumption at the level of the individual female body. Relative to the present day, however, dieting was not a major obsession during the postwar period. In fact, diet books written in the 1950s and 1960s talked about keeping the diet a secret, "as if a fat woman's diet should be as furtive as her eating. Her failures, like her shame, would be private" (H. Schwartz 1986, 210). I suggest that because women were seen as expert consumers, dieting, while symbolically logical, represented a failure in the management of consumption. Accordingly, there were no popular schemes for quick weight loss at the time, no "fad" diets; rather, "the dieter's life had to be one long unending struggle, with one eye constantly on the scales, a life of unceasing vigilance" (227). In contrast, dieting today is a practice that signals an increasingly individualistic relationship to consumption and zeroes in on body fat as a dynamic, "productive," and ever-renewable energy resource. The cultural construction of fatness has been altered: no longer an intractable problem, fatness can always be worked off in preparation to consume again.

If women—and girls "in training" to be women—were seen as expert managers of domestic space in the postwar era, and dieting was therefore a furtive activity, I suggest that this situation has gradually become inverted. Today dieting and exercise, along with individual achievement in the world of paid work, represent success in the management of consumption; this mastered, other forms of consumer management, such as domestic caretaking, will ideally fall into place without difficulty. "I can bring home the bacon, fry it up in the pan, and never let you forget you're a man," promises today's svelte superwoman.[25] But when women work to become fit, they appear to do battle with their own natures, with continued imperatives to engage in seemingly less-productive forms of consumption work: namely, to serve food for others and for themselves. Contradictory injunctions to diet and to prepare tempting foods are everywhere presented to women. One woman's magazine after another juxtaposes the latest fad diet with recipes for delicious and fattening meals and desserts, presumably to be prepared and served by the reader. Most women and girls experience this contradiction as repeated failures in weight control and bodily control, failures that are a constant call to try again. Anorexia is one version of "success" in this endeavor. We have seen how Maude harnessed weight loss to achievement so thoroughly that food refusal itself came easily; she had folded the threat of failure into a practice that appeared to transcend it through sheer persistence and unending work. Maude's anorexia ensured that she would not fail, would not have to "try again"; so much so that, in her case, the work of anorexia did not even feel like perpetual effort. Maude was not willfully transcending failure, but neither was she the passive victim of anorexia. Rather, she enacted and embodied a specific cultural logic, one that tethers the idea that fitness requires body work to the idea that the female body is an obstacle to fitness.

I now examine one patient's struggle with clinicians in the hospital to show how these cultural discourses about the body operate in the treatment program. Recall that clinicians view patients' struggles against treatment protocols as misguided, but promising, assertions of autonomy that can be marshaled to serve the ultimate goal of treatment, which is for patients to "will" health as the treatment program defines it. Clinicians encourage patients to accept biomedical criteria of health but to experience this acceptance as an internal transformation. These ideas about treatment are in keeping with culturally dominant notions of feminine fitness: pressures for women and girls to gain weight—to know their bodies as consuming bodies—are, ideally, to be internalized and to be controlled by individual effort and willpower. At the same time, because imperatives to gain weight in the treatment program are represented as objective medical facts, patients' experiences of their bodies as intractably other to the goal of achievement through body work are intensified. As Bordo (1993d) points out, a crucial question arises in treatment: Whose body is this? And whose will it become?

"Defined by Numbers": A Case Study

Rebecca, age eighteen, had a three-year history of anorexia when she was admitted to the hospital because of a low pulse, caused by over-exercise at a low body weight. During her hospital stay, Rebecca gained enough weight to reach her exercise weight (i.e., it should have been medically safe for her to exercise). However, Rebecca's pulse remained low, even though she was not exercising while in the hospital, and this situation posed a problem for the clinicians working with Rebecca. Clinicians often use a patient's exercise weight as a cutoff point for discharge from the hospital, because they consider it a minimally safe weight to maintain. So those responsible for Rebecca's care were considering raising her exercise weight in the hopes that her pulse would improve, thus requiring her to gain more weight before she was allowed to go home. But they disagreed about this plan, because they had already raised Rebecca's exercise weight several times in the past. As an outpatient, Rebecca did not respond well to increases in her exercise weight: she ended up intensifying her exercise regimes, which made it difficult for her to maintain the new weight and was also the probable cause of her chronically low pulse.

In other words, Rebecca had been engaging in a "legalistic" form of resistance to treatment that exaggerates its terms. She experienced her exercise weight, which is official permission to exercise, as an *imperative* to exercise. On one occasion, when she was told her exercise weight would go up, she responded, "Okay, if you want me to take up sumo wrestling!" Early on in her hospitalization, Rebecca told me that once she reached a given exercise weight, she would try to strike a balance between caloric intake and exercise, but she was always tempted to "work harder," that is, to exercise more (and, occasionally, to eat less). She said she tries to maintain her exercise weight to stay healthy, but "the whole idea of gaining weight is so scary. I just picture my body getting bigger and bigger. It seems like the number I have to get to for exercise weight . . . [is] just so big. So I avoid the number" (meaning she feels compelled to stay below it).

In this way, the criterion of exercise weight literally creates the body as an objectified other: a number, an amount of weight, an obstacle to fight against with the work of exercise. Of course, this experience was already familiar to Rebecca through anorexia. She said that because of her experience with anorexia, her identity was, in general, "defined by numbers": her weight, her body size, the number of calories she ate in a given day, and the number of calories she burned off through exercise. As she put it, "Some days, when I say, 'Oh my God, my thighs,' I comfort myself by saying, well, I know it can't be getting worse right now, because . . . I'm doing the exercise, and *maybe* the exercise will make it better. . . . You say to yourself, it has to be getting better with every pound [lost]." Thus "big numbers" meant that Rebecca had work to do: she was compelled to transform the "bigness" of her body through exercise. I suggest that Rebecca's lived experience of being defined by numbers materializes a dominant cultural discourse of the female body as a stubborn resource for the crafting of identity.

While Rebecca was increasingly critical of her clinicians' insistence that she achieve various exercise weights, she had learned in therapy to attribute her difficulty with this treatment strategy to a deficiency of "self," a deficiency that had led to adopting anorexia as a "superficial identity," or a "false sense of self." So, on the whole, Rebecca viewed her exercise weight as appropriate support from her caretakers, as leverage for fighting anorexia. As she saw it, because a powerful part of her current sense of self was anorexic, and because the treatment team represented health, she and the team were at war, but the fight was necessary. Rebecca put it this way: "I guess the exercise weight personifies the people here who keep me healthy and tell me I need to be here [in the hospital]. . . . You could [identify] dichotomies, columns of things that work against each other, because you have the exercise weight and the medical doctors and psychology and the people who want me to get up to this weight, and then you have the part of me that feels you have to restrict [calories and continue to exercise]." For Rebecca, her "true self," a healthy self, would learn to incorporate the opposition: "Somewhere along the line, I'm just going to have to make their goals line up with my goals [of thinness and rigorous exercise], in terms of my health."

However, as we shall see, the treatment team's opinions about Rebecca's care were themselves contested. But the clinicians kept their disagreements from Rebecca. The team's claim that their opinions were unified and unambiguous—or "objective"—participated in dominant cultural discourses that represent feminine fitness as an elusive ideal requiring tireless and vigilant work. At the same time, the contradictions embedded in the treatment team's assessments created a space for Rebecca's struggle and resistance, pointing up the contingent character of psychiatric assessments of the body and person.

Disagreements among clinicians about Rebecca's treatment plan were expressed when the treatment team met in rounds to review patients' progress and discuss treatment options. Those regularly present when Rebecca was an inpatient included Ellen, the pediatrician working on the unit that month; Bob, a psychiatrist assigned to all eating-disordered patients during that time, and the medical director of the unit; Sally and Martha, both psychologists; Ann, the nutritionist; two psychology interns; and one intern in psychiatry. In addition, two or three staff members who were on duty at the time the team was meeting also attended. Occasionally, Rebecca was present, as well: once a week, rounds were called "miniteams," and patients attended part of these meetings (after their progress and treatment plans had been reviewed and possibly revised in their absence). Patients could affect the direction of these discussions by submitting requests and questions in advance, but the main reason they were invited to miniteams was to practice "negotiating" with adults (while in reality, the team's decisions, once they were made, were rarely altered). What follows is an account of two of these meetings, as they relate to decision making about Rebecca's care, and Rebecca's reactions to these meetings.

When Rebecca reached her exercise weight and still had a low pulse, Ellen suggested that instead of raising her exercise weight again, they tell Rebecca she could not exercise at all for a month. But Ann, the nutritionist, insisted that Rebecca needed something more concrete to work with, so her exercise weight should be raised. Ann's plug for "concreteness" won out among the treatment team as a whole, because patients are considered to be "concrete thinkers": they need to know that, at a certain weight, they can exercise. This tactic avoids overwhelming patients with too much responsibility for their care, an issue of particular importance in Rebecca's case, as she had just turned eighteen and therefore had the option of leaving the program at any time without parental consent.[26] At the same time, the concept of an exercise weight ensures that patients will take *enough* responsibility for their health, because it is linked to a specific form of body work that patients can control.

In other words, according to the nutritionist and those who supported her view, the trick was to define health in such a way that Rebecca would "will" to incorporate it into her identity through body work. When Rebecca was invited to join this discussion, Bob—the medical director and the designated spokesperson for the team that day—attempted to create a will to health for Rebecca by suggesting that she, too, is an expert who can observe herself as a patient and has an interest in her health as the treatment team defined it. Rebecca asked Bob if her exercise weight would be raised. Bob asked her what she thought, and Rebecca said she did not know, but that she was afraid it would be raised. Bob asked, "If you were a doctor—," and Rebecca interrupted with, "I don't ever plan to be." Bob continued: "and you really wanted to support your patient, what would you do?" Rebecca said she would take into account the fact that her pulse was normal the previous day, and that it had been normal at her current body weight in the past, even when exercising. Bob then asked, "Okay, given this, how much would you raise the weight, to support your patient, but not overwhelm them?" In this rhetorical move, raising Rebecca's exercise weight became the only option. The only question left was "By how much?" Rebecca guessed the amount the team had specified. Bob told her she would make a good doctor, that maybe she *should* consider it. In this way, the team's decision, made without Rebecca's input, was explicitly presented as Rebecca's own desire. Creating an alignment between official medical criteria (her new exercise weight) and Rebecca's will to health was a goal in its own right; the team told Rebecca she could not exercise for a month anyway, regardless of her weight.

Also note that a contested decision-making process within the treatment team was put forth as a unified, expert opinion. This representation of a healthy body for Rebecca as an objective fact—a representation that papered over a negotiated and unstable agreement—had specific effects on her. Instead of responding to the team's decision with a "will to health" that integrated compliance and independence, Rebecca experienced a split between being told what to do and having to choose what to do. Rebecca explained to me that she and her therapist had been talking about her active choice to stay in the hospital as an example of fighting the desire to have others tell her what to do. But now that her exercise weight had been raised again, it was less clear to Rebecca that staying at Walsh was her choice. "They're saying: These are our 'suggestions' and our 'recommendations,' and it's your choice. It's like, Aaaa! It makes me frustrated and scared," because, as she pointed out, the team's "recommendations" are powerful; in practice, she would try to do what the team said, because, she said, she was vulnerable and needed the support.

Of course, there is no question that Rebecca needed support. What is at issue here is the treatment team's participation in patients' perceived dependence on others even as they seek self-control. In keeping with the special efforts that feminine fitness requires, the imperative that Rebecca "choose" health in the face of seemingly unambiguous, expert advice created an overwhelming rift between the expert power of the treatment team and Rebecca's individual identity, a rift that, for Rebecca, highlighted the power of anorexia to generate internal conflict: "When I'm in the hospital, anorexia doesn't completely take me over, because the staff are *making* me eat and keeping me from exercising. But toward the end of an admission, I say to myself, OK, there's the anorexia and the hospital [program], but what am *I* going to do? . . . When you get out, it's just you and the problem again. You can check back in, and going to clinic is very important in helping you to control it, but ultimately it is up to you; and especially when you get out, you really feel that."

One week later, the treatment team was in an even greater bind to preserve its own authority as well as Rebecca's responsibility. Rebecca had reached her newest exercise weight but still had a low pulse, and her case continued to generate conflict within the team. At this point, Rebecca was very close to reaching her final goal weight, or her "target weight." As opposed to a patient's exercise weight, the target weight is considered immutable; once patients reach and maintain this weight, they are considered "cured." During this week's team meeting, Ellen (Rebecca's pediatrician) argued that Rebecca should be told that she needed to reach her target weight. But several other members of the team strongly disagreed with this idea. Clinicians never use target weights as inpatient goals, in part because patients "prove" they are healthy by reaching this weight on their own, outside of the hospital. The target weight marks the end of a struggle toward health; a patient cannot internalize it as part of her identity along the way. In arguing her case, Ellen pointed out that Rebecca had almost reached her target weight anyway, and that it was time to face up to the fact that Rebecca's real problem was her refusal finally to reach and maintain this weight. By this point, Rebecca's case had thoroughly disrupted the treatment team's categories and familiar strategies for engendering patients' sense of responsibility in their health. It was almost too obvious a point that Rebecca needed to reach her target weight: this was tantamount to saying that she was anorexic.

Bob agreed with the idea of specifying Rebecca's target weight as her discharge weight but suggested that the team simply rename her target weight her "medically safe weight." Ellen countered that if they dropped the authoritative label of "target weight," Rebecca might feel justified in trying to stay below this weight in the future. Bob responded, "Rebecca has been unable to process the idea that she has to reach a fixed weight," and he argued that the team should therefore show "flexibility in its categories." The implication here is that Rebecca's "pathology" had been the cause of difficulties with her treatment, in spite of the fact that it was the treatment team who were unable to agree on and maintain a fixed goal for Rebecca. In this way, Bob explicitly displaced collective ambiguity about Rebecca's care as a problem that was internal to Rebecca's eating disorder.

The team eventually took up Bob's idea, and once again, they presented their decision to Rebecca as a unified and unanimous one. When Rebecca joined the meeting and was informed of the decision, she asked why her medically safe weight had no official name and why she no longer had an exercise weight (it had become, for now, the same as her target weight, or medically safe weight). Bob replied that the team was acting in the interest of her health, that she should not be exercising anyway, and that she would have an exercise weight eventually (once her heart problem resolved). In other words, the team couched the answers to Rebecca's difficult questions in terms of her responsibility to stay healthy.

Let me pause here to note that Rebecca's case was unusual in its disruption of the team's status quo procedures. Normally, goal weights are not manipulated in this way. However, Rebecca's case reveals constructions of health and displacements of conflict among clinicians that are quite common at Walsh. Note also that while the manipulation of the terms of treatment that we see operating here might seem blatantly unfair, some clinicians would argue that such tactics are necessary at times, and possibly lifesaving.[27] Even so, problems and conflicts within the treatment team were consistently grafted onto "anorexic" bodies and psyches, which were therefore represented as sites of failure. While there is always the potential for resistance against this process (on the part of clinicians and staff as well as patients), dominant discourses that create "the anorexic" as a clinical and pathologized entity usually succeed in masking the fact that clinical decisions are active and contested constructions (even manipulations). Any of patients' experiences of anger or betrayal are often muted, as well.

For Rebecca, the team's new decision about her care confirmed her identity as anorexic, precisely the opposite of its intended effect, but consistent with a logic that located conflict over her health as *her* problem, as a problem of anorexia. Rebecca felt that any other potential identity for herself was erased, that she was now "defined by an even heavier number," and that "with each number increase it's like, more and more out of my control. . . . and what that makes me want to do is go back to the anorexia, and take control over myself." She said that with people at Walsh telling her what to do in this fashion, "All of a sudden it comes back to me and the anorexia, and it feels like we're the same." She added, "I don't know what I'll do with the number when I get home. I want to lose the number . . . I started making weight loss plans for home."

Recall that in the previous week, Rebecca experienced a split between being told what to do and needing to choose what to do. This week, when the treatment team's criteria were more disrupted and more thoroughly collapsed into Rebecca's responsibility for her own health, she completely internalized the contradictions of her treatment. The so-called expert criteria for her health kept changing, with no explanation save the "failures" of her own body, a body that, to her, now seemed medically sanctioned as a stubbornly resistant resource in her efforts to achieve health. Faced with the requirement to will her own health in this context, it seemed to Rebecca that her only recourse was achievement through anorexia, that familiar practice of fighting the body's perceived failures with willpower.

In many ways, Rebecca's hospital experience was similar to the "medically identified and sanctioned symptom persistence" that Alexander found among hemodialysis patients (Alexander 1981, 307). Using "double-bind" theory (Bateson et al. 1956), Alexander shows that hemodialysis patients and their caretakers are caught in destructive paradoxes. For example, the fact that patients are dependent on hospitalization and are *also* encouraged to become independent ultimately promotes chronicity (failure to become independent is internalized in an institutionally sanctioned way). Likewise, the requirement that Rebecca willfully incorporate the treatment team's criteria ultimately reinforced her anorexia.

At the same time, however, Rebecca did not accept this situation quietly; the contradictions of her treatment created room for critique. Rebecca directly implicated the treatment program in reducing her identity to numbers, implying that her hospital experience participated in creating her anorexic identity: "[When I'm in the hospital], I feel like a number of calories, a unit of weight, a measurement, not a person. Through this whole thing, I begin to feel like a vital sign. Kinda losing the personality, the identity just as a person through this. It's like, I feel like people look at me and they know my weight and everything. . . . [The numbers] are taking over . . . especially the weight. My weight is just painted on my forehead. It's kinda like the scarlet letter, only different." But Rebecca also believed that her own "anorexic way of thinking" was responsible for what we can identify here as an experience of bodily objectification in the hospital. While Rebecca thought that Walsh's focus on numbers was conducive to anorexia, she also concurred with the opinion that—as the clinicians working with her often put it to me—her negative "interpretation" of treatment practices was a "projection" of her "pathology" (although Rebecca herself did not use these particular words). Rebecca expressed her mixed feelings on the matter in this way:

> I think the *feeling* of being a number, a vital sign . . . comes from me, or comes from the anorexic way of thinking. It comes from myself. But the daily things that we do here—from that, the anorexia can basically [take over. When there's] something you're very sensitive about . . . even just in light conversation [at Walsh], something can be easily interpreted as hitting me in the face with a number again. In some way. And it's like they're insulting me, only they're not, they're just saying, 'Well, your weight today is . . .' And if I don't like the weight, it's like they're . . . insulting me, or hurting me in some way, stabbing me. . . . The focus on the numbers and everything here, it's very easy to turn it—every day I do, I turn it to myself, it kind of, like, says something about myself. And I think it's a real hard process here. Because I think in one way you have to use the numbers, you have to

get the numbers. But since I've been here, the numbers have been very hard to take. Daily.

I suggest that here Rebecca is expressing what cultural theorist Stuart Hall (1986) has called "contradictory consciousness," a phrase Hall uses to describe Antonio Gramsci's theory of subjectivity. Gramsci (1971) draws a distinction between "common sense," or sedimented popular belief, and "good sense," which is an intuitive, if inchoate, awareness of the constraints and relations of power that common sense entails. Rebecca's idea that her "anorexic way of thinking" was generating her criticisms of the treatment program is an example of common sense, and her fleeting awareness that the treatment program participated in specifying her identity as anorexic is an example of good sense. Rebecca's contradictory consciousness can be read as a challenge to the treatment team's claim to uphold and promote a form of subjectivity that is noncontradictory—in other words, "healthy."

In this way, Rebecca's case differs from those of the hemodialysis patients in Alexander's analysis. Alexander draws an analytic distinction between the double binds she explored in her research, and contradictions, "which are generative of oscillation and alternation rather than behavioral paralysis" (Alexander 1981, 313). While showing elements of a double-bind scenario, Rebecca's case is one of contradictions. Both Rebecca and members of her treatment team were able to escape paradox through critical consciousness and disagreement, which are disallowed in a double-bind situation. Although the treatment team presented a unified front to Rebecca in official contexts, Rebecca was aware that there were disagreements within the team. Also, members of the treatment team were aware among themselves, to a degree, that they were undermining their own goals by continually raising the bar for Rebecca's discharge. Notably, it was Rebecca's resistance to treatment that led to the team's internal conflict and shifting criteria, which, in turn, generated Rebecca's critical consciousness.

Conclusion

Rebecca's case underscores the fact that anorexic patients do not resist treatment protocols in a fully oppositional way. Instead, patients' resistance operates in the interstices of medical discourse, pointing up its instabilities. These instabilities, in turn, point up both the contingent character and the real effects of discourses specifying the female body as a problematic resource in the making of fitness and health.

While psychiatric understandings of health in the treatment of anorexia import and naturalize culturally and historically specific ideas about feminine fitness, these ideas are not simply imposed on patients' bodies. The young women on the unit are active participants in efforts to craft fit bodies and subjectivities in the treatment process. However, this is by no means to say that differentials of power are absent in the treatment of anorexia, as some theories about the "fragmentation" of coherent bodies and identities in an advanced capitalist context might lead us to believe (e.g., Kroker and Kroker 1987). The deployment of psychiatric expertise is constitutive of problems in the clinic, and corporeal experiences in the hospital are not "fragmented." At the same time, I have shown that fitness as a cultural dominant is not a seamless and unitary discourse; feminine fitness in particular contains contradictions. Because of these contradictions, patients diagnosed with anorexia are able to disrupt ideals of fitness and the process of treatment, even as they support both. My analysis shows that anorexic patients are not just victims of cultural and medical molding, or simply sites of resistance to these processes. Rather, they are agents who both author and unsettle ideals of bodily fitness, consumption, and control.

If norms of fitness at work in the treatment of anorexia are understood as multiply determined and contradictory cultural practices, it is difficult to conceptualize the body as pregiven material for the construction of fitness.[28] As the rhetorician Judith Butler (1993) argues, the creation of normalized bodies does not occur in a top-down fashion, operating on material reality we can assume to exist a priori. Rather, while feminine fitness as a cultural dominant can have real, top-down *effects,* it is in fact a multifaceted, contested, and contingent set of practices—which themselves produce certain kinds of bodily experience. Borrowing terms from Stuart Hall (1986, 1988), we can say that fitness is a "commonsensical" cultural story that is institutionalized—made true—through a variety of crosscutting discourses (e.g., gendered ideas about consumer management and cultural ideals of self-control), discourses that come together to form a powerful, and yet unstable, specification of bodies as natural objects and resources for the construction of fit identities.

In their struggles over the terms of feminine fitness, patients and clinicians are (largely unwittingly) engaged in a form of cultural work.

In the clinic, at the very moment when "objective" psychiatric representations of health explicitly naturalize dominant cultural norms, these
norms produce problematic embodied effects: fitness, sickness, and
health converge in anorexic bodies. As a result, discourses of fitness are
more visibly open to contestation than they otherwise might be.

TWO

Minimal Mothers and Psychiatric Discourse about the Family

The idea that the treatment team is a "sub-stitute family" for patients came up again and again during my fieldwork. Parents are asked to entrust their teenagers to the treatment program, particularly when their daughters are on the inpatient unit, and they are told to remove themselves from struggles over their daughters' bodies so that the treatment team can take over with these struggles. Parents are given very little information about their daughters' prog-ress in treatment, and they are asked to re-frain from conversation about food, eating, and weight.[1] Staff and clinicians believe that with this transfer of authority, they are able to "break" and therefore challenge destruc-tive patterns of interaction and behavior in families. As a pediatrician at Walsh ex-plained to a new medical student: "My ad-vice to parents is to get out. It's a battle they can't win. And probably, the parents tend to be overbearing." And as a psychologist put it to me once about an outpatient: "She'll have to be admitted at some point, just to break the family system."

Once a patient has been admitted to the hospital, the treatment team works to model corrective parenting for them, and also for the patient's family as a whole through family meetings. In chapter 3, I describe the workings of what I dub the "therapeutic family" in some detail. In this chapter, I focus on psychiatric constructions of illness and health within the "natural" family. I argue that the treatment team's attempts to transform familial relationships through the provision of a substitute family hyperbolize dominant constructions of "ideal" families—and of motherhood in particular—in the United States today.

I begin this chapter by locating the therapeutic strategy of familial "substitution" within shifting social expectations about ideal family forms. I then outline changes in therapeutic discourse about families that are in keeping with these shifting expectations, focusing on certain psychiatric representations of maternal caretaking from the 1950s to the present. Next, I write about one case of familial substitution at Walsh over the course of two hospital admissions, showing how contemporary constructions of ideal mothering articulate with the therapeutic goal of facilitating patients' individuation within, and separation from, their families. Throughout, I argue that ideal motherhood in the 1990s is a minimized, or a "whittled-down," version of the 1950s ideal. In addition, I show that assumptions about what I call "minimal motherhood" today justify excluding mothers from many aspects of the treatment process—an exclusion that, paradoxically, helps to create mothers' perceived (pathological) "overinvolvement" in their daughters' lives and psychiatric care. In the final section of this chapter, I discuss the absence of an elaborate discourse about fathers and fatherhood in the treatment of anorexia, in spite of a new social and therapeutic interest in father-daughter relationships.

Substitute Families in a "Postmodern" Society

Many staff view the therapeutic family as an ideal family of sorts. They even claim that for many patients, the therapeutic family is the best family they have ever had. Nursing staff often say that they could have done "a better job" as the parents of these patients than their "natural" parents have done. As one psychologist who is critical of this assumption put it to me, "Supposedly, we're good parents. So, what are we saying: the family is bad?" But at the same time that the therapeutic family is represented as an ideal family, staff also stress that the therapeutic family is a stand-in: it is not the real thing. If it were the real thing, patients might become too dependent on hospitalization. And of course, a "real" family cannot monitor and control adolescents' bodies with the same degree of impunity exercised by the treatment team. Parents are routinely told that the reason they are asked to "get out of the loop" when their daughters are in treatment is to allow the treatment team to be "the bad guys," and home a "safe haven."

So the logic of surrogate parenthood allows for two kinds of excess with respect to so-called families of origin. On the one hand, members of the treatment team are often seen as better parents for these patients. On the other hand, staff are not parents at all, which allows them to do their job. There is a paradox at work here: the family can and should be remade, through the artifice of substitution, but at the same time, there is no real substitute for the "natural" family. Families must be open to change but still retain a kernel of authenticity that distinguishes the family from any other set of relationships. The idea that the family should be both flexible and immutable is not new: ever since the industrial revolution, dominant descriptions of the nuclear family have represented it as both a natural "haven in a heartless world" (Lasch 1977) and the primary environment for creating individuals who will be capable of leaving the nest. But this paradox has taken on a new form, one that the current treatment of eating disorders exemplifies.

It was not until the late 1970s, when family therapy became well established as a therapeutic modality, that families routinely became the objects of therapeutic management. Family "systems" theory, which has influenced most (some say all) of the major family therapy models, holds that families communicate and express states of illness and health in ways that are self-regulating and semiautonomous from the individuals, roles, and hierarchical structures that make up the family.[2] In this view, families can be altered as "units" unto themselves. For the treatment of anorexia, caregivers almost always recommend family therapy, or at least family meetings, especially for hospitalized adolescent patients. In fact, as we shall see, new ideas about effective treatments for anorexia played a significant role in the shaping of systems thinking more broadly within the therapy world. Although the program at Walsh did not offer formal family therapy, family meetings were strongly recommended one to two times per week, and these meetings had a therapeutic (as well as an informational) component. More generally, and more importantly for my purposes in this chapter, family systems theory makes possible the notions at Walsh that a substitute family can be therapeutic and that a hospital admission will help to "break the family system."

The idea of breaking the family system is particularly strong within structural family therapy, which was developed in the 1970s by Salvador Minuchin and his colleagues.[3] Structural family therapy is, arguably, the most influential model of family therapy for the treatment of anorexia, and it is a popular model at Walsh.[4] Often, a central goal of this therapy is to minimize, or pare down, family structures—"dysfunctional" roles and patterned lines of authority—in order to support the "individuation" of family members. "Therapeutic [strategies are] focused on *de*structuring the family's rigid patterns, and *re*structuring them according to more functional parameters"—which include "clearer boundaries" around both individuals and "subsystems" such as the husband/wife subsystem—and "increased flexibility in transactions, [and] conflict negotiation" (Colapinto 1991, 420). Family therapy for anorexia, especially, is designed to counteract a perceived overprotective, domestic "enmeshment" to facilitate anorexic patients' heretofore thwarted attempts to achieve autonomy. Enmeshment is a widely used concept in structural family therapy; it refers to a "low level of individual differentiation and autonomy" within a given family (426). More often than not, the aim of structural family therapy in the treatment of anorexia is, according to psychologist Lynn Hoffman's 1981 analysis of this approach, to create "a set of stairs up which the [anorexic] daughter would, one hope[s], march on her way out" (270).

This vision of flexible families and individuation within families articulates with a relatively new, purportedly gender-equalizing ideology of individualism in American society. Judith Stacey (1990) documents the increasingly powerful idea that family structure should be as flexible as possible, reduced to a scaffolding of support for the individuals within it, and that autonomy for girls and boys alike should be promoted. She traces this "postmodern" view of the family to a reorganization of work and relationships within an advanced capitalist economy. With the expansion of the service economy in the 1980s and the accompanying massive rise in female employment, full-time domesticity has been in decline, and families have become more fluid and mutable. Blended families (families including stepparents and stepchildren) and single-parent families have proliferated. The ideal family form no longer contains a male breadwinner and a female homemaker;

the two-income family is now an accepted norm, and the family is seen with greater relativity, with an eye to maximizing individuals' social mobility.

However, as Donna Haraway points out, women's (continued) "enforced status as mothers" in this socioeconomic context engenders a double exploitation for them, given the rising divorce rate, the dismantling of the welfare state, "the homework economy where stable jobs become the exception, and . . . the expectation that women's wage will not be matched by a male income for the support of children" (Haraway 1991a, 167). But a gender-inclusive ideology of individualism not only ignores a lack of affordable child care in the United States and the effects of this problem on mothers in particular. It also implies that women, even poor women with children, can (indeed should) "do it all" (both work for pay and raise children).[5] So while families have become "flexible" in the past few decades in the name of freeing up more (middle-class) women to join the paid workforce, the burden of parenting for many women has increased, even as the obligations of motherhood are less visible in the dominant cultural imaginary than they were in the 1950s and 1960s era of the "happy homemaker."

At the same time, a conservative backlash romanticizes the "traditional" nuclear family (Faludi 1991). In addition, as Stacey points out, many people—conservative and not—still see family relationships as a bulwark against perceived social fragmentation and individualism. Stacey argues that even with its diversity of forms, the family provides emotional "glue" in these changing and uncertain times. This idea appears in psychiatric representations of so-called anorexic families at Walsh: even while clinicians strive to increase autonomous individualism in families, many clinicians and staff also concur that a fundamental problem with anorexic families is that their rigid patterns of interaction preclude genuine, spontaneous, unconditional love. Here, "natural" familial attachments are valued right along with "flexibility" in family structure.

But familial attachments are not timeless and unchanging bonds. Rather, they are themselves mutable, and constituted within the wider sociocultural processes that are so often represented *in opposition* to family ties, within both psychiatric discourse and popular culture. I disagree with Stacey's view that people's continued investment in the emotional attachments of family life is a *response to* the reorganization of work and the concomitant breakdown of the "traditional" nuclear family form. This formulation misses new cultural specifications for caretaking in family relationships. I will show that with the debunking of fixed "gender roles" in the family, and particularly the idea of a prescribed maternal role, the construction of familial nurturance in the treatment of anorexia now operates at the level of individual desire. There is an insidious form of naturalization at work here: mothers, like fathers, are now imagined to be free to "choose" a caretaking role in the family, but this choice is thought to tap into and mobilize deep-seated "instincts." While ideas about maternal instincts—or incitements to realize them—are certainly not new, the idea that one *chooses* to realize these instincts is new. Familial love is now coded as a matter of individual desire, which conceals its cultural production as a natural phenomenon in a way that is historically unique.

In her book *Reproducing the Future,* cultural anthropologist Marilyn Strathern (1992b) writes about recent cultural constructions of imperatives to become a parent, in light of new reproductive technologies (NRTs) that seem to destabilize the idea of "natural" parenthood by offering reproductive choices. Until recently, the naturalization of parenthood has been figured almost exclusively through the idiom of sexual difference, seen as functional to reproduction and to "healthy" nuclear family structures. Strathern argues that NRTs help call this idea into question, apropos of the diversity and "flexibility" of family forms that has recently been sanctioned (in some quarters). For example, with NRTs, single women, lesbian and gay couples, and "infertile" heterosexual couples can bear children. However, Strathern shows that the naturalization of parenthood per se has not been destabilized; rather, it has been pared down from a structural/functional vision of familial health and reinscribed as personal desire, which is invoked and enabled by the "choices" that NRTs provide. New reproductive technologies embody a "prescriptive consumerism: namely the idea that if you have the opportunity to enhance yourself you should take it" (Strathern 1992b, 36—37; see also Franklin 1998). Strathern's larger point is that NRTs help to create the reproductive "needs" they appear only to serve. Her specific point is that NRTs posit these needs—in the relatively minimalist form of individuals' desires—as resources for the marketing of reproductive "choice." In creating choices that will fulfill the seemingly natural desire to have a child, these technologies invigorate the status of reproductive desire as "natural" (and the proliferation of new reproductive choices and diverse family forms appears to prove the point. Note, however, that NRTs also reinscribe heteronormative family ideals, since there are many legal, social, and economic barriers for lesbian and gay couples who wish to make use of them).[6]

Like NRTs, family therapy is only a few decades old, and it also seems to challenge the naturalness of the family, given therapists' willingness to question and restructure family relationships. Until relatively recently, mental health professionals viewed the family as part of individual patients' "natural environment." During the 1950s and 1960s, the decades in which family therapies were first beginning to take shape, therapy meetings often did not include direct clinical interventions. But, during the 1970s, therapists began to see the family as a system of patterned, interpersonal interactions that they could work to alter. However, even with such a therapeutic "destructuring" (and reconstruction) of the family, the naturalness of motherhood in particular is retained. Therapists at Walsh posit a particular version of maternal caretaking as the core of familial health (which is the professed *goal*—supposedly not fully predictable—of family work). So, as with discourses surrounding parenting that are linked to NRTs, family therapy helps to create the maternal "natures" they appear only to serve. And like contemporary representations of reproductive desire, maternal nature appears in a form that is ideologically minimized.

I suggest that the logic of excluding parents from active participation in their daughters' care at Walsh rests on the assumption that a requisite degree of "natural" mothering is indestructible. Clinicians ask parents to "get out of the loop," but they still expect that most parents—usually their mothers—will be attentive enough to their daughters' lives that they can provide the treatment team with information if need be (about a given patient's "mood" when she is at home, her eating habits, etc.) and will, at the very least, arrange for their daughters' outpatient clinic visits. But perhaps most importantly, once parents hand over their daughters to the treatment team, and once patients begin the process of "separating and individuating" their identities within both their "natural" families and the therapeutic family, clinicians expect mothers to realize, on their own accord, a health-promoting, unconditional love for their daughters. This expectation is one illustration of the fact that current approaches to family dynamics represent caretaking in the family as a natural female desire, as opposed to a "gender role." Just as patients should acquire a will to health in the course of treatment (discussed in chapter 1), mothers are expected to manifest a will to care for their daughters. While there is a focus on separation and individuation within families, especially for mothers and daughters, family "support" is required for daughters to achieve this goal, and it is coded as a maternal value.

In chapter 1, I show that individual patients' resistance to treatment is considered a sign of health. Note that this idea does not apply to patients' parents, who are expected to comply with Walsh's rules and regulations, even though parents are figured as other to the treatment team in a more thoroughgoing way than are individual patients. The contradiction here for mothers in particular can be viewed in the following way: the essence of "healthy" motherhood is located outside the ambit of treatment, but at the same time, clinicians often view mothers as very much in need of, if resistant to, change. This contradiction is largely due to the fact that, since the beginnings of family therapy in the 1950s, motherhood and family "pathology" have often been elided in psychiatric discourse. In the following section, I trace part of the history of this elision to show that ideas about the naturalness of motherhood in the treatment of anorexia today are linked to therapeutic discourses of the past (especially those tied to schizophrenia, an important illness for the creation of family therapy)—even as they articulate with ideas about substitute parenting in a way that is historically specific.

Psychiatric Constructions of "Pathogenic" Mothers from 1950 to the Present

During the decades after World War II, the psychiatric literature was replete with "pathogenic" mothers. In particular, therapists blamed mothers for causing schizophrenia in their children. Schizophrenia had been very difficult to treat and manage prior to this time, and in the late 1940s, the psychiatrist Frieda Fromm-Reichman (1948) coined the phrase "schizophrenogenic mother" in her search to identify a new cause of the problem.[7] She described such a mother as, on the one hand, rejecting of her children's needs and, on the other hand, overprotective of her children to the point of confusing their identities with her own. These ideas about "schizophrenogenic" mothers were taken up within the family therapy movement in the 1950s and 1960s. Family systems theory was developed in the 1950s largely through an attempt to understand schizophrenia in family context (Guttman 1991; Hoffman 1981), so representations of "schizophrenogenic" mothers in this literature can tell us quite a bit about psychiatric theories of the family as a whole during this time.

During the 1950s and 1960s, prominent therapists such as Theodore Lidz and his colleagues at Yale, and a group of therapists at the Mental Research Institute in Menlo Park, California, led by the anthropologist Gregory Bateson, routinely described the mothers of schizophrenic patients as oppressive of other family members' individualities (in spite of the fact that systems thinking eshews linear causality).[8] These mothers were thought to be overnurturant, causing "the development of a kind of symbiotic relationship between mother and child in which the two egos become so fused and intermingled that the boundaries never become clear" (Reichard and Tillman 1950, 237). At the same time, these mothers were thought to withhold nurturance in a selfish and hostile way. Lidz et al. (1958) write of two mothers in particular who "completely dominated the lives of their passive husbands and children," and whom they consider "typical 'schizophrenogenic' mothers in needing and using their sons to complete their own frustrated lives" (308–9).

In the psychiatric literature of the 1950s and 1960s, "mother" was often taken as a synonym for "family" or "family environment," and I suggest that ideas about schizophrenogenic mothers were bound up with contradictory representations of the "ideal" family form that were widespread at the time. The twin ideas that mothers essentially define "the family" and are capable of pathological overparenting were linked up with a new social vigilance to naturalize women as mothers. Women who had worked outside the home during World War II were encouraged to return to full-time domestic caretaking.[9] From this standpoint, therapists were diagnosing an excess in maternal caretaking that was, arguably, culturally mandated. At the same time, however, the idea that pathogenic mothers were selfish and rejecting revealed a lack of faith in the naturalness of the family, in the wake of its dismantling during the war. Here, the larger questions were, *Are* mothers "naturally" mothering? And how does mothering affect individualism in the family?

Of particular concern were the perceived suffocating effects of mothering on men and boys in the family. Postwar efforts to reconstitute the family as a stable institution with fixed gender roles produced a heightened ambivalence about the dual mandate of families: ideologies about the family naturalized motherhood as a quintessentially nurturing role and kept women out of the postwar workplace, and the family therefore represented the antithesis of market individualism; but families were also responsible to create individuals—gendered male—who could engage in competitive market individualism. The idea that schizophrenogenic mothers both smothered and rejected their sons highlights this contradiction. Neill (1990) points out that social discontent with the "bureaucratization of work, the rise of the corporate 'man in the gray flannel suit,' [and] the demise of individualism" during the postwar era lay at the feet of mothers, who were said to be "emasculating" of their sons and husbands. One can see why the male schizophrenic was considered to be the paradigmatic psychiatric disaster: schizophrenia was seen as the antithesis of the autonomous, indivisible self that defined the essence of male personhood (see Barrett 1996 on notions of individualism at work in constructs of schizophrenia).

Psychiatric ideas about "schizophrenogenic" families also point to the social construction of the family as a natural environment that was almost entirely outside the ambit of therapeutic intervention at that time. There was no cure for the mother, and hence the family, of a schizophrenic patient. Prior to the deinstitutionalization of mental hospitals in the 1960s, many psychiatrists believed that the only way to manage the "pathological" effects of a schizophrenic patient's family was to separate the patient from his or her family through institutionalization (Haley 1959) or alternative family care (Barton and Davidson 1961). This stance was due, in part, to the fact that in the days before family therapy was (widely considered) a legitimate treatment modality, family meetings could be justified only as research projects (as opposed to clinical interventions). "Observation of a family as a basis for treatment would have been a direct challenge to the prevailing sanction against a therapist's contact with anyone in the family other than her or his own patient" (Goldenberg and Goldenberg, 1991, 74). But the fledgling status of family therapy was by no means the complete explanation for the belief that schizophrenogenic families were incurable. Lidz et al. (1958) capture well the ways in which psychiatrists represented these mothers not only as "lost causes" but also as disruptive to the therapeutic process, even as the psychiatrists washed their hands of the mothers they identified as the cause of the problem: "We could never really understand these mothers, for their incessant talk was driven and mixed up, displaying unbelievable obtuseness to any ideas not their own . . . two major private psychiatric hospitals had refused to keep [one schizophrenic patient], not because of his behavior but because they could not stand his mother's incessant interference" (309).

After the deinstitutionalization movement, family therapy became more established as a valid form of therapeutic intervention, and more and more therapists began organizing family therapy meetings as part of the treatment of schizophrenia. However, most therapists still viewed the schizophrenic family as essentially unchangeable, or hopelessly "homeostatic" (Jackson 1968): "Our goals at the moment are limited. Our main goal is to get the family to live apart. Now, this doesn't mean that we want to ship, say, one to Chicago and another to New York. We simply want them to be able to live in some sort of autonomy so that they can live together. This is very difficult to achieve. . . . They just don't seem to be able to do without each other when the patient is living at home. . . . We try mainly to get the family to see how much they intertwine with each other. We are not attempting to bring about profound personality change" (Jackson 1968, 206). Many viewed the family as a pregiven structure that contains, and constrains, individuals. Deinstitutionalization, then, posed a problem: "After having been judged to be responsible for their offspring's illness by one segment of the psychiatric community (family therapists and psychoanalysts), the parents, especially, were being asked to assume total responsibility for the care of the patients by another segment (community psychiatrists). One might assume that general confusion in such families could follow from such an odd set of contextual messages" (McFarlane 1983, 5). But we have seen that this contradiction informed family therapy thinking about schizophrenia from the beginning.

In sum, family therapy was born grappling with the problem of schizophrenia—that "archchallenge of psychiatric theories" (McFarlane 1983, 1)—and pitted healthy, masculine individualism (the antithesis of schizophrenia) against the family. The family, in turn, was represented as a naturalized *environment* out of which (masculine) individuals emerged, and the maternal role both constituted and carried the burden of this contradiction. Mothers had recently been enjoined to return to full-time homemaking, and family therapy monitored mothers' abilities to produce autonomous individuals. This new therapy focused on "the spaces between people," examining relationships within the family (Armstrong 1983, 101). But this focus on relationships, and specifically on people's ability to differentiate their identities within

the family, *assumed* "the family" as the given context for this identity work. So at the very historical moment that the family became an
object of therapeutic analysis to be examined and questioned, family
structure was naturalized as a feminized environment—the context for
the analysis.[10]

Beginning in the late 1970s, however, change in the family brought
about by therapeutic intervention was (and is now) both expected and
desired. And once again, an illness that is particularly difficult to treat—
anorexia nervosa—was quite influential in these new developments.[11]
Salvador Minuchin (Minuchin, Rosman, and Baker 1978), the founder
of structural family therapy, and Mara Selvini-Pallazoli (1974), who
pioneered the Milan systemic approach to family systems therapy, both
use anorexia as a primary example, arguing that it requires new theoretical developments to analyze and treat. Whereas schizophrenia in the
postwar period seemed to pose the question of how to create masculine
individualism almost in spite of the family (note that since that time,
treatments for schizophrenia have gradually focused more and more
on pharmacological therapies; see Tomlinson 1990), family therapies
for anorexia, in contrast, work to reconfigure family structures, coali-
tions, and belief systems to free up young women and girls who experience anorexic symptoms from the perceived constraints of family life.
An example from structural family therapy, mentioned earlier, is therapists' attempts to reduce "enmeshment" in so-called anorexic families,
or strengthen "boundaries" around individuals and roles in families (a
goal that can be found in a wide range of therapeutic approaches).
Because this goal applies to all family members, it is in keeping with
supposedly gender-inclusive ideologies of individualism in the United
States today. However, even though systems therapists do not overtly
adhere to "traditional" ideals of motherhood that seem to compromise
individualism, I suggest that these therapies reinscribe motherhood as
the essential, but now relatively invisible, core of family life. Therapeutic ideas about individuation for anorexic daughters are not modeled on a postwar version of (masculinized) "escape" from family ties;
rather, as we shall see, individuation is to be mediated through minimal
mothering.

Most therapists no longer assume that there are predetermined gender roles in the family, and it is difficult to find a "pathogenic mother"
in today's literature on anorexia. As the psychiatrist George Hsu noted
in the early 1980s: "Attempts to identify a typical anorexic mother . . .

have produced no consistent findings . . . more recently, several authors have described a typical anorexic family interaction pathology" (Hsu 1983, 232). The consensus in the past few decades among mental health professionals is that family dynamics, understood and analyzed in supposedly gender-neutral terms, usually play a role in creating and supporting anorexia, but no specific causality can be determined, whether one is talking about particular family members or familial patterns of behavior (see Neal and Herzog 1985; Reiff and Reiff 1992). However, as a number of feminist psychotherapists have been pointing out since the late 1970s, as long as family therapists maintain a stance of gender neutrality in their work, powerful sociocultural discourses that are steeped in gendered inequalities will continue to operate unchallenged (whether implicitly or explicitly) in families and in family therapy.[12]

Indeed, in spite of claims of gender neutrality, it is not uncommon within family systems thinking about anorexia today to find a focus on the mother-daughter relationship both as a central problem and as the key to the daughter's health. Consider Minuchin's construct of enmeshment in this light. While Minuchin is clear that any family member can engage in enmeshed interactions (e.g., by speaking for or controlling another family member), in practice, enmeshment is almost always coded as maternal. Systems therapists concerned with reducing enmeshment in families often focus on reforming mothers. At the same time, enmeshment has an ambiguous status within family therapy, because as the opposite of individualism, it represents family cohesion, some of which therapists would like to retain (Kog, Vandereycken, and Vertommen 1985). While systems therapists are to "support individuation and challenge enmeshment," they are to do so in ways that do not challenge "the value of family 'togetherness,' which can be a functional characteristic" (Minuchin, Rosman, and Baker 1978, 98). Too much autonomy can look like rigidity and isolation (Colapinto 1991), and not surprisingly, "togetherness" is usually feminized. A brief discussion of Minuchin's reported casework will help illustrate these gender politics in his work (which is, again, still quite influential in family therapy for anorexia today).

Minuchin, Rosman, and Baker (1978) describe a therapy session in which the parents of an anorexic patient (Deborah) try to convince their daughter to eat. They are not successful (as expected). The therapists tell us that the mother and father undermine *each other's* efforts in this task, suggesting that both parents are to blame for their failure (4). They write: "Mother pleads, Deborah refuses, Father enters with a firm demand, Mother intervenes to soften Father's demand, Deborah refuses, and so on" (4). However, Minuchin and his colleagues focus primarily on the ways in which mothers thwart fathers' efforts. The mother in this case is described in the following way: "Mrs. Kaplan is desperate. But she is equally incompetent. She is a woman who has devoted her life to being a good wife and mother in accordance with her values. But her futile reasoning [and] her mindless repetition of ineffective interactions . . . all lend credence to her hints that she is part of the problem" (9). The father, however, is described thus: "The intensity of [his] authoritarian statements is impressive. But so is their lack of effect. He presents a clear demand, but he always undercuts his own position by a long monologue that delays the necessity to act. . . . [he is unable] to give a simple command" (9). One gathers that the father has learned to undercut his own position through interactions with the mother. In reference to a similar case study, Minuchin and his colleagues write: "Typically, the father insists on action and change, while the mother tries to find reasons to understand and justify the symptom" (71). Minuchin often pathologizes mothers' roles in this way and naturalizes both fathers' "action orientation" and mothers' "enmeshment" (or collusion) with their daughters. Fathers are described, at times, as overly controlling, but because the ultimate goal within family therapy is that everyone "learn to fend for himself " (102), some fathers' excesses in this regard—spilling over to the control over others in the family—is read as one effect of an enmeshed "system" that requires, first and foremost, that the mother change.[13] Only then will (masculine) individualism balance with (feminine) connectedness. But the implication is that the mother is dysfunctional from the start and is always a potential threat to the goal of separation and individuation within the family, even though a minimal, "functional" mothering remains as a requirement of familial health.

In sum, as with therapeutic constructs of motherhood in the 1950s and 1960s, mothers today are seen to be responsible for both health and pathology in families, and both the values and the dangers of motherhood are naturalized. At the same time, however, the promises and problems of maternal caretaking are now folded into the therapeutic process—family roles *appear* to be denaturalized, to an extent, because the family is no longer bracketed from therapy, from the possibility for change. Again, the family environment—objectified as such in the postwar era and feminized through its ideological opposition to market individualism—has now become an object of direct therapeutic management in order to facilitate the making of healthy, individuated selves, both male and female. In the process, the family has become more of a dynamic resource for the creation of persons; family structures are minimized, and the dichotomy of family/individual appears to be less rigid than it was in the 1950s and 1960s. Minuchin sees the family as a "laboratory," reducing its status as a "natural environment" to a "matrix" that produces individuals. He writes: "The family imprints its members with selfhood. Human experience of identity has two elements: a sense of belonging and a sense of being separate. The laboratory in which these ingredients are mixed and dispensed is the family, the matrix of identity" (Minuchin 1974, 47). But in spite of the new therapies' claims to gender neutrality in their analysis of the "matrix of identity" that is the family, therapeutic ideas about the family continue to represent familial enmeshment as quintessentially feminine. Minimal mothering retains a core "nature" that, while perceived as dynamic, is still imagined to be in an oppositional relationship to individualism.

Case Study of Familial "Substitution"

Substitute Mothering, Day One of Admission

I now turn to a specific case of familial substitution at Walsh. First, a brief description of Walsh's "typical" family profiles is in order.[14] Most patients diagnosed with anorexia and hospitalized at Walsh in the mid-1990s were living in white, middle-class nuclear families. Some families were blended, most were two-career, and the majority included one or two additional children. A significant number of patients' mothers (approximately one-fourth) did not work for pay on a full-time basis (and many did not work for pay at all). The majority of patients' fathers were professionals: engineers, doctors, architects.

The family that is the main case study for this chapter includes a professional father, a so-called stay-at-home mother, and two daughters. Maude, the sixteen-year-old patient discussed in chapter 1, is a member of this family and was admitted to Walsh twice during the time I was conducting my fieldwork. I followed her treatment very closely over the course of about three months, a period of time covering both of these admissions and many outpatient clinic visits, as well. I also got to know Maude's parents, Carol and Peter, very well. Near the end of Maude's first admission to the hospital, I met with her parents and her sister Joan to ask them about their experiences on the unit. Maude's mother, Carol, recounted a series of events that had had an enormous impact on her. She started off by saying that it is difficult to understand why Maude stopped eating, especially when, somehow, she was able to eat in the hospital. Carol then said that on the day that Maude was admitted, John, the admissions coordinator, had told her that it would be helpful if Maude drank some Ensure (total liquid nutrition) in the car on the long drive to the hospital from Maude's hometown.[15] But Maude did not do so; she wanted to wait until she arrived at the hospital. Carol continued the story, addressing me: "Then once we were here, you brought her that cup of warm Ensure, and she drank it right up." Thinking back on that event, I said: "That *was* me, wasn't it?" Carol said, "It's one of the few things I remember from that day."

Carol's memories encouraged me to think about deployments of the treatment team as a "substitute family" and my own participation in this construction. For Maude and her mother, parental substitution operated very strongly on the first day of Maude's first admission to Walsh. Before Maude arrived, nursing staff were alerted to the fact that I was hoping to get to know Maude and her family well, and to track the details of her treatment from its beginning. When Maude and Carol showed up on the unit, Richard, her assigned nurse for the afternoon, introduced himself and me, and then we all went to Maude's room. Maude moved her frighteningly tiny body slowly and deliberately, quietly allowing Richard to weigh her and take her vital signs, while Carol watched, smiling nervously and appearing to be in shock. Meanwhile Elsie, a nurse, poured a can of Ensure into a cup and warmed it up, explaining to me that Maude was almost certainly hypothermic (dangerously below normal body temperature) and should not drink anything cold. To my surprise, Elsie handed me the cup of Ensure and said, out of Maude's and Carol's earshot, "She has to be watched drinking this, and she has to drink every drop. It's medicine. It's a calorie a cc.[16] Of course, she's not a seasoned anorexic; they try to wipe it on their shirts, dribble it, et cetera. She'll probably drink it up fast." Both excited and unsettled by my assigned task, I brought the

Ensure to Maude, who was now in her bed with a bed warmer. Meanwhile Elsie turned to Carol and said, "When kids eat, parents are not to be in the room. It's just to avoid conflict." Carol said OK, and left the room. Elsie was right: Maude drank the Ensure quickly while I sat by her bedside, so that moments later I joined Elsie and Carol in the hallway. Carol was explaining that she had tried to get Maude to drink Ensure at home, but to no avail; Maude had kept saying she would wait until she was admitted to the hospital.

What we see happening here is a direct substitution of the treatment team for Carol in the role of nurturer. Maude arrived with her mother in a state of starvation, refusing food; she was then given a new room, tucked into bed, and "fed" once her mother left this space. At the very moment that Maude was most in need of others' care, this nurturing took a ritualized and medicalized form: her food was "medicine," it was measured out and warmed (just as her body was measured and warmed), it was administered in a formalized way, and it was deliberately *not* received from her mother. The substitution "worked": Maude drank the Ensure, and she drank it quickly. Excluded, Carol experienced this event as Maude's eager acceptance of nurturing from someone other than herself. The substitution was supposed to be a "lesson" about how to nurture Maude—that is, Maude *will* eat, just not in front of her mother.

However, in an important sense, this kind of hospital care cannot be compared to mothering at all—it is not "the real thing." Part of the reason Maude drank the Ensure quickly was because, in a hospital context, Ensure seems like "medicine," not "food."[17] As a form of liquid nutrition, Ensure can be digested very quickly and easily, and for a person close to death from starvation, it is not merely life sustaining but also lifesaving. In this sense, and in this case, providing Ensure is a medical intervention. In addition, Ensure is medicine in this context because it is offered in the same spirit that a cast is offered for a broken bone; the institutionalized aspects of feeding here grant it an air of inevitability that is specific to professional medical care, as opposed to the care of mothering. Maude seemed to recognize and even embrace the inevitability of drinking Ensure in the hospital—and to experience this act as fundamentally different from receiving Ensure from her mother—when she insisted on waiting until she arrived at Walsh before taking the liquid into her body.[18] The fact that I was given the role of providing food for Maude threw into relief the formal aspects of "substitute" nurturing: even the resident anthropologist can do it. Elsie told me the rules and what to expect; that is all that was required.

But at the same time, caregivers at Walsh *did* represent the provision of Ensure in the hospital as a form of "mothering" for anorexic patients, and a superior form at that. In an interview with me some weeks later, Elsie told me that she wanted me to give Maude the Ensure because she was aware that I would be trying to get to know Maude well during her stay, and it was a "symbolic role" for me to have. The symbolism here is not difficult to decipher, and Carol certainly felt it. I was, seemingly, Maude's substitute mother. Lorna, another nurse at Walsh, once told me during an interview that Ensure was comparable to mother's milk, particularly when one considers the way it is used at Walsh. Lorna said that because anorexia embodies a "developmental arrest," patients need re-parenting in treatment, so they begin hospitalization with a diet of 100 percent Ensure not only for medical reasons but also to relive a developmental transition from liquid to solid food in a way that is health giving.[19]

Many consider the feeding of children to be a uniquely maternal gesture. Note that on the first day of Maude's initial hospital admission, Maude's father, Peter, was absent. In general, staff and clinicians see much more of patients' mothers than of their fathers (to my knowledge, there were only two patients whose mothers were uninvolved in treatment during the time I was conducting my fieldwork). While there is an expectation on the unit that fathers will visit their daughters and take an active part in family therapy (and Peter soon became more involved in his daughter's hospital experience than most fathers do), no one on the treatment team is surprised by, or concerned about, fathers' relative unavailability. In general, Walsh lacks an elaborate discourse about fathers and fatherhood, a topic I address at the end of this chapter. The point I want to emphasize here is that parental substitution at Walsh is figured primarily as substitute mothering.[20]

For Maude and Carol, the process of (maternal) substitution continued throughout Maude's five-hour admission process. Cecilia, Maude's assigned nurse for the evening, interviewed Maude and Carol together about what had brought them to the hospital. Then Cecilia asked Carol to leave the room so that she could ask Maude the same questions in her mother's absence (I was present for both interviews). Cecilia explained to Maude, "Sometimes patients don't feel comfortable saying things in front of their parents." Then, after reviewing some of the unit's rules, Cecilia told Maude: "Conversations with me, staff, and doctors are between us. We won't tell your parents. We won't tell them how much you're eating, or how much you weigh. It's up to you to share what you want, and your parents get information through family meetings. And this is because with kids who have a chronic illness, a life-threatening illness, like you have, studies show that you need to grow up a bit faster, take charge. This is a part of that." Here, the hospital program is represented as a new, healthier environment that will take the place of Maude's family environment. An important measure of healthiness is individuation; the unit allows for a patient's "separation" from her "natural" family so that she can "grow up a bit faster" (here again we see the notion of developmental arrest at work). Contrary to standard ideas about medical help, Cecilia told Maude that the treatment team will *withhold* information from Maude's parents. This withholding goes beyond preserving Maude's confidentiality: it is part and parcel of treatment, allowing for individuation. Apart from family meetings, there is no systematic way for parents to receive information about their children's treatment. Also, family meetings are, in part, (informal) family *therapy* meetings, which makes them part of treatment, not just a forum for providing information about treatment. In these meetings, therapists offer parents only very general information, and parents are usually considered to be part of the problem.

At the same time, data flows freely in the opposite direction: the treatment team seeks information from parents about patients. Carol was interviewed extensively on that first day (and on other occasions as well) by nursing staff; by Martha, Maude's individual and family therapist; and by Ellen, Maude's pediatrician. These (and other) clinicians believed that Carol, as Maude's mother, had important knowledge about Maude that the treatment team should take into account. But also, clinicians seek to draw out information from parents about family life because most of them believe that when it comes down to it, a real "cure" will happen outside of the hospital, back in the "natural" family environment. When she was orienting Maude to the unit, Cecilia said, "You'll find a lot of this is up to you and your family. We'll guide and help, but mostly, the hard work is up to you." And as Martha, Maude's individual and family therapist, put it once in an early family meeting, "Parents need *some* information [about their children's progress]; *you're* the caretakers of your daughter, and we're consultants to you." Recall that while the treatment team is put into place as a substitute family, clinicians also believe that the "natural" family is irreplaceable. One of the goals of hospitalization is to create a wedge between patients and their families, opening up possibilities for change by providing a different model of the family. But paradoxically, in the very separation of "individual" and "family," these categories seem to be given and relatively fixed (and therefore resistant to change).

Problems with Motherhood Are Dynamic

How is it that mothers remain a focus of intense therapeutic concern in spite of a shift away from 1950s- and 1960s-style mother blaming? I now turn to examine the so-called "interaction pathology" of Maude's family to address this question. Apparent in this example are problems within (mainstream) family therapies that a number of feminist critics have identified—for example, the pathologizing of stereotypically feminine roles and modes of interaction. But I am also attending here to the presumption that a minimized (and feminized) family environment is the necessary (if also devalued) context for the making of autonomous individuals.

Several members of the treatment team told me that problems in Maude's family were "typical" in many ways. They described Peter, Maude's father, as a problem solver interested in concrete answers to his questions, an approach that put Maude under pressure to explain herself "rationally." One clinician characterized Peter as a "meter reader"; in other words, he was focused on external signs of improvement, such as weight gain and matter-of-fact assessments of Maude's level of independence.[21] Peter was somewhat self-conscious about these issues in a range of contexts in his life (Martha, Maude's individual and family therapist, said that Peter's consciousness was rare for fathers in her experience): he wondered about a family habit of pleasing others by appearing to be "together" and self-controlled, and he cited his own accommodation to others at his job. But on the whole, members of the treatment team saw Peter's thinking about Maude's road to health as overly individualistic and rationalistic. For example, he wondered when Maude would "take charge" of her health as he had seen her do in other areas of her life. As Maude put it, "I think it's hard for dads to understand that it's a thinking process. He just wants to fix it." One effect of Peter's rationalism and his "quick-fix" desires, as a few people saw it, was to mask his own participation in Maude's approval seeking and therefore in her anorexic experience of isolation, extreme self-reliance, and perpetual effort (both in shaping her body and in her academic work). In contrast, Maude's mother was said to be overly preoccupied with the interpersonal "causes" of Maude's anorexia, picking up the slack for Peter here and thereby helping to perpetuate Peter's stance. Everyone in Maude's family described Carol as a "super-caretaker," and Carol often said that she felt a lot of guilt about Maude's eating disorder, because as a full-time mother, it has been her job to "raise the kids." In addition, Carol's mother had been ill and bedridden for some time, and as Peter put it, Carol "has taken on half of [her father's] burden" in caring for her own mother. Martha's take on the situation was that Maude got the message to care for herself, both from her father's idea that she should take charge of her own life and from the fact that Carol was so overwhelmed with her caretaking roles. At the same time, as Carol's daughter, Maude was invited to play the part of someone in need of care while Carol's guilt led her to try even harder in her caretaking. This situation had reached the point where Maude felt like such a burden that she had become "invisible" in the family, engaging in what Martha calls a "disappearing lifestyle."

In keeping with contemporary therapeutic discourse about families, Martha considered a variety of relationships and alignments in Maude's family—for example, the relationship between Carol and Peter, and Maude's relationship with her sister Joan. However, Martha focused on Maude's relationship with Carol. But instead of describing problems in this mother-daughter tie in terms of maternal oppression, as a family therapist in the 1950s might have done, Martha thought about its "dynamic" qualities. As she put it to me once: "The problem between Maude and Carol is abstract. It's an interaction, a dance. . . . it's a pursuer/pursued dynamic. If you feel someone pursues you, you go, 'Oh!' and turn and go away. And it gives Maude power: the power of invisibility." Martha's job, as she saw it, was to help Maude and her family question those imperatives embedded in the "dance" of their interactions that support the eating disorder. In particular, for Martha, Maude could not be independent in a healthy way until the burdens surrounding caretaking between Maude and Carol were reduced. There was one familial imperative, however, that Martha chose not to question. After Maude's first family meeting, Martha said to me, "It's Mom's job to take care of Maude. Everyone agrees with this." So at the same time that Martha critically examined many working assumptions within Maude's family—for example, gendered assumptions about the way mothers and fathers are expected to act—she was willing to leave intact the expectation that Maude's mother is the primary caretaker of her children. Also, several members of the treatment team, including Martha, concluded that Carol was more "emotionally available" than Peter (rather than focusing on the mutual construction of Peter's rationalism and Carol's caretaking). The general consensus was that Maude had a better chance of developing a healthy (individuated) relationship with her mother than with her father.

Here we can see clearly that psychiatric discourse about family dynamics in the treatment of anorexia both recycles and refigures contradictions surrounding individualism and family life that were present in representations of "schizophrenogenic" mothers in the 1950s and 1960s. Mothers like Carol are no longer blamed outright, but they still carry the burden of these (revised) contradictions. I suggest that "healthy" motherhood today is constituted in therapy as a kind of natural resource for the creation of individual patients' healthy selves. Even while motherhood is minimized (for example, Martha works to reduce the burdens of Carol's caretaking), it is also made available to be continually "used up" in the service of patients' individualism (it is Carol's job to take care of a properly individuated Maude).[22] The next section shows in some detail how minimal mothering is created and deployed in the treatment program at Walsh by examining Maude's experiences of "separation and individuation" from both her "natural" and "therapeutic" families in the course of her treatment. I describe how Maude moved from an alignment with the treatment team, and a growing separation from Carol and Peter, to a clear differentiation between her sense of self and the "therapeutic family," as well. As her therapy progressed, her parents' roles—particularly her mother's role—remained ambiguous. Was Carol to align herself with Maude or with the treatment team? Or was she to take an independent stance as a mother, allowing her daughter to "separate" from her?

Separating and Individuating

When Maude was first admitted to the hospital, she was very trusting of the treatment team and quite relieved to be in their hands. Although for weeks she was confined to her bed and was always observed when eating, she complied happily with her treatment program. Whenever I asked her how she felt about various aspects of her treatment, she always said, "They know what they're doing." This compliant phase is the norm and is unsurprising given patients' compromised medical conditions, and staff encourage it. Cecilia, one of Maude's nurses, told Maude on her first day that "it's important to trust staff as much as possible. Especially in the beginning. It's tempting not to." Maude replied that she would try to trust staff, and added, significantly, "I have no choice." Cecilia told her she *did* have a choice—that she would find she has a lot of control at Walsh, though it did not seem like it early on in treatment. Meanwhile, as I have suggested already, Carol was given the message that *she* had no choice but to comply with unit rules. Clinicians and staff stipulated specific conditions for her relationship with her daughter, as long as Maude was in the hospital. On the first day of Maude's hospitalization, when she was found to have a dangerously low pulse and body temperature, Carol noted with dismay that visiting hours were limited to 6:00 to 8:00 P.M. (on weekdays). Carol asked Cecilia if she could stay later than 8:00 that day, until she was sure Maude was safe, and Cecilia said no. Carol nodded solemnly but said she was uncomfortable leaving. Cecilia told her that the program is conservative, and that all their patients get better, though treatment sometimes takes a long time. Again we see that, beginning with day one, parental (maternal) care is almost fully replaced by hospital care; parents are taken out of the loop. This is the first step toward crafting a new "self" for patients.

For some time, Maude aligned herself with the treatment team and said she did not need her mother to visit her so much. Because Maude's family lived a few hours' drive from Walsh, Carol was temporarily staying with some relatives who lived near the hospital, and as Maude put it, "She's here every day at 6:00; I think they set the clocks by her." When Carol would ask for something on Maude's behalf, such as a brief opportunity to get out of her bed, Maude would defend the treatment team by saying, "I have no complaints." Carol began to feel shut out by Maude as well as the treatment team. I sat in on a family therapy session for Maude and her parents that took place after Maude had been in the hospital for three weeks; the conversation revolved around Maude's desire to be self-reliant and free of her parents' sympathy. Maude's parents said they experienced her attitude as a rejection of their care. But Maude did not, at this point, feel any overt conflict with her parents on this score. She simply felt she was not in need of their concern and wished to unburden them of any obligation to care for her

emotionally. After the family session, I spoke with Martha (the therapist) about her impressions of the meeting. Martha said that Maude was
expressing an independent "sense of self" to her parents, and Martha
also wondered about conflict around caretaking in Maude's "natural"
family (which was not discussed in the family meeting). Martha said
that Maude seemed to be requesting a certain kind of support, support
"that's not about worry, sadness, et cetera; but also, she's not letting in
support at all. . . . there are paradoxes here about caretaking. Someone
tries to caretake, and the caretakee gets pissed, and the caretaker is mad
about caretaking. And the paradox is that Maude's [response of self-
reliance] has gotten her into the opposite of what she wanted: now she
can't get rid of people" (i.e., her parents and the treatment team).

Eventually, Maude became aware of these conflicts around caretaking. She first articulated them in her relationship with the treatment
team only, in part because her "natural" family had been substituted by
the treatment team. About one month into her first stay in the hospital,
Maude began to question her compliance with the treatment program
and to separate out a sense of self that was resistant to the program's
rules and to her caretakers' control over her progress. During this time
in Maude's treatment, I sat in on an individual therapy session that
both Maude and her therapist Martha thought of as a turning point in
this regard. In this session, Maude and Martha objectified the treatment
program as an entity they called "structure," an entity that took care of
Maude but also seemed to deprive her of her individuality. Because
Martha thought that Maude's conflict with the treatment team reflected
conflict with her parents (particularly her mother)—familial conflict
that Maude did not recognize at the time—Martha encouraged Maude
to explore the effects of hospital "structure" on her relationship with
her parents, and on her eating disorder more generally. In this way, the
treatment program became a vehicle for the objectification, projection,
and exploration of Maude's struggles around independence, dependence, and caretaking in her "natural" family. At the same time, Martha
took seriously the idea that hospital treatment might be generating
some of Maude's conflicts with her parents. Martha's approach to therapy was unusual on the unit, in that she considered the idea that dominant cultural notions about the family and about personhood can appear unquestioned within institutions such as Walsh and can influence
people's experiences of problems in a negative way. She worked to
develop a therapeutic language with patients that reified (and some-

times personified) problems and institutional arrangements that support problems, disassociating both patients and herself from these objectified representations in order to create an analytic space for new formulations of patients' identities.[23] This process began for Maude with conversations about "structure."

At the start of the therapy session in which "structure" was named, Martha and Maude were exploring how "self-reliance" (a term that Martha had also objectified) was "convincing" Maude that she had no particular interest in her parents visiting her, an idea that was having a negative effect on Maude's family relationships. Carol in particular was very upset that Maude was noncommunicative when she and Peter would visit. Maude explained to Martha that it was not the case that she actively did not want her parents to visit; rather, she did not *need* them to visit and would not be disappointed if they stayed home. Martha said, "What I'm hearing is that the self-reliance is saying, 'well, you know, people can come or not. . . . I won't be too disappointed. It's OK, but it's not necessary.' You know what I'm saying? . . . does that ring true, that self-reliance would speak in those words?" Maude said that this phrasing made sense to her, but that she remembers always being that way. Martha concurred and then continued to explore the effects of self-reliance on Maude's family visits in the hospital: "I'm kinda thinking, if I were [your parents], and I came around and, you know, and there was all this incredible—you know, there's Maude, but then there's also all this self-reliance that's indicating to me, gee whiz, I can come or not come, and basically the self-reliance is kind of convincing Maude of this. I'm just wondering what I might be thinking. I might think, 'Gee, I'd like to see Maude, but there's all this self-reliance in the way!' " Maude replied, "Part of it is I'm tired of visiting people in this atmosphere." It was at this point that the conversation took a turn toward the effects of hospitalization on Maude and her parents. Maude said that it was difficult to "kick back" and relax with her parents in a hospital environment, and that the structure of visiting hours made visiting a tense time: "It's like an unusual situation because, I mean, you have set visiting hours, and then you're just expected to like sit and talk because that's all the time you have, whereas . . . at home . . . you talk and stuff but you're usually doing an activity. I mean, [at home] there's never a set time . . . when your schedule is 'visiting hours.' "

From here, Martha and Maude developed the concept of "structure," which consists of hospital rules, the program's schedule, and clinicians' "preconceived ideas" about Maude's eating disorder and the trajectory of her treatment. For example, Maude talked about how the program's rigid schedule and protocols made it impossible for her to think for herself about what she wants and needs in her struggle toward health. Martha suggested that "structure" invites "self-reliance" to step in and convince Maude that as long as she is in the hospital, she can't "be herself," and therefore she cannot relate to her parents. By representing Maude's conflict with her parents as an effect of "structure," Martha was attempting to create an analytic (and experiential) separation between this problem and the people involved. At one point, she said, "I'm just wondering if the hospital structure is sort of convincing you that it's all-powerful. That—that it's got you." And later she added, "It feels like the structure sort of, um, sneaks in and grabs . . . grabs your Maudeness." Maude agreed with this idea, saying that structure does not want her "to be an individual here." Martha then suggested that they find ways for Maude to fight the effects of structure so that self-reliance did not interfere so much with Maude's relationships. Maude pointed out that structure was also having an effect on her parents—it wasn't just "self-reliance" that was disrupting family visits. She remarked that her parents were anxious when they visited her; that they thought "all the time has to be filled up with talking"; and that there was inequality in the fact that her parents could come and go, but she could not. Martha thought out loud about the effects of structure on Maude's parents: "[Structure is] saying, 'You can't take your daughter home.' That's pretty powerful to say to a parent."

One of Martha's goals here was to align herself, Maude, and Maude's parents against the negative effects of structure. At this point in Maude's therapy—now that Maude was no longer happily compliant within her substitute family—Martha wanted to help position Maude's parents "on her side" in her struggle "to be an individual." This move is one way to position the treatment team (minus Martha) as "the bad guys" when the treatment process becomes uncomfortable, and therefore to begin transforming relationships in Maude's family. Martha said to Maude, "We need to get [this conflict surrounding structure] out of the way somehow. We shouldn't allow the structure to be so powerful. . . . it might be good to get some of [your parents'] input on this. To see how we can take some of the power out of the structure. Get some of their input and help."

However, Martha also believed that Maude's struggles with structure mirrored problematic relations with her parents, which meant that Maude's parents and structure could not be neatly dichotomized. At the same time that Martha and Maude were talking about the treatment program (structure) as other to Maude and her family, as a set of constraints that all parties needed to resist if genuine family connections were to flourish, Martha also conceptualized Maude's treatment trajectory as a crystallized version of historical developments in caretaking relationships within Maude's family—in particular, Maude's caretaking experiences with her mother, Carol. Martha's views on this topic were apparent in the therapy session about structure, in response to Maude's reflections about her independence before and after hospitalization. Toward the end of the session, Maude said that while it had been necessary for her to give in to structure when she first arrived, after a while, it was destructive to give up her individuality to structure.

> [Before I was admitted to the hospital] my independence kind of got me into trouble, you know. So I came here . . . and it's like, "Let's take that away from her." . . . You misuse it once, and you get it taken away from you. And then you're gonna get it back, you know, a long time later, and like, what good does that do? . . . Some of the things here don't seem like—they seem like the reverse of what help would be. . . . I mean, how does it help not to have what got you into trouble? Because it's a very useful tool. You misused it once. So you're not gonna learn how to reuse it right again if you don't have it. . . . At first, you really need to be here. . . . At first, the structure was helpful. . . . But after an extended period of time, I think it becomes really unhealthy being in the structure. . . . I think it only goes to a certain point of helpfulness, and then it starts kind of a reversal, and it's not helpful.

Martha engaged Maude on these points by talking about structure as if it were a strict parent (read: mother) taking care of a developing child. As Martha put it to me in private, after the session: "It's like parenting. Mothering is good when you're a baby, but then it becomes overprotective mothering when you're an adolescent. It's like, strict parents can do fine with young kids, but then they can't with adolescents. . . . Maude's struggle with the hospital parallels her struggle with caretaking issues [at home]." During the therapy session, Martha had said to Maude: "As I was listening to you, [the structure] sounded like, um, very punishing. . . . 'Okay, you messed up with [your independence], we're gonna take it away.' The structure's saying, 'And determine when you can have it back. If you've been a good girl, then you can get this.' . . . So at first the structure was helpful . . . it sounds like at first, the structure is very, has a very sweet voice, a very nice voice. It says, 'Let me make sure you're safe, let me make sure you get healthy,' and then somewhere along the way it turns into a mean voice."[24] Martha then summarized Maude's more recent feelings about structure, and the subtext here was about how Maude's experience of structure might resonate with her (as yet unrecognized) feelings toward her mother: "You're too containing. You're pinching a little bit . . . you're telling me I can't be Maude. Because Maude is independent and on her own, and how can I do that while you're telling me what to do?"

To recap a bit here: while Martha encouraged a clear distinction between "structure" and Maude as an individual, her distinction between structure and Maude's family was not as clear. Again, at this stage of treatment, while Martha was seeking to align Maude and her parents against structure, she simultaneously thought about Maude's struggles with the treatment team as a recapitulation of struggles in her family. This example shows how parents occupy a difficult "middle position" in the treatment program.

On the one hand, parents are patients of a sort. In this view, family problems are bound to become visible in, and intertwined with, the treatment process. Also, treatment team members are seen as experts, and parents are expected to comply with the team's recommendations. On the other hand, parents represent a "natural" human environment that the treatment program can never replicate, and they maintain ultimate authority over their children. In this view, parents can be represented as other to the treatment team, and they can legitimately resist medical authority. However, as I have already suggested, parents can never resist medical authority to the same extent that patients do (in the eyes of the treatment team). Resistance is an expression of individuation, which is a treatment goal for patients more so than parents. So, ideally, where do parents stand, ultimately, vis-à-vis the treatment team? I have argued that it is clinicians' primary goal to help effect patients' separation and individuation from their families while still expecting a degree of authentic family "togetherness" to emerge in the process. This goal can be achieved once patients' parents align with the treatment team to the extent that they willingly relinquish control over their daughters' medical care. Martha once told me that when parents reach this stage, patients will "deal with their own struggles" both in the hospital and at home, rather than envisioning themselves as victims of psychiatric control (a mind-set that can easily result in their returning to old patterns at home). The idea here is that parents will parent well at home once they have learned to give up control over certain areas of their daughters' lives (e.g., control over their daughters' bodies and eating habits).

The team imagines that parents must go through a few stages before they (and their daughters) reach this point. Early on in treatment, parents are shut out in a way that is not conducive to patients' individuation within their natural families, or to parents' alignment with the treatment team: we have seen that at first, members of the treatment team deliberately set up a split between patients' so-called natural families (to be seen as safe havens) and their new, substitute family (the new arena of bodily control and psychological monitoring). This split was at work in Maude and Martha's formulation of hospital structure constraining both Maude and her family relationships. Carol and Peter felt this split, as well. Although they had handed over Maude's care to the treatment team, they had thought of this move only in terms of a medical emergency and were surprised to learn that they were to be excluded from knowledge about, and participation in, Maude's care. Both of them talked to me about how difficult it was to get any information about Maude's treatment trajectory. As Carol put it, "Parents are left in the cold, unless you're assertive, which I try to be." She also commented, "They can't wait to get Maude's sister in here, to get their hooks into her" (there was a bit of a delay before Maude's sister Joan could attend family meetings). Here we can see that (for a time) Maude's parents felt themselves to be separate from—and, at times, "victims" of—the treatment program, as did Maude after she had spent a few weeks in the hospital.

But eventually Maude and her parents were no longer united in their disagreements with the treatment program. As Carol put it to me once: "I thought [Peter and I] were on the same side [as Maude], but I can see that in some ways we're not. We want Maude to gain weight; she doesn't." It was during Maude's second hospitalization, once Carol and Peter were more aligned with the treatment team, that Maude and Martha began to articulate differences not only between Maude's "self" and the treatment team (a process they had begun during her first admission with their conversations about structure) but also between her self and her family. At this point in Maude's therapy, Maude and

Martha no longer talked about Maude's parents as unambiguously "on her side." This change took place gradually. Martha told me about a therapy session I missed in which Maude had a conversation with her "eating disorder" and "the treatment team" as if they were entities that were present in the therapy room. Implicitly invoking Maude's relationship with her parents, Martha told Maude that she seemed to speak to each as if she were a pleasing and placating child. A few weeks later, Maude took up Martha's characterization of her as a challenge: when Maude was an outpatient once again, she began to resist gaining weight, because she felt she was gaining just to please the treatment team, that she was taking the team's side. In addition, she began to feel it was important that her parents stay out of these outpatient struggles altogether, that they not "take sides" (either hers or the treatment team's). Martha viewed Maude's independence from her parents in this regard as a healthy step toward reducing parental involvement, a step that could be credited, in part, to the parent/child idiom she and Maude had been using to discuss Maude's struggles with her eating disorder and with the treatment team. Martha's support here of Maude's parents' relinquishing control to therapists was also apparent in her conversations with Maude about her family meetings with her new outpatient therapist in her hometown. Maude told Martha that she dreaded these meetings, because her parents would just "talk and talk." Martha pointed out to Maude that if her parents can anticipate these family meetings, it probably helps them to "back off" from her at other times.

Indeed, Maude's parents, like most parents in the program, had taken to heart the treatment program's injunction that they remove themselves from Maude's struggles with anorexia as much as possible. Several clinicians had consistently conveyed this message to them. Martha disagreed with the idea of telling parents to "stay out" altogether, preferring a middle road that combined parental separation and involvement. She talked to me about some of the unintended and paradoxical effects of telling parents simply to stay out. She said this policy conveys "totally the wrong message," because it participates in the problem by imposing silence and secrecy. In talking with Maude's parents, I could see that their positioning as outsiders in the treatment process (to the extent that they were positioned as such) generated for them a passionate, but subterranean, interest in the details of Maude's life. In this way, the strategy of taking parents out of the loop actually produces seemingly problematic forms of parental interest. Carol and

Peter became extremely attentive to Maude's eating habits, work habits, social life, and so on. They tried not to reveal this interest to Maude, talking about it quietly between themselves, and also occasionally to me in the clinic. As Peter put it once, because Maude shared so little with him and Carol, "Sometimes you try to guess what she's thinking. It's almost like a contest." Not surprisingly, Carol was particularly susceptible to this kind of "underground" involvement in Maude's life, given the conflicts around caretaking between herself and Maude, and given the goal of "separating" from Maude's struggles while at the same time somehow remaining a caring, concerned, and supportive mother.

The requirement that parents separate from their daughters leaves them uncertain about how to conceptualize their relationship with the treatment team. One afternoon in the outpatient clinic, I spoke with Carol and Peter about this issue while they were waiting in the seating area outside the clinic for Maude's appointment to end. Carol said she relied emotionally on clinic visits—it was helpful to her to look forward to Maude's outpatient appointments. "For example, if Maude isn't eating very much at home, I can say to myself, 'It's OK, I'll check in at clinic.'" But at the same time, she and Peter both felt pressure to disidentify completely with the treatment team, to carve out a space for themselves that, as Maude had put it, did not "take sides," neither Maude's nor the team's. Peter said that on the way to clinic that day, he had told Maude he wanted to go up to the inpatient unit to say hello to Maude's former caregivers. "But Maude said, 'Why do *you* want to go up there? That's *my* place.' She drew the line." Carol added, "I'm working on separating from the eating disorder. In our [outpatient] family session, we talked about how this is hard [for me] given the long drive here. But I'm moving farther down the hallway [from the clinic as I wait for Maude's appointment to end]. It's a visual image of progress." Carol's comment about the long drive speaks to her feelings of being taken for granted as a minimal mother; in spite of the fact that she was to "separate" from Maude, *and* assert parental difference from the treatment team, she was still expected to support Maude's treatment.

A few weeks later, Carol and I spoke at length about the contradictions of her position as Maude's mother delivering Maude to the clinic. Our conversation seemed to encapsulate several dilemmas embedded in psychiatric constructions of maternal health as it emerges through the process of familial substitution. Carol told me that the previous week, Maude and her pediatrician had decided she should come to the clinic twice a week instead of just once a week, since Maude was not gaining enough weight. Coming once a week had put a lot of pressure on Maude to monitor her own progress. Maude announced the new plan to Carol, who responded, "Oh, so less pressure on you and more on me." Carol had just told Maude on the way to the clinic that day how much better it felt to drive to the hospital just once a week, now that Maude was an outpatient (when she was an inpatient, Carol visited several times a week). But what was more significant for Carol was that Maude had announced the new plan, rather than asking her about it; Carol was not included in the decision, and there was no dialogue about it between her and the treatment team. Carol felt like a mere vehicle for Maude's treatment, a situation which, paradoxically, led her to focus attention on the probable details of Maude's thinking, a tendency she had been asked to resist. Carol told me she thought that Maude saw the new plan as a way to relinquish responsibility to gain weight, and that Maude "figured out two times a week works [for *her* schedule].[25] She can do her homework in the car on the way up and sleep on the way back." But at the same time that Carol felt "used" as a mother with this arrangement, she also felt guilt about her resentment. She wondered, shouldn't she, as Maude's mother, just be willing to go along with whatever the treatment team thinks will be helpful to Maude? In a triple bind of commitments to the treatment program, to Maude, and to herself as a "separating" parent, Carol usually privatized the contradictions of her position, doubting herself as a mother and feeling responsible for "mother-daughter conflict." Here we can see the institutional production of a maternal "condition" that is all too readily imagined to lie at the heart of the problem that is anorexia.

The Construction of Minimal Mothering

We have seen that throughout the extended process of articulating distinctions among patients' senses of self, their natural families, and their substitute families, patients' mothers in particular can never be sure whether to align with the treatment team. The requirements of minimal mothering are too vague to provide guidance. Many mothers wonder if they should try to help repair damage they feel they have caused, or stay "out of the loop," as they are asked to, separating from their daughters. But how can they stay out when their daughters return home?

Opinions about Carol as a mother at the time Maude was first admitted to Walsh are telling. Before Maude's admission, she was seeing a therapist who told Carol not to intervene in Maude's treatment, and Carol complied, even though Maude continued to lose weight. Several staff members at Walsh doubted Carol's ability to be a good mother because she went along with this therapist. But at the same time, the staff expected Carol to hand over to *them* control of her daughter's health. Martha pointed out to me one day that no matter how Carol acted in these situations, she could be seen as a "bad mother." When a mother listens to an expert she is, like a good mother, acting in the interest of her child; but often mothers listen to experts because they worry that they are *not* good-enough mothers, since they need experts to help them.

What is a "good-enough" mother? As part of my fieldwork experience, I participated in a seminar on developmental psychology for residents and interns in training at Walsh. During this seminar, the instructor explained a popular theory about "good-enough" mothering, as put forth by the psychologist D. W. Winnicott. Winnicott is a well-known object relations theorist whose work has helped to shape new individual therapies that have been influential in treatments for anorexia since the 1970s (see note 22). Arguing against the structured set of expectations for mothers that had developed out of Freudian theory, Winnicott proposed a minimalist theory about motherhood, suggesting that most mothers are "good enough" (Winnicott 1965). Good-enough mothers provide a "holding environment" for their children's individuation. Winnicott further proposed that mothers who are *not* good enough cannot be taught; they must be treated. In other words, motherhood is a natural quality of personhood that cannot be formally specified.

Often treatment team members imply that a good mother will know what is best for her daughter intuitively and will "choose" what is best even in the face of conflicting and compelling alternatives. One afternoon, I was in the charting room on the inpatient unit when Sally returned a phone call to Beth, the mother of a former inpatient of hers, named Lila. Lila was scheduled to come in to the clinic that week and wanted to cancel because of pressure at school (it was a long drive from Lila's hometown to the clinic). Sally recommended to Beth that Lila come to the clinic or at the very least see a local doctor. She said, "It's hard, I know. You have to prioritize: school, or health." Their conversation continued for some time, and then Sally said, with some exasperation, "We *consult* to you; you, as a *parent*, decide." After she hung up the phone, Sally explained to me that in the past, Beth would tell Lila that the treatment team "made" her agree with their recommendations to avoid asserting her own authority as a parent against Lila's wishes. Karen, a psychology intern, told me a similar story about discussions in the outpatient clinic that led to Maude's second admission to the hospital. Maude was upset about the prospect of another admission, and Carol asked about the consequences of keeping Maude at home, against medical advice. Martha told her that the treatment team would not hold such a decision against them, but their insurance company might refuse coverage in the future. They decided to admit Maude, and after Maude left the room, Carol said to Martha, "She really needs to come in. She needs this." While telling me this story, Karen rolled her eyes about Carol's failure to assert what she thought was best for Maude in Maude's presence. Karen said, "Carol's afraid of Maude's anger; she wants the team to decide." But she then added an acknowledgment of the power of experts: "You know, it's hard [for her], because she's been jerked around by professionals, she's really unsure of what is best." The idea in both of these stories is that mothers should "naturally" know what is best or at the very least choose willingly what the treatment team "knows" to be best—this in spite of the fact that parents are told to "get out," and to let the treatment team be "the bad guys." So good mothering, or good-enough mothering, is imagined as an intuitive set of ideas and practices that transcends medical advice but is at the same time so underspecified that the judgment of medical professionals can articulate or usurp its content.

Let me step back a moment from the production of minimal mothering in the process of treatment to explore one form of its expression outside of the hospital setting (as reported at Walsh). Early on in Maude's first hospitalization, during a family meeting, Carol spoke about the negotiation of independence and dependence between herself and Maude and cited a kind of competitive housecleaning that had developed between the two of them over the past few months as an example of conflict in this area of their lives. Carol noticed that Maude began to clean and tidy up the house every afternoon, and that specific tasks, such as straightening the linen closet and arranging magazines in the living room, had become routinized and rote for Maude. Although Carol felt that Maude was "compulsive" about these tasks, Maude herself attributed no particular significance to this house-work; in fact, she did not remember doing it with such regularity. But other members of her family thought she was asserting her independence over her mother's caretaking, and even taking over Carol's caretaking work. As Maude's sister Joan put it, "She was doing mom's job!" The situation made Carol uneasy. As she explained, "Here's [the need to please] in me: since I knew [Maude's] routine, I'd try to do it before Maude got home [from school]." Martha asked if this strategy worked. Carol said, "No; if I turned the magazines one way, she'd turn them another. I feel Maude was controlling of me on this one." Martha described this situation as one of "dueling caretaking" and said she had seen it before—Carol and Maude were by no means alone in expressing this kind of conflict.

What can we make of this ritualistic, competitive attention to household chores? And how are we to understand its furtive quality? Several other patients I interviewed also recognized their participation in "dueling caretaking" with some surprise and spoke of it as an almost underground activity. One way to shed light on dueling caretaking, and its relationship to anorexia, is to locate it historically. Recall my earlier discussion about the fact that in the postwar era, women—and girls "in training" to be women—were seen as "expert" managers of domestic space, and their dieting was often kept a secret. In chapter 1, I suggest that this situation has gradually become inverted: fitness (dieting and exercise) has replaced domestic caretaking as the primary arena for the expression of women's skills in consumer management, and in this scheme, domestic caretaking should ideally fall into place without difficulty. While women continue to be the primary domestic caretakers in families, this job has lost much of its institutional and ideological support. Many mothers of adolescent girls today grew up with the assumption that their primary role in life would be domestic caretaking, and they now struggle to raise "independent" daughters who, for the most part, still plan to become wives and mothers. I suggest that dueling caretaking points to conflicting constructions of feminine identity at this historical juncture: both Maude and Carol were trying to assert "autonomy" (that is, "competitiveness" and a refusal of the other's help) *while* (furtively) caretaking the other. Dueling caretaking exaggerates, almost parodies, the idea that domestic caretaking is a necessary but "underground" practice that should manifest itself as an effect of—that is, as secondary to—individual effort. Patients who engage in dueling caretaking with their mothers show that their own caretaking work is subsumed within ritualistic practices that display their autonomy, implicitly protesting the "dependency" implied in their mothers' more "traditional" caretaking roles, even as they perform domestic chores.

This conflict is often experienced as *individual* mothers' and daughters' problems with "interpersonal dependency." As much contemporary psychiatric theory would have it, these mothers and daughters are expressing pathological enmeshment, or difficulty with "separation and individuation." Many patients and their parents are embarrassed about their perceived problems with interpersonal dependency and imagine that these problems would be solved if patients were more autonomous from their families, and from their mothers in particular. Most clinicians at Walsh agree with this idea. But as we have seen, the treatment program itself creates experiences in which mothers and daughters appear to have difficulty "separating." Consider the following story. During Maude's second admission to the hospital, her experience of being oppressed by the treatment program outweighed her desire to be independent from her parents. She called her mother frequently and begged her to take her home (against medical advice). In a sense, Maude was caring for Carol by letting her know that she wanted her to be her primary caretaker. But at the same time, as Carol pointed out, Maude knew that she was asking for something that Carol would not give her. Carol was very upset and torn by these phone calls. As she put it to me, "It's hard when what your child wants to do is the *worst* thing for them. It's hard for a parent." Maude never asked Carol for anything—never let her "be a mother"—and here she was asking for something that Carol felt she could not provide, for two reasons. First, the treatment program had almost certainly saved Maude's life, so Carol did not dare contradict the treatment team. Second, Carol feared that the ultimate reason she had no choice but to rely on the treatment program was that she had been deeply flawed as a provider: she had been unable to ensure that her daughter would eat, and she felt that this was the most fundamental aspect of her "job" as a mother. There is a parallel here with Maude and Carol's "dueling caretaking" over household chores: the desire of each to care for the other was, paradoxically, produced through assertions of separateness. Carol's caring for Maude in this case was to "get out of the loop," to give up her caretaking work to the treatment team. When Maude was asking Carol to take her out of the hospital, knowing full well that Carol would not do this, she was invoking her mother's desire to care for her by reminding Carol of the specific ways that she had, seemingly, "failed" in her maternal caretaking. Similarly, Maude's housework both invoked and usurped Carol's "job" as a housewife. In both cases, mother-daughter "separation and individuation" was enacted in reference to maternal lack.

The idea of a maternal lack naturalizes a notion of motherhood as it should be; an ideal form of maternal caretaking appears as an absent referent. Many mothers I interviewed felt that they were to blame for their daughters' eating disorders because of a deficit in their mothering abilities. Carol talked with me about her fear that she had been a "bad mother" (and had therefore caused the anorexia), since, she felt, she herself had not been mothered well. Most of the mothers I spoke with combed the past to find "answers," retrospectively imagining themselves as ever-present caretakers who somehow missed something vital or did something wrong. A therapist on the inpatient unit described the mother of a new patient this way: "Mom feels there's a 'right' way to handle this, and that she lost competence as a mother. She feels guilt about how she's handled it." Maude's father Peter, her sister Joan, and her mother Carol had this to say about Carol's retrospective engagement with the problem, comparing it to Peter's more "pragmatic" approach:

> *Peter:* Moms and dads are different. Fathers don't take as much responsibility for it. Or maybe that's just me.
>
> *Joan:* My dad, he sees problems as, "well this happened, it's done. Now what?" It's a problem-solving approach. My mom, she goes back over stuff in the past. "What if x, or if we'd done y?" Basically, dad is forward looking, and mom backward. But, I think it's *natural* for moms.
>
> *Carol:* Thank you, Joan. As I said, it's been my whole job, raising the kids.

I have argued that by focusing on mother-daughter separation and individuation as the solution to "enmeshment," the treatment program itself produces both of these extremes. In particular, the provision of a substitute family allows for separation and individuation through parental exclusion, which generates guilt and involvement, which, in turn, seem to confirm the problem of enmeshment. Janet, the mother of a young woman named Heather who had been an outpatient in the program for many years, talked to me about this issue in an interview:

"I feel very excluded [from the treatment process]. . . . Ed [Heather's father] says it's [Heather's] problem, there's nothing we can do. . . . She's been very close to me, and I can see it wasn't always good for her. . . . The question of the parents' role: I blame myself. There's been no illness in the family before. I didn't know how many questions to ask [of the treatment team]. In hindsight, I should have been more involved medically. I should have let them know I resented the exclusion. But they'd say, 'You're overinvolved,' so I don't know." During an interview with Beth, whose daughter Lila was an outpatient at the time, I asked Beth to say more about the low level of communication she noticed between herself and the treatment team. She said, "It has to be OK with me, because it wouldn't work otherwise. I have to step out; I can't fix it. If I knew information about her treatment plan, she and I would be arguing all night. Through this whole process, I've needed to learn that I can't fix it. And it's been kind of a relief." So the ideal of an ever-present, "fix-everything" mother is rejected. At the same time, re-call that Sally, Lila's therapist, thought that Beth was relinquishing *too* much responsibility to the treatment team. However, there is no explicit advice for parents about how to help their daughters at home. It seems that the ideal of motherhood that the treatment program promotes rests on a notion of natural maternal feeling that will perform invisible healing work. What is more, mothers are in the impossible position of being "responsible" for having these natural feelings, and ensur-ing that they have good effects. One day in the clinic, I interviewed a woman whose daughter Elaine had been in and out of the program for several years. She said, "All they do here is pull things apart; no one tells you how to put it back together. When Elaine left the hospital, I asked for advice about what to do at home. They told me: 'You just love her. You just love her, and leave her alone.' Later, my daughter lost weight again, so I brought her in. The first thing they say to us is: 'you were supposed to be eating 3,500 calories a day. You didn't. And Mom, you let her do this?' I told them I resented that; no one had told me any-thing. So on the one hand, you're the cause, and on the other, you're not supposed to do anything." In this way, maternal love is conjured up as a "structure of feeling" (Williams 1977) that should somehow naturally fall into place once the separation and individuation that is promoted by the treatment program has taken effect.

Even those parents at Walsh who regret changes in the "traditional family" identify seemingly enmeshed mother-daughter relationships as a primary focus of therapeutic concern. George is a case in point. He was one of a very few fathers who regularly accompanied his daughter, Laura, to the outpatient clinic. George was a seasoned parent in the program; when I met him, Laura had been in and out of the hospital many times over the course of several years. Laura was an outpatient during the entire time I was conducting fieldwork, and George and I met to talk on several occasions during their clinic visits. He began our first conversation by telling me that "parents are mushroomed: kept in the dark and fed shit. This is the way you feel. They do a good job here; they do what they have to. It's the way it has to be. But parents are taken out of control . . . 'out of the loop' is the phrase I use . . . they are given very little information." Like many parents in the program, George was bitter about this situation, and he felt that the treatment program gives too much control to individual patients at the expense of parental authority: "Parents are advised to relinquish all control. . . . *we* are being controlled by our fifteen-year-old daughter." George explicitly linked this aspect of treatment to the decline of the "traditional" family: "Discipline isn't possible anymore: my wife's a teacher. Kids do what they want. Earlier, things were more simple; families were more traditional, so discipline wasn't as much of a problem. One thing they say here is, nurses are surrogate parents. Society says parents can't do what needs to be done with these kids; but *they* can do it, under the auspices of treatment. I mean, if we strapped our kid to her bed, or watched her when she went to the bathroom, we'd be put in jail.[26] . . . And I'm not saying all families are OK; some are abusive and need to be kept in check. But it's gone too far in the other direction. Families are out of control these days."

Note that George valorizes "the traditional family" when speaking about both himself and his wife being positioned "outside of the loop" vis-à-vis the treatment team. But when he turned to address his wife's role in the family, his position shifted. After talking about the decline of traditional family authority and the inordinate control afforded to both the treatment team and his daughter, George added, "I'm not saying our family is fine. Something's wrong for it to have gone this far." He identified overnurturance as the primary difficulty, feminizing their family's "pathology." His representation of the problem was aligned with contemporary theory on the matter (in which George was well versed): he pointed to mother-daughter enmeshment and said that taking mothers in particular "out of the loop" did seem helpful: "In families, I think women have the control. And moms pass it on to daughters. I've noticed, and not just with us, that these girls tend to have more conflict with their moms. And moms have a harder time pulling back, because, you know, parents are asked to get out of the loop. This is harder for moms. Moms are trained to nurture, and feed, that's thoroughly socialized. It's really hard for [Laura] to eat in front of us, and this disrupts normal family structure. This disturbs the wife more than the husband."

So when focusing on his wife's role in the family, George agreed with the idea promoted in treatment that mother-daughter enmeshment is problematic and obsolete and supported the idea of his daughter gaining autonomy. Like clinicians and staff at Walsh, George identified mother-daughter enmeshment as a contemporary social problem, suggesting that families need to "modernize" in this respect—even as he valued an imagined past that supported more authoritarian, "traditional" families. In some ways, then, George's version of traditionalism is implicitly masculine; he seems most concerned about the loss of his own control and authority over his daughter. Which brings me to psychiatric concerns about fatherhood.

Psychiatric Discourse about Fatherhood

Given that the cultural logic of minimal mothering is linked with shifts toward "postmodern" family forms that question gender roles within the "traditional" (postwar) nuclear family, why is it that psychiatric discourse about the family is relatively silent about fathers? I have suggested that just as mothers are expected to reduce their "enmeshment" with their daughters, so fathers are expected to participate actively in family therapy and to show concern for their daughters' well-being. But while fathers are, ideally, to challenge traditional ideas about paternal separation from the family in this way, it is no surprise to anyone working on the unit when they do not. I have argued that ideas about maternal caretaking rest on the assumption that women will naturally choose to nurture their children. Ideas about paternal involvement are coded differently: fathers' choices in this regard are seen as extracurricular. Popular images of working fathers who spend time with their families depict *extraordinary* men (see Thompson and Walker 1989). Paternal agency in the postmodern family is represented as heroic in part because it is seen to be fighting an uphill battle against maternal enmeshment. As I suggested earlier in this chapter in my discussion of Minuchin's analysis of "eating-disordered" family dynamics, fathers' "ineffectual" interactions with their daughters are often implicitly attributed to maternal pathology. Hence, while the role of fathers in "anorexic families" is taken into account today, it is not of major psychiatric concern.[27]

Before the 1980s, father-daughter relationships were largely ignored in the psychiatric literature. Recall that analyses of "schizophrenogenic" family dynamics in the 1950s and 1960s describe fathers in relationship to their wives and sons only. These fathers are represented as "unusually passive" (Lidz et al. 1958), weak (Haley 1959), inadequate, and submissive (Barton and Davidson 1961). As I suggested toward the beginning of this chapter, these characterizations invert the postwar ideal of competitive, instrumental, and task-oriented masculine identities, which were figured in opposition to women's expressive and relational natures (Parsons and Bales 1955). Strong, competitive fathers were thought to be good role models for their sons.[28] They were also thought to help temper the threat of maternal enmeshment with children (both boys and girls), but this presumed benefit was seen as incidental to mother-daughter relationships. In the postwar era, interpersonal problems in the family that affected daughters were represented almost entirely as the mother's responsibility.

In contrast, and in keeping with gender-equalizing ideologies of paid work and of family life that have emerged in the United States over the past few decades, the family therapy literature of the 1980s began to examine critically paternal "distance" from family ties. A critique of "narcissistic" and "type A" fathers appeared, with a particular focus on the negative effects that workaholic men can have on their daughters.[29] Popular books such as *The Wounded Woman: Healing the Father-Daughter Relationship* (Leonard 1982) chronicle the psychological harm that women suffer growing up with distant, critical, and overworked fathers. Family therapy literature that examines the qualities of fathers in "anorexic families" focuses on similar themes and also criticizes these fathers for their narcissistic, appearance- and achievement-oriented attitudes toward their daughters (Bemporad et al. 1992; Gordon, Beresin, and Herzog 1989; Guidano and Liotti 1983).

In short, competitive masculine individualism has been applied to supposedly more equal-opportunity "gender training" in the family, and has been found wanting. As discussed in the case of Maude and her

father, fathers' workaholism and "type A personalities" seem to participate in daughters' approval orientation, and therefore in their experience of isolation and perpetual effort in the pursuit of fitness (physical
or academic fitness). The basic critique of fathers, then, is that they do
not know how to temper individualism and competitiveness with nurturance; they are not skilled in helping to create the minimal familial
support that is required to produce feminine autonomy. As Karen, a
psychology intern on the unit, said about one father: "He is very 'do-
oriented,' productive, high-powered. He doesn't get it."

I suggest that if ideal fathers of the 1950s and 1960s were breadwin-
ners, or material providers, fathers today are expected to participate in
emotional provision for the family.[30] When a clinician at Walsh characterized Maude's father as a "meter reader," she was describing him as
inappropriately focused on "hard facts," and as emotionally unavailable. Karen continued in her description of the "do-oriented" father in a
similar vein. With some exasperation, she said, "He's an epidemiolo-
gist; he wants statistics and psychometrics." Karen described another
father to me in the following way: "He's not cuddly. He's really competitive with his son and doesn't know how to cuddle. I think Joan [his
anorexic daughter] needs cuddling." This idea that fathers should be
emotionally available for their daughters articulates with a new social
discourse about sensitive men, men who reject postwar specifications
for their identities by attending to significant relationships in their lives
and "expressing their feelings" (Neal and Slobodnik 1991; M. White
1992). Some analyses of anorexia suggest that in the absence of such
paternal sensitivity, girls who are achievement oriented model "masculine" behaviors from their fathers and embody a kind of androgyny
through their anorexia.[31] This idea participates in popular discourses
about "sensitive men" that conflate sensitivity and femininity: if only
men were more feminine, fathers would be better role models for their
daughters.[32]

Ultimately, sensitive men are extraordinary men because interpersonal nurturance is still seen as, primarily, women's domain. For fathers, emotional expressiveness is additive to essentially unemotional
"natures," and it is hard work willfully chosen. A 1990 article in *Newsweek* on this topic describes one therapist's belief that "the focus of
family therapy now ought to be on showing men how to take a more
equal family role, something extremely hard for them to do because
their own fathers were so often emotionally unavailable to them. . . .

Many men genuinely want to change their role but don't have enough emotional underpinning" (Gelman 1990, 43). It is important to emphasize that maternal and paternal choices in this realm are figured differently. Recall that mothers in the treatment program are expected willfully to enact their minimal maternal "natures" by giving up supposedly outdated forms of maternal caretaking (overmothering). Nurturing fathers, on the other hand, are choosing to *enrich* their family lives.

In addition, while fathers in the treatment program are criticized for their emotional distance from their daughters, they are also praised for their clearheaded and "rational" perspective on the emotional entanglements of mothers and daughters, the perceived core problem within "anorexic families." As John, the intake coordinator, said about Maude's father (as compared to her mother): "He's very rational; he's with the program." Karen, the psychology intern quoted earlier, remarked that Joan's father (the one who did not know how to cuddle) was rightfully embarrassed by his wife, who was, after all, responsible for making sure their daughter was well fed. The implication here is that if Joan's mother were a good mother, it would not be so important for her father to develop nurturing skills. In this line of thinking, fathers' emotional effects on mother-child relationships—while seen as more than incidental, which is how they were depicted in the 1950s and 1960s—are only of secondary importance. In a family "systems" version of postwar ideology about gender roles in parenting, fathers are considered sufficiently "sensitive" toward their daughters when they actively intervene in the mother-daughter relationship. Ron, a psychiatrist, talked to me about several "pathological mother-daughter dyads" in families with emotionally absent fathers, and his main point was that these fathers do not take the responsibility to pull their wives away from their daughters when maternal enmeshment rears its ugly head. An example from the outpatient clinic will illustrate Ron's view.

During a discussion one day among several clinicians and staff, Ron described a couple, Sally and Ed, in relation to their anorexic daughter. Ron offered that "if you just go into the waiting room and have a look at Sally, [her daughter's] problem is obvious." He characterized Sally as "anxious, labile, hysterical, a juggernaut," and as "difficult to maintain." Ron said that when Sally pressed for information about her daughter, she was "attaching her own fury" to the psychiatrists and therapists. In contrast, Ron depicted Sally's husband Ed, who did not ask the team many questions, as "the more reasonable of the two." While Ed "harbored resentment"—a sign of distance and detachment—Ron suggested that "with what Sally dishes out, it must be rough on him." I interviewed Ed, who had the following to say: "I've read just about everything I can get my hands on about [anorexia], so I don't have a lot of questions [to ask the treatment team]. I'm probably unique in this respect; not a lot of people come in with the kind of knowledge I have. I know my wife gets upset; she doesn't understand half of what they tell her. I try to tell her: 'It's OK, I've read about this.'" Ed's "rational" approach to the situation seemed to offset Sally's "overemotional" state, and the treatment team requested nothing more from him. In contrast, a pediatrician in the clinic recommended that Sally receive counseling because "she doesn't understand anything, and [her daughter] won't talk to her [about her anorexia], which is common."

At times, perceived problems with fathers are explicitly deflected onto mothers. Bruce, the father of an outpatient in the program, had requested a new family therapist after a few months of therapy, which Ron saw as part of a general pattern of his avoiding conflict raised by women (the family therapist was a woman, and Amy, Bruce's wife, was beginning to raise "difficult" issues about gender roles in the family during the therapy sessions). The team decided that they should not change therapists but rather "empower the mother in the system." This plan seems to steer away from mother blaming. However, Ron had in fact decided that the father would probably not change his ways; Ron suggested to the family therapist that she empower the mother to help their daughter assert herself *behind Bruce's back*. Ron called this a "women plotting behind the scenes" maneuver, joking about the "eternal conspiracy of women." Thus even in this situation, it is the mother who must change, and the images invoked in connection with how this should be accomplished are those of a malleable, yet naturally nurturant, mother who quietly and covertly stabilizes the family behind the scenes. So while some contemporary literature in family therapy criticizes "traditional" paternal roles, encouraging fathers' emotional involvement with their daughters, a therapeutic focus on minimal mothering ultimately lets fathers off the hook.

Conclusion

In this chapter, I have argued that seemingly progressive understandings about "postmodern" family forms in the treatment of anorexia are situated within shifting social and symbolic constructions of maternal love. "Traditional" family forms of the 1950s and 1960s have been dismantled to facilitate individuation in families, and ideal motherhood is, accordingly, a "minimal" form of motherhood. Compared to expectations for mothers in the postwar period, less seems to be required of mothering today. What is required is unconditional love, structural and financial support, and a clarification of "limits" and "boundaries" around individual family members—not full-time service and sacrifice to one's children and husband. In this light, mothers' continued "enmeshment" with their daughters seems to confirm the idea that individual women have difficulty negotiating postmodern family roles. But seemingly outdated, overinvolved mothering is in fact produced through increasing pressures for individual women to "do it all" (maintain both a career and their families). It is also produced at Walsh, through the very unit practices that are designed to minimize mothers' involvement in treatment: mothers' intense interest in their daughters' lives and psychiatric care is encouraged by their exclusion from the treatment process. The creation of a substitute family in the treatment of anorexia invokes a perceived excess of concern on the part of mothers, an excess that is seen as part and parcel of the family's "pathology" and a central object of therapeutic work. "Natural" maternal desire is then mobilized as a resource for the creation of a more minimal form of family support. In turn, a feminized family environment is reduced to a resource for the creation of individualism within the family. Invoked and yet reduced to a perceived bare minimum, maternal caretaking has been, paradoxically, both eroded and intensified within therapeutic discourse about the family since the 1950s and 1960s.[33]

Ideal mothering today, then, appears both as a form of liberation from "the past" and as a natural, timeless quality of persons who are mothers. Minimal mothering is seen as the core feature, the essential nature, of motherhood as we have always known it—it is a taken-for-granted, unspecified activity and structure of feeling. There is a new expectation that fathers will be involved in the treatment process, but this expectation is minimal. Fathers are still encouraged to maintain a critical distance from caretaking in families to help ward off the perceived threat of mother-daughter enmeshment.

I have shown that the ideal of minimal motherhood is contradictory: it is motherhood reduced to a perceived bare minimum and represented as a matter of choice, but it is also thought to be a natural instinct (stronger than any paternal equivalent) that will naturally perform healing work. Because this healing work is to take place largely outside the ambit of treatment, the contradictions of minimal mothering do not usually challenge or disrupt treatment practices. However, in the next chapter, I will show that ideals of minimal mothering are at work *within* the "therapeutic family" as well, and are thereby rendered (somewhat) more problematic.

THREE

Hierarchy, Power, and Gender in
the "Therapeutic Family"

In the previous chapter, I suggest that psychiatric discourse surrounding health and pathology in "anorexic" families highlights contradictions within dominant cultural ideals of motherhood and thereby actively produces some of the problems that are diagnosed in these families. Clinicians expect mothers both to separate their identities from their daughters and to create, through domestic caretaking, a form of family togetherness that is a platform for individuation but also carries the risk of sabotaging this goal. Meanwhile fathers are expected to facilitate healing by participating actively in family life, but also, ideally, they are to retain a critical distance from emotional ties between mothers and daughters. In this chapter, I show that relationships within the "therapeutic family"—those among members of the treatment team, and between team members and individual patients—are also embedded in cultural contradictions that inform psychiatric constructions of patients' problems. While clinicians claim to model "healthy" family relations for patients and their parents, the sexual politics of caretaking in treatment accentuate similar kinds of gendered inequalities that appear within the "natural" families taking part in the treatment program.

Female caretakers at Walsh nurture patients in ways that call on, and yet carefully control, their "maternal instincts," which are constantly bordering on becoming antitherapeutic in the eyes of the treatment team. This caretaking work is produced as a counterpoint to more assertive and detached clinical interventions that take place at Walsh, interventions that appear in their most dramatic form through the actions and words of male psychiatrists. Often, the hierarchy of professional statuses at Walsh reinforces these gendered patterns of caretaking; for example, relatively less powerful female staff perform most of the day-to-day, "maternal" caretaking work on the unit. At the same time, however, hierarchies of gender, patterns of caretaking, and professional status levels do not always line up neatly. Most of the various status levels on the unit include both women and men. The upper status levels include psychiatrists, pediatricians, and psychologists (seven people total). Although all of the psychiatrists at Walsh are male and hold the most decision-making power there, they share much of this power with female and male pediatricians, who are the most detached and distant members of the treatment team (and therefore represent a "harder"—read masculine—science). During my fieldwork, all the psychologists were female and had considerable influence, but little or no direct power. In addition, psychologists and psychiatrists supervise a total of four interns in training at any given time. Interns are both male and female. Finally, more than twenty nurses and milieu counselors at Walsh exercise little to no programmatic decision-making power, and the vast majority are women. Staff power at this level inheres primarily in ongoing emotional and interactive labor with patients, labor that is almost always coded as maternal. However, an important part of these everyday interactions involves a distant and "professional" stance as well, which is viewed as the opposite of (untempered) maternal feeling.

In general, feminized caretaking labor on the unit, whatever its location in the status hierarchy—psychologist versus psychiatrist or pediatrician, staff versus the upper levels of power—is described as a crucial, even defining, feature of the milieu at Walsh but is simultaneously perceived as a risky therapeutic resource. As a result, this caretaking work, particularly for nurses and milieu counselors, seems to require a form of "minimal mothering" that is akin to the ideal for patients' mothers that I describe in chapter 2. But minimal motherhood for hospital staff is difficult to achieve (as it is for anyone). This difficulty is more noticeably a product of specific institutional arrangements and relations of power than it is for patients' "natural"[1] mothers. Even so, the problematic sexual politics of caretaking at Walsh are often displaced onto the perceived personal problems of staff.

Therapeutic "Fathers" and "Mothers"

I begin with an account of the basic model of a healthy therapeutic family for patients at Walsh. Patient-caretaker interactions involve shared rules and spatial boundaries that are, at bottom, nonnegotiable but are never *presented* in a top-down fashion. The idea here is that patients should be able to express their individual feelings about, and experiences of, these boundaries and rules, and that healthy families of origin operate in a similar way. One patient's father remarked during an interview that nursing staff in particular seem "specially trained" to have a combination of hardness and compassion, firmness and flexibility. Rather than assuming an authoritative stance, staff usually state what "needs to happen" in a casual way and strongly suggest through their tone of voice and body language that patients should want it this way, too. If a patient presses the issue, staff will "put it back on them." For example, if a patient is refusing to finish her calories for the day, staff might point out to her that she will only stay in the hospital longer this way, because her weight loss will show up on the scale. Also, staff attempt to provide a range of "choices" for patients within an essentially nonnegotiable structure. Patients can request small changes in their programs (e.g., to have vital signs taken less frequently), and these requests are sometimes granted; they vote on a limited range of options for recreational outings; and they choose the specific foods they will eat (although there are certain food group requirements, and they cannot choose the number of calories they will eat). In addition, staff will, as a rule, phrase interventions in terms of "choices." For example, if a patient is supposed to be observed for a period of time and tries to retreat to her room, a staff member might tell her that "this is not OK," and that she can either sit in the community room or by the nursing station until the next activity. At all times, patients are encouraged to express their feelings and complaints about the program. As one staff member put it to me, "We do not try to control their mood."

Overall, these approaches to patient care are designed to model a kind of parenting that patients have presumably lacked: the provision of a predictable and consistent "environment" that is in the interest of patients' safety (both medical and emotional safety), coupled with an encouragement for patients to express themselves freely, and, in particular, to voice disagreement with, or resistance to, authority. Wendy, who had been a nurse on the unit for close to ten years, put it this way: "No one makes a unilateral decision. With [the structure of the program], the kids feel the weight of the program. This is a basic philosophical fundamental about how to relate to kids. It's reasoned and consistent, logical and not capricious. This is to mirror a normal functional family. So, we have our rules; and then, the eating-disordered patients being who they are, they will [do with those rules what they will]." Notice the explicitly hierarchical structure depicted here: clinicians, and healthy parents, create rules, and their value is beyond question. And whereas these rules are not (usually) imposed by force, patients—who, as "kids" in the system, are relatively powerless players—"feel the weight" of collective agreement on the part of those who have power over them. Wendy went on to talk about the value of patients' resistance and discontent (which, however, never really alters clinicians' firm, "united front"): "We tell them what to do, but we let them fight like heck! And a lot of this is allowing them to fight back. . . . we do let them ask for things. And in a very autocratic family, that doesn't happen. [Here] they can protest, they can be mad, they can cry, they can demand, you know that's fine. And nobody punishes them for that. So [while] I think there's a united front—and I'll tell you, sometimes I think that the only reason that we have any success with these patients is they know that every single person on the team thinks that they have to do what they have to do—it's also, I think, the *way* that it's done [that is important]."

Richard, a nurse, also spoke with me at length about how the treatment team balances enforcing unit rules with a willingness to negotiate with patients. He too described the treatment team as an idealized (surrogate) family in which hierarchies of age predominate but are tempered by the freedom to maneuver within these hierarchies:

> Part of it is, we're surrogate parents, I view it that way. In a professional surrogate parent role, we give them the rule, and then we begin to negotiate the rule with them, and show them that power can in fact be—understanding, individualized. Basically what we're trying to establish, and this is going on with the parent work too, is we want the

parents to be strong parents, to be able to feel entitled in making decisions for children that are positive, healthy. . . . [We want to show patients] another structure for dealing with adultness, with parents, and working anger out, working situations out. How to negotiate, which they're usually really bad at. . . . And I think there is a loving part of the program; we all respond as adults to children in a fundamental archetypal way. And [treatment here is] part of that. [We're archetypal parents], working that out.

However, at another point in the interview, Richard described the power dynamics of the treatment program as necessarily aversive, even opposed to "family values":

There are a lot of aversive features to how we treat. Being in a hospital is an aversive experience, and we want it to be that way. And you'll hear that in rounds: "This is not a country club." . . . you'll hear [some] more honest than others say, We want to make this painful. . . . We're working on changing habits. And how do you change habits? Behavior modification works very well with that. It's not necessarily lasting, but it does give you short-term benefits. But we're good because we [also] work with the family. We do look at underlying causes, at relationship. And that's why we're pretty successful. But it takes a long time.

Here we can see a tension between the time-consuming process of creating a healthy natural family and the "short-term benefits" of behavior modification, which embodies the raw edge of power in the treatment program that seems necessary to transform individuals.

Like most clinicians and staff, both Wendy and Richard talked about the combination of relatively autocratic and (nominally) permissive features of care at Walsh as a general characteristic of the unit environment that all staff and clinicians promote in equal measure. It is true that nurses, psychologists, and psychiatrists alike interact with patients in ways that are both hard-edged and nurturing. But in fact, these features of treatment are gendered hierarchically, in ways that often mirror and reinforce hierarchies of professional status in the treatment program. Generally speaking, male psychiatrists engage with patients in "tough," even provoking ways, and female staff and psychologists are more soothing and protective of individual patients.[2] In turn, female staff (and sometimes female psychologists) are perceived to be at risk of overnurturing patients and must learn to keep nurturing practices in check: specifically, they are expected to "keep their boundaries" so that they do not re-create the presumably harmful effects of "mother-daughter enmeshment." As one (female) milieu counselor put it to me, "For some reason, these kids are really enmeshed with their mothers. One reason staff needs boundaries is so kids won't try to get real enmeshed with female staff." However—as with so-called mother-daughter enmeshment in the natural families that take part in the treatment program—the same nurturing relationships between patients and staff that the treatment team tries to curb are *produced* in relation to unit practices that are designed to promote the opposite: separation and individuation. As suggested during my interview with Richard, these individuating unit practices are sometimes aversive, controlling, and painful. They are also gendered male and are strongly associated with the prestigious status of psychiatrist on the unit. Almost invariably, women who work on the unit "come to the rescue" as patients' nurturers. Before I provide a few examples of how this gendered dynamic can play out within the therapeutic family, let me describe some of the lines of power that delineate hierarchical relationships among psychiatrists, psychologists, staff, and interns at Walsh.

Talking with Bob in the charting room one day, I asked him about his role as medical director of the unit. He talked about the responsibilities involved and then discussed patients' "fantasies" in viewing him as an authority figure. Bob claimed that he had no "real" power in relationship to patients on the unit, although he had the last word about patients' care when he was serving a term as head psychiatrist. In contrast, Bob considered it very important that the lines of power between himself and staff were clearly drawn, even as he espoused a practice of "democratic" decision making within the treatment team. Most people who worked at Walsh acknowledged differentials of power among clinicians and staff that seemed to compromise the goal of shared power when it comes to patient care. In fact, a number of staff members likened their roles in shaping unit policies and procedures (relative to the head psychiatrist and pediatrician) to those of patients themselves. As one milieu counselor put it to me when I asked him to describe the therapeutic family: "The [head psychiatrist and pediatrician] on service . . . are to us as we are to the patients. They talk a good line about our participation in decision making . . . and they want feedback from us, and they want to know how we feel. But when it comes down to it, the buck stops with them."

The structure of authority within the therapeutic family is often figured in terms of heterosexual nuclear family relations. At one point in my interview with Bob about his role on the unit, he referred to himself and Sally, a prominent psychologist at Walsh, as "a powerful couple." As we continued talking, it became clear that he meant "couple" in the sense of "mom and dad of the unit," a phrase I had heard staff use many times to refer to Bob and Sally, and to Mark and Martha, as well (who are the most senior psychiatrist and psychologist "pair" affiliated with the unit). Bob's "children" (though they were not called children) were staff and interns and included patients only indirectly. (Usually, only female members of the nursing staff refer to patients as "kids," and themselves as "moms" to patients.)

For the most part, the heterosexual and nuclear character of the therapeutic family goes unremarked; it is an assumed norm. But a former psychology intern expressed this idea explicitly during a conversation with me over lunch. She described a discussion during rounds one day in which Steve—a psychiatrist who worked on the unit before I arrived—defended his position that interns should not be given more direct decision-making power about patients' care. Steve said that to allow such a thing would disrupt the "proper heterosexual relationships" that pertained between himself and interns (only a psychologist, or symbolic "wife," would ever be allowed such a degree of influence— never the "children"). Note that Steve is gay, and he did not conceal his sexual orientation from other members of the treatment team.[3] Clearly, Steve maintained a sharp distinction between his personal life and his professional position as a heterosexual "father" on the unit. Such a distinction highlights the institutional production of masculine, heterosexual power within the therapeutic family. In his capacity as a therapeutic father, Steve had been one of the most powerful people who worked at Walsh, but according to several people I interviewed, he disavowed any "personal" involvement in his positioning as such. Like Bob, the medical director, Steve even claimed that he held no real power with patients but instead took on, as Richard put it earlier, an "archetypal" meaning for them.

In contrast, female staff, clinicians, and interns are considered vulnerable to blurring this boundary between their personal and professional lives. One psychiatrist talked to me about (female) staff members' "neediness" in their desire for affirmation and attention from their superiors, and he doubted that he could ever address these needs to the staff's satisfaction. He went on to suggest that this problem is reflected in staff members' occasional "overinvestment" in patients' care and is due to their unresolved issues around caretaking and nurturance in their personal lives. Many staff members would agree with this latter point, a topic to which I will return. But as a number of staff members and several interns and clinicians saw it, the way female workers at Walsh were sometimes treated by their superiors (relative to male workers) strongly shaped their experiences as highly invested caretakers on the unit. During a discussion in the charting room with two psychology interns (Shelly and Karen) about this issue, Shelly told me that, in general, psychiatrists and pediatricians on the unit were very lenient toward Josh, an intern who "says some empty lines about patients: 'I haven't seen her yet today,' et cetera. This is no problem [in rounds]." Karen agreed, "He's a golden boy." Shelly added, "Whereas we [women], who have a lot to say about our patients, are dismissed. And it spills over to us. Whenever I work with Josh, I do all the work." When women compensate for work that is left undone on the unit, it looks very much like the seemingly overinvested forms of engagement that patients' mothers express when they are cut off from connection with, and information about, their daughters. Many unit practices create a need for caretaking, gendered female, which is then attributed to "poor boundaries" and is criticized and "cut down to size" (or minimized) accordingly.

Let me say a word about male nursing staff and milieu counselors, who are never thought to be too personally involved with patients. There are not many male staff on the unit; the ratio of male to female staff is about one to five, and several men work only part-time. More often than not, male staff are assigned to work closely with (non-eating-disordered) boys on the unit who are hyperactive and/or "acting out." But they do have occasion to interact with eating-disordered patients. Significantly, men who work on the unit are seen as "sensitive men": they temper masculine strength with a feminized softness. As a former milieu counselor put it to me, "This is a female unit . . . each shift has one strong male counselor to absorb the acting-out boys. But the men are ectomorphic—quiet, not aggressive. They are feminized men." As I discuss in the previous chapter, sensitive, feminized male role models are considered healthy for anorexic patients, but a mixed blessing. Wendy, a nurse on the unit, once talked to me about anorexic patients' "hostility" toward Bill, a milieu counselor. Wendy said that Bill is "a father figure who's kind and gentle and nurturing. . . . It's interesting because you'll see some of the girls who've had very difficult fathers just give him enormous flack. They detest him, won't allow him in their rooms, be very nasty to him. Which is always kinda funny because he's the mildest-mannered person. But I think that's a lot of what it is, they just can't tolerate a nice guy." While Wendy's main point here is that patients and their families are insufficiently flexible to accept a gentle and nonauthoritative man, she also implied with her tone of voice that Bill was a little strange, a little "unmanly." As Cecilia, a milieu counselor, put it, laughing: "The male staff are—how can I put it? They lack testosterone." I have suggested that therapeutic male role models for anorexic patients are thought to require a "harder," more provoking style. But whether the men who work with anorexic patients are only nominally nurturing (simply by virtue of their location on a therapeutic team), or "sensitive," these qualities are not seen as a threat to their professional "boundaries" with patients.[4]

In contrast, sensitivity from a female worker can always be read as a threat to appropriate care. I now turn to an example of such a perceived threat from a female clinician, and its production as a counterpoint to an assertive intervention (on the part of a male psychiatrist) during a miniteam meeting. Recall that in these meetings, the treatment team discusses patients' progress, and then patients join in on the discussion one at a time. One day, the team was talking about a patient I will call Valerie, who was considered an "old-timer": she was an eighteen-year-old anorexic patient who had been in and out of the program for many years. Martha was Valerie's individual therapist and was very close to her after working with her for all that time. Martha once said to me, "You may have noticed, I'm pretty protective of Valerie. That's because when a patient has been here so many times, and is difficult to work with, it's easy sometimes to start punishing them." This miniteam discussion can be seen as a case in point. Mark, the head psychiatrist for eating-disordered patients that month, said he planned to ask Valerie if she was using laxatives to "help along" her recent bout of diarrhea. No one thought it was likely that Valerie was using laxatives; Mark's question was designed as an exercise in confrontation with Valerie about the intimate details of her health (to counteract the secrecy surrounding these matters within Valerie's family). Martha was alarmed: "Oh . . . *be nice.*" She and Susan, a milieu counselor, wondered if the team should test Valerie's stool first. Mark replied, "No, we're not going to do what her dad does [i.e., act indirectly and behind the scenes]; we're going to do what *we* do. In your face. You have to ask." Bob added, "It's *supportive* to ask." Martha said, "It's the *way* you ask." Bob then said, "Martha's being mom here. She's saying, 'Don't hurt my Valerie.' " At this point, Mark began reading a "joke" version of Valerie's written requests for miniteams, pretending that Valerie had written about her gratitude to the team for helping her (Valerie was well known for her bitter criticisms of caregivers). Martha got out of her chair and walked over to Mark, saying, "You want me to read it?" John, the intake coordinator, said in a half-joking way that he was going to have to get between Mark and Martha. Bob quietly repeated his remark about Martha playing the role of "mom" and suggested that Martha was "using" Valerie as a substitute for her little boy (Martha is the mother of a small child). Notice that, in contrast, Mark's role as "dad" was completely unmarked as such; it was taken simply as a dramatic form of treatment.

When it was time for Valerie to join miniteams, Martha left (which is unusual—my guess is that she decided she could not serve as an advocate for Valerie and simultaneously support Mark's approach with her), and Ann, the nutritionist, moved to the far side of the room. Sally, a psychologist, exclaimed, "Whoa, this kid's anger is powerful!" suggesting that Valerie was the "cause" of the discomfort in the room. Mark did broach the issue of laxatives gingerly: "I'm not accusing, just asking. . . . I'm the only one who's suspicious. So I ask: Laxatives? Then when you say no, I settle down." Mark thereby incorporated Martha's "tempering" influence. While psychologists at Walsh, in their roles as symbolic wives, rarely exercise power within the treatment team directly, they often influence the upper levels of power. In this case, Martha's caretaking work was, in her absence, folded into a confrontational, suspicious approach to Valerie that Martha seemed to consider antitherapeutic.

Male psychiatrists and pediatricians frequently express their roles as powerful players on the treatment team, and as therapeutic fathers, by confronting and provoking patients in this way, and less-powerful female psychologists and nursing staff quietly smooth over these interactions. At lunch one day, Karen, a psychology intern, talked to me about one such situation involving a patient of hers named Lila. Bob (the medical director) took the time to have minitherapy sessions with Lila when she was on the unit. Karen was not consulted about this cotherapy arrangement, and though she was open to the idea, she had mixed feelings about it: "We're a good team, I think. Bob is more provocative and aggressive; I'm more nurturing and supportive. . . . Bob makes her furious, and then I sort of help Lila deal with that, the feelings around that." Karen added that while she may be "too nurturing" with patients, she *did* know how to "set limits," and that Bob was nurturing too, "in his own way." Here Karen was representing a gendered hierarchy on the unit (between herself and Bob) in terms of (somewhat) equal mixtures of masculinized and feminized qualities, both within Bob's and Karen's cotherapy arrangement and within each of their approaches as individual therapists.

After a while, however, Karen became frustrated with the situation: "I think Bob seeing patients for therapy is confusing, because he only sees some, the ones he's interested in. . . . And it's ironic, because Bob has such rigid boundaries—but not when it comes to something *he's* interested in. . . . is he the medical director or a therapist? It's confusing, and invalidating to individual therapists." Karen then talked about Bob's need to find "the brilliant thing to say" about patients: "The implication is, *you* can't find it. Maybe it's my own lack of self-confidence, but I'm rarely willing to say I'm sure I'm right. I may be wrong. And I think it's devaluing to tell patients what they think. I mean, even if you *are* right. It's disrespectful. . . . I think he's a good therapist one-on-one, very insightful. But I know he pisses them off." Another (female) intern who found herself in an almost identical situation with Bob also talked to me about Bob's "poking" her patients: "They come to me with it. Mark [a psychiatrist] does that too. I'm a lot more like Martha [a psychologist], definitely [i.e., nurturing]. It works well in some cases, but the part about cotherapy that feels weird is, it's not talked about in advance. . . . it's because we're below him that he feels he doesn't need to ask. It's pulling rank, really." Interestingly, Lila—Karen's patient—had a very similar take on these cotherapy arrangements. During a conversation with me, Lila said about Bob: "He says he knows what I feel. He's smart, but I don't like that. He'll say I feel something, and I'll say, 'No, I don't!' And then I'll get confused. . . . it makes me mad." I then asked: "So, Karen is your therapist. Is Dr. [Bob] Peters, too?"[5] Lila said, "I'm not sure *what* Dr. Peters is. But Dr. [Mark] Blevins I guess is . . . I don't know who he is. But I guess he has a big say in my program, so I better be nice to him." I then explained to Lila that while Mark was often the psychiatrist in charge on the unit, Bob was in this role for her care, so he had the final say. Lila responded, "Oh, so that's what he meant when he said he's above Karen. I thought, 'Well, I don't care, I like Karen.' He said, 'Karen's your therapist? Well, I'm above Karen.' I thought, 'Well, thanks for that little piece of information.' "

Female caretakers and patients sometimes resist such gendered expressions of professional power at Walsh. In the next section, I show how these forms of resistance challenge, but also underscore, the treatment program's ideal of therapeutic family unity. Like patients' resistance to weight gain explored in chapter 1, women's and girls' resistances to gendered constructions of power in the therapeutic family operate within the interstices of psychiatric discourse. They both unsettle and help to constitute ideas about a united front among staff and clinicians on the unit.

The Creation and Disruption of Therapeutic Family Unity

I remember well the extreme discomfort in the room when Sally, a psychologist, brought one of her patient's mothers into a miniteam meeting. The patient was leaving the hospital that day and so felt that she should not have to attend miniteams, which terrified her. Some members of the treatment team took her resistance as evidence that she needed to be confronted, in a public forum, about maintaining her weight outside of the hospital. However, she was refusing to come in. Sally left miniteams to talk with her about it and returned with the patient and her mother. Bob, the spokesperson for miniteams that day, barely knew what to say. The patient's mother asked a lot of questions about how to care for her daughter at home, which clearly annoyed Bob as being beside the point of miniteams. He answered her questions nervously and curtly, and the patient and her mother soon left. Sally shrugged and said, somewhat defiantly, "It's the only way I could get her to come in." Several people muttered about the "inappropriateness" of having a mother in miniteams, and the meeting disbanded. Later, a psychology intern told me she thought the discomfort in the room was due to the fact that people did not want to "beat up on" a patient in front of her mother.

This event allowed for some critical commentary about miniteams: How are patients treated in this context? Who is excluded from the room, and why? But Sally's resistance to status quo procedures also buttressed standard protocols by inciting a perceived need to establish (formal) unity within the therapeutic family. Bob in particular left the meeting convinced that it was inappropriate for parents to appear in miniteams; he stated that it would not happen again.

More often than not, powerful male figures (usually psychiatrists) articulate the terms of the treatment team's united front. Assertions of difference, which are usually expressed by female psychologists and staff, are frequently seen as a sign that the (masculinized) unity of the therapeutic family needs to be reestablished. But it is not enough to say that resistance within the treatment team is co-opted by the discourse of family unity. Rather, women's expressions of difference or disagreement are continually created and *mobilized* in the construction of this unity. The united front that staff and clinicians present to patients both conceals *and* produces inequalities within the treatment team. In other words, the production of feminine difference on the unit is part and parcel of the making of the status quo on the unit.

This difference is asserted against (masculinized) positions of power, which are, in turn, reformulated as points of "consensus" that paper over difference. So, as with patients' resistance to treatment protocols, resistance within the treatment team does not lie "outside" of the normalizing effects of psychiatric "health." Talking about her own resistance on the unit, one female psychologist said to me: "I often wonder, do I stay in the hierarchy, just go with the [head psychiatrist]? Or do I push it? If I push, I push *very* quietly, or it wouldn't work. I start with: 'I agree with you.' I *survive* here . . . by not challenging the hierarchy, not pushing too much. Others who pushed are outta here. I push *from within*."

One of the ways that women who work on the unit "push quietly" is by talking behind the scenes about opinions that (male) psychiatrists and pediatricians do not support, supporting each other for having these ideas and for trying to assert them (though rarely directly). Conflict over the timing of patients' discharge from the hospital often leads to this kind of resistance. Toward the end of one patient's stay at Walsh, almost everyone but Bob thought that the patient, Elaine, had earned the right to be discharged. Bob had decided on a particular litmus test for Elaine's readiness to go, which she had not passed: although Elaine had met her weight criterion, the pH balance of her urine was slightly higher than normal range. Urine pH, which can be used to assess whether a patient is vomiting, is not normally a part of discharge criteria, but the team had been monitoring Elaine's because it was so far outside of the norm when she was first admitted to the hospital. Eventually, Bob himself came to doubt the importance of this test for Elaine's discharge, but he nevertheless insisted that the team maintain the discharge criteria that had already been established for her, lest the team risk representing unit protocols as arbitrary. Elaine's therapist, Margo—a psychiatrist in training who was under Bob's supervision— felt strongly that Elaine should be allowed to go home. In the charting room one afternoon, Margo explained her position to me: Elaine had worked very hard to meet her discharge criteria and often felt that her efforts to achieve her goals (e.g., in school) were not validated. Margo felt that the team should not participate in this pattern in Elaine's life. Besides, she argued, urine pH is less reliable as an indicator of vomiting once it is close to normal range. I asked Margo what it was like to be Elaine's therapist in this context. Margo said it was quite difficult: because of the politics of team unity, she did not share her opinions with Elaine; instead, she told Elaine that the "team decision" requiring her to stay must be hard for her. Meanwhile Margo and Gayle, a psychiatry intern, were talking behind the scenes about how Margo might convince Bob to change his mind.

Later that afternoon, I was talking with Gayle in the hallway just outside of Walsh when Margo approached us to tell Gayle that she was not sure how to handle the question of Elaine's discharge in rounds, because she has difficulty speaking up with Bob about her opinions. Gayle said that as Elaine's therapist, Margo should definitely speak up. Gayle offered that *she* would speak up, but she did not want to contradict Bob. Realizing that this concern would be a problem for Margo, as well, Gayle told Margo about a "trick" she had learned from psychologists on the unit: she suggested that Margo present her opinion as "information," so that if Bob changed his mind, it would look like his decision. Margo tried this approach in rounds the next day, but Bob responded by suggesting that Margo was caught up in Elaine's "pathology"—that she was allowing Elaine to "split" her from the treatment team when, after all, a decision had been made. Margo acknowledged the hierarchies of the system by pointing out that she had not discussed the issue with Elaine but had brought it to rounds instead for the purpose of her own edification, because she was in training and trying to understand. Bob replied, "Well, apparently, you don't." Gayle stepped in to say that Bob's litmus test was very subjective. Bob agreed that the test "isn't perfect" but said that the problem here was that Elaine *wanted* it to be perfect. He argued that the treatment team should not cater to that desire; the best the team could do was make a decision and stick to it. The following day, Elaine wrote a two-page essay for miniteams (an unusual gesture) expressing her anger and confusion about why she could not go home. Bob said that the team should not respond, because Elaine was obsessing. Martha, the spokesperson for miniteams that day, did respond to Elaine's essay when Elaine joined miniteams. She told Elaine that the program is not perfect and implied that Elaine should not ask it to be perfect. Later, Gayle (referring to Martha) told me that she could not believe what comes out of people's mouths sometimes; that "they say crazy things, since they have no real power in the system as psychologists and as women."

Occasionally, gendered and hierarchical difference at Walsh creates ruptures in therapeutic family unity that are articulated as such publicly. Negotiating the care of very "difficult" patients can have this effect. Sandra, whom I discuss in more detail in the next chapter, was one such patient. Sandra required a good deal of individual attention and had run away from the unit a few times. Several clinicians and staff believed that a locked unit was more appropriate for Sandra, but a number of others argued otherwise and believed that Sandra was discriminated against in this regard. Bob was one person who thought that Walsh was not the best treatment environment for Sandra. After Sandra was discharged from a hospital stay and became an outpatient, Bob suggested in rounds one day that she should never be readmitted to the hospital. Martha and Sally, the two psychologists present, asked Bob to clarify his position. In a tone that was unusually sharp, Martha asked: "So, the bottom line is, Sandra doesn't get admitted? Even if there is a bed [available]? That's important for us to know. And I have a question: should she be seen in [the outpatient] clinic [at all]?" As someone who works with patients in a "maternal" caretaking role, Martha was asking Bob to think through the practical implications of his proposal, which involved a refusal to treat.[6] In response to Martha, Bob said, "That's a good question. Being seen in clinic, that was Mark's plan. I *never* thought it was a good idea." Here Bob is pointing to the infighting between himself and Mark, who is the head psychiatrist at Walsh, regarding Sandra's treatment. After rounds, Sally told me that many of the staff were upset with Mark for authorizing Sandra's most recent admission, because Sandra is such a "difficult" patient, and because

Bob had suggested that she would not be returning to the unit. Sally pointed out to me that "it upsets staff when Mark and Bob disagree, because they feel it comes down on *them*." As the primary caretakers on the unit, staff negotiate patient care on an hourly basis, and the difficulties of this job seem exacerbated when the therapeutic fathers are in conflict over the terms of treatment. During the discussion in rounds about Sandra's status as an outpatient, Karen, a psychology intern, named this particular conflict publicly. She suggested that "the divisiveness here in talking about Sandra shows that we are acting out her stuff," meaning that Sandra's "pathology" had gotten the better of team members in their dealings with one another. Even though Karen was pinning the blame on Sandra for the conflict over her care, the fact that she explicitly identified this conflict at all was threatening to unit hierarchy, particularly for Bob. Karen told me a few days later that after rounds that day, Bob criticized her for her "problem with her role boundary," because it was, according to Bob, *his* job to offer "interpretive remarks" about disunity within the treatment team.

Clearly, Bob can be an abrasive and difficult individual when his authority is challenged. But it would be a mistake to reduce the meaning and effects of psychiatrists' interpersonal stances to the individual qualities of the men concerned, or even solely to the institutional power of psychiatrists at Walsh. Constructions of professional hierarchies and of gendered inequalities among clinicians and staff on the unit are part of a larger field of intersecting discourses at work in the treatment of anorexia. Although women sometimes express direct disagreement with, or point to ruptures within, the unified front that is presented to patients, we have seen that women's caretaking practices at Walsh are also configured and expressed as supportive ground for aggressive, masculinized forms of psychiatric intervention. As supportive ground, these caretaking practices are both summoned up and "used up"—that is, deployed as resources in the treatment process.

In previous chapters, I write about the resourcing logic of discourses about fit bodies and minimal families: stubbornly unfit bodies and purportedly overinvolved, outdated forms of maternal caretaking are produced, and then worked on, to create more streamlined bodies and families. Similarly, within the therapeutic family, female staff, patients, and clinicians—and, peripherally, patients' parents (usually mothers)— often provide material that becomes an important part of masculine psychiatric performances. Mark (the head psychiatrist on the unit), speaking one day to a gathering of interns that I attended, said that his own occasional, dramatic therapeutic interventions on the unit would not be possible without "his" staff being there to "pick up the pieces" once he was through. An example from a miniteam meeting in which Mark was the spokesperson will serve as a case in point.

Several people had mentioned to me that Mark is a real "performer" in miniteams. Though many felt uncomfortable about his provoking style, most described him as a "master." On this particular occasion, Susan, a milieu counselor, was presenting new information about a patient named Heather (Susan was Heather's staff advocate). She reported that Heather's mother had found several empty bottles of laxatives in Heather's room at home. Mark said, "Bingo. She's slippery," meaning that she hides such information from the treatment team. There was agreement among the team to search Heather's hospital room for laxatives. Then Mark asked Susan, "Mom didn't tell us this with a seal of confidence, did she?" Susan hedged, and Mark said firmly, "She can't." Susan agreed immediately, and Mark continued, "So we'll raise it as an issue, and we'll be delighted to search her room. With this one, come down like a ton of bricks; accuse and confront her. Let her know we don't trust her any further than we can throw her, which isn't very far. She has a history of deception and slipperiness. . . . This usually happens when there are secrets in the family, when a family member is vulnerable and needs to be protected." When Heather joined the discussion, it seems to me that Mark's strategy with her was to be as *in*vulnerable as possible, making *Heather* vulnerable to exposure, and to shame. Talking with Heather about her stay on the unit thus far, Mark was very flip and jocular, even though Heather was visibly angry about his tone. Mark then said, "We've got the dibs on you. It's something your mama told us that we're worried about." After a dramatic pause, Mark told her the team knew she had been abusing laxatives. Heather turned beet red, a look of panic coming over her. Softening a little, Mark said, "Now, we don't know *for sure* . . ." Heather said, with some desperation, "I tried one, and then I couldn't stop." Several women in the room murmured supportively. Mark asked Drew, a pediatrician, to speak about the dangers of laxatives. When Drew finished speaking, Mark added, "So we don't like it one bit. But it's nothing we can't fix." Heather protested feebly, "I'm not taking them here." Mark replied, "Maybe that's true, maybe it's not. Our job is to be suspicious; we're going to search your room." Frightened, Heather said, "OK."

Mark turned away from her and said, with sarcasm, "Thanks for coming by." As Heather was leaving, Lorna (a nurse) and Martha walked with her somewhat nervously, reaching out to her. Lorna said quietly, "We want to support you. If you have laxatives, give them to Susan, and she's going to help you search your room."

In this powerful example, Heather, her mother, and her staff advocate provide "data" for Mark's aggressive intervention, and in turn, female clinicians and staff surround the intervention with support for Heather. Notice also the location of the pediatrician as the most distant authority figure, providing a different kind of data for Mark ("factual" medical information). In this case, and also in the earlier example involving Mark's confrontation with Valerie about possible laxative abuse, there is a gendered logic of discovery, exposure, and analysis at work. Feminist scholars of science such as Ludmilla Jordanova (1989) and Evelyn Fox Keller (1985) write about a long cultural history expressed within some forms of scientific practice in which a feminized "nature," materialized in the female body, has its secrets wrested from it by the masculinized, probing work of scientific inquiry and experimentation. At Walsh, this feminized nature is produced through a variety of gendered practices, which articulate with additional axes of power, as well (e.g., hierarchies of professional status, and differentials of power between adult doctors and adolescent patients).

The female body, then—the primary object of some feminist analyses of "masculine science" (e.g., Merchant 1989)—only *appears* to be the "original" site of masculinized psychiatric performances. There is a persistent tendency in some critical feminist scholarship of science to represent the female body as a pregiven object that is acted on. Throughout this book, I have suggested instead that dominant understandings and experiences of the female body precipitate out of a multiplicity of discourses—about individualism, mothering, consumption, caretaking. Anorexic bodies and (potentially) healthy bodies on the unit are *constituted through* these many discourses. As Butler (1993) suggests, the embodiment, or "materialization," of power occurs through the repeated enactment of various cultural practices, a process that produces a "naturalized effect." In the case involving Heather and the exposure of her laxative abuse, representations of Heather and her body emerged in such a way that her body and her emotions materialized as focal points that could serve to mobilize—and valorize—therapeutic unity in the team's approach. Before Heather joined miniteams, Mark said, implicitly addressing unit staff, "Look out for abuse, you gotta wonder who else hates her body" (besides Heather herself). At the same time that Mark was representing his own impending intrusiveness with Heather as categorically different from any abuse she may have suffered in the past, he was also representing Heather as a victim who needs protection (to be provided by female staff). After miniteams that day, John, the intake coordinator, suggested to me that Heather's heated and shamed blushing (her reaction to Mark's exposure) was "purely psychosomatic"; that is, a physical expression of what would ordinarily be hidden emotion, or a physical revelation of secrets inside of Heather—a revelation that is diagnostic of her "pathology" (Mark had guessed that family secrets shape Heather's eating disorder and believed that these secrets must be brought out into the open). In sum, while the "scientific" status of Mark's psychiatric intervention conjures up the idea that his approach with Heather was simply an effective method for uncovering the "truth" about her, I suggest that, in fact, Mark's intervention helped constitute the reality he was diagnosing (with the help of information from Heather's mother and through the calling up of staff care); and in turn, Heather's "psychosomatic" reaction appeared as an embodied manifestation of this truth, and as physical evidence of the need for "maternal" (staff) protection.

So the making of a feminized nature as supportive ground for masculinized action and for therapeutic family unity articulates patients' bodies, natural mothers, therapeutic mothers, and the supportive milieu more generally at Walsh. In the next section, I focus on the complex processes that create "feminine nature" among female staff. How do staff members understand and practice "maternal caretaking" in their work at Walsh? How is it that their seemingly personalized labor is both highly valued and viewed as risky for patient care? We will see that beliefs about so-called families of origin, which are very powerful within psychiatric discourse about patients' pathologies, are strongly implicated here.

Natural and Unnatural Families:
Blurring the Personal and the Professional

My interviews with nursing staff and milieu counselors about their everyday caretaking work were quite extensive. Female staff in particular were interested in talking with me in some detail about the dilemmas of developing caring and nurturing relationships with patients in a hospital setting; for many, perhaps two out of three hours total of interview time were taken up by this topic. Because staff have far more contact with patients than any other kind of professional caretaker at Walsh, they feel acutely in their work a tension that physician and medical ethicist Howard Brody (1992) suggests is endemic to medical practice, a tension "between care and work—between the individualized demands of compassion and sympathy and the impersonalized, routine demands of the efficient workplace" (66). Medical sociologist Renée Fox (1989) analyzes this dilemma as it relates specifically to nursing care: "The nurse is simultaneously an employee of the institution who is expected to abide by its policies and rules, an assistant to the physician whose orders relating to the patient's diagnosis and treatment plan she is expected to follow, and a primary patient caretaker and advocate" (60). Fox argues that this latter aspect of nursing care, as I have already suggested in this chapter, can seem strongly antithetical to the "routine demands of the efficient workplace." Because nurses are obligated to other parties who hold more power and authority, they are sometimes kept in their places in the status hierarchy by being told that they are "too emotionally involved" with their patients (Rostain 1986, quoted in Fox 1989, 61), even though intense emotional involvement with patients is an integral part of nursing work:

> Part of the tension that exists between nurses and physicians derives from the character of the nurse-patient relationship. In their daily, hands-on, continuous care of patients, nurses deal with some of their most basic and intimate physical, emotional, and not infrequently, spiritual needs. They come to know patients in these inner and outer ways—especially how patients are reacting to and dealing with their illness and treatment. Nurses also have considerable contact with close members of patients' families. Under these circumstances, they often become identified with their patients as persons: with their feelings, values, relationships, life histories, and how these bear on what the hospitalized patient is experiencing. In fact, the nurse is ideally expected to do so, and to translate this identification into patient advocacy when it is called for. (Fox 1989, 60)

Female staff at Walsh often spoke to the challenges and difficulties of their jobs in terms of an intimacy and closeness with patients that could seem excessive. But rather than presenting their dilemmas in terms of their own (gendered) location in the hierarchy of professions at Walsh, female staff linked these difficulties to similar dilemmas in their own personal histories as mothers and as daughters. In this way, the care in their work was not "individualized," as Brody suggests; rather, it was articulated to seemingly personal (and feminized) discourses about "natural" families.

Many staff members I interviewed said directly that their work on the unit often brings up feelings for them about their own families. On the one hand, these feelings are to be expected, and they signal an appropriate "maternal" involvement in the therapeutic family. Amy, a milieu counselor, put it this way: "I bring to nursing my experience as a mom with three kids. I bring skills and feelings from this. . . . Sometimes, patients just want a hug. I feel this job is very nurturing and mothering." Lorna, a nurse on the unit, implied that marriage and motherhood are prerequisites for quality psychiatric nursing. She told me that she became interested in her current work through questioning and challenging her early experiences as a medical nurse working with a "nurse Ratchet," who Lorna noted was "an unmarried woman." Lorna then described how she combined her training in psychology with caring for her young daughter.[7]

But however appropriate it seems for staff to link maternal feelings with patient care, they are also thought to risk an unhealthy personal investment and overinvolvement with patients when they do so. Negotiating the positive and problematic aspects of maternal feeling is central to many staff members' experiences of their work. Susan, a milieu counselor, had this to say about the issue:

> When you work with [other staff] for a long time, it's likely to delve into your own . . . family issues. Because you see people here more than your own family: eight hours a day, four days a week. . . . and kids are seeking you out to re-create their family of origin, and interactions with other staff re-create unresolved stuff in your own family of origin. . . . Kids you've worked with a long time, it's real easy to feel maternal towards them, and protective of them. You have to really watch those feelings; they might reproduce something that's not necessarily in the best interest of the child. . . . There's a way to make it therapeutic. . . . Maybe redirect it to why relationships at home are not working, rather than allowing your relationship [with the patient] to feed [the problem].

These dilemmas speak to the fine line that is created on the unit between natural and therapeutic families, and the crucial mediating role that female staff play in finessing this line.

Significantly, Susan identifies families of origin as the families that contain problems. This idea is rooted in three decades of thought and practice within family therapy, which points to the family of origin as the cause of pathology. But Susan also references her *own* family of origin as one cause of difficulties with her role in the therapeutic family. I will return shortly to the question of why staff members' families of the past might be represented as problematic for their nursing or counseling work. I want to stress a broader point at this juncture: in citing her own family of origin as a potent source of insight about her job performance, Susan highlights the fact that many of us locate the strongest of human feelings (of any kind) within natural families. As cultural anthropologist David Schneider ([1968] 1980) has pointed out, within Euro-American kinship ideologies, blood is always thicker than water. Hence if problems appear within the caretaking practices of the therapeutic family, clinicians and staff will almost invariably trace them to natural families, rather than the hierarchical and gendered politics of therapeutic relationships in the present.

Staff consider the meanings of more than one kind of natural family of their own. Every female staff member at Walsh had children of her own, and the *positive* aspects of maternal caretaking on the unit were often associated with staff's skills as natural mothers within their families of procreation, as in Amy's and Lorna's cases quoted earlier. Susan's mixing of generations (in the foregoing quote), along with her mixing of natural and therapeutic families, is striking: she is at once the daughter of a problematic family of origin, a wife and mother, and a surrogate mother to patients. How do these different families relate to one another? Many staff members and clinicians I interviewed told me that people become interested in nursing through a desire to rework themes around maternal caretaking that have been salient in their own lives through time. Lorna described her own fraught career trajectory in such terms:

> I was programmed to be in nursing very early. . . . [My mother] began talking to me as an adult when I was fourteen, telling me all of her problems. . . . I may have been as young as ten. My sister was nine years older than I, and she left home when I was nine, and clearly

my mother started using me. She had used my sister to tell her all her problems. So I think she trained me to be a nurse, to listen to people. . . .

[When I first started in nursing], I wanted to work with teenagers, because I had a very problematic teenage life, and I thought I could understand them. And I'm sure I could, but I was too close to it. So [senior] nurses, probably appropriately, wouldn't let me do that.

It was not until Lorna had her own child and studied psychology that she felt she had sufficiently "worked through" problems she had experienced in her own family of origin and could begin working with teenagers.

When Lorna and other staff members talked to me about how their jobs today relate to their relationships with their own children, they often drew a contrast between the ways they were raised and their own approaches as natural and therapeutic mothers. For example, Susan characterized her upbringing as constrained and autocratic and then described her different approach with patients through the analogy of negotiating an appropriate bedtime with her daughter: "I tell her I don't care what she does, as long as she's reasonably cheerful in the morning. [This kind of negotiation] is important for [the anorexic kids on the unit], who need to have control, but know the limit to this freedom." Similarly, several staff pointed to positive developments in their nursing practice that resulted from parenting in their private lives. For example, Wendy, a nurse, told me that she felt more empathetic toward parents' hospital experiences once she became a parent: "Now that I have a kid that age, [I can see] it would make me crazy, it would be incredibly painful. . . . you're not ready to turn over, just hand over a thirteen- or fourteen-year-old kid. . . . It made a lot more sense to me early on [in my career] that these folks would just drop their kids off and let us do it. I've developed a lot more sensitivity to that. I just know it would make me nuts."[8] In a similar vein, Amy (a milieu counselor) suggested that Mark, the chief psychiatrist on the unit, has become less "patriarchal" and aggressive in his approach to patients over the years because of his "wonderful wife and daughters" (in keeping with contemporary ideologies about sensitive men, discussed in the previous chapter, marriage and parenthood are here seen to affect Mark positively in an almost extracurricular way: through the "softening" influences of females in his family).

If staff often liken positive aspects of their work at Walsh to their own natural parenting experiences, they are equally likely to claim that their families of origin haunt relations within the therapeutic family in troubling ways. In fact, many staff members I interviewed remarked that they grew up struggling with issues that affect many eating-disordered patients on the unit. Susan put it to me this way: "Our eating-disordered population tends to be very rigid and perfectionistic, and a lot of our staff, including myself, have a lot of the same qualities." She went on to say that her sister had been anorexic and that she could very easily have "ended up anorexic" herself. A few staff members I interviewed discussed their own adolescent histories with dieting and bodily control. Some staff members talked with me about growing up with parents who were similar to many parents they meet on the unit. For example, Wendy remarked, "I've had to deal with my own family-of-origin issues. There was alcoholism in my family, and addiction; and in many of these families, you'll find that, and it goes down through the generations. So those issues have come up for me, and I've had to think about them more, in working with these kids, because of the nature of the work."

I have already suggested that a focus on problems within natural families turns attention away from the politics of caretaking relationships within the therapeutic family. Let us take a closer look now at an important question: Why do staff focus on problems within their own families of origin, rather than on their roles as "natural" mothers, when considering the difficulties of their jobs? On the surface, the answer seems obvious: staff want to represent themselves as good maternal caretakers in their private lives. Also, it seems likely that if staff view the problems they experience with their roles in the therapeutic family as stemming (in part) from their status as daughters in their own families of origin, it would be easier for them to imagine that the same is true for patients themselves. But there is also a cultural logic at work here that is more subtle, and that—like ideas about motherhood within natural families—points up contradictions within contemporary American visions of the family.

In chapter 2, I show that one purpose of the therapeutic family is to destructure, through the artifice of substitution, seemingly outdated forms of parenting (particularly mothering) in patients' natural families. This therapeutic goal is in keeping with contemporary ideals of family life: modernist family conventions should be transformed into postmodern arrangements that are minimal, allowing for greater individualism and choice among family members. Writing about these kinds of changes in dominant European and Euro-American ideas about kinship since the 1950s, Strathern (1992a) shows how an increasing valorization of cultural pluralism, diversity, and individual choice appears to undermine older family forms, with their relatively fixed gender roles. This historical shift signals a particular representation of, and relationship to, the past. The past becomes outdated "nature" (the "traditional family"), and the present becomes progressive "culture" that is "postnature" (and, more recently, "postmodern"). Strathern argues convincingly that these relationships of past to present and nature to culture are specific to capitalist "enterprise cultures," in which nature is construed as a resource in the production of culture. Strathern further suggests that while a "natural past" is often imagined as a point of contrast to the apparent newness of any given "present," the present is, in fact, constructed in and through this imagined past and through a reconfiguration of this past.[9]

In family work at Walsh, natural families (patients' families of origin) are strongly marked as such (in contrast with the therapeutic family), and problems in these families are conflated with so-called traditional (modernist, outdated) families of the "past." The artifice of the therapeutic family, then, works to streamline (destructure) patients' families to fit into a social world that appears to transcend familial nature as we have known it; but it also posits this nature as a point of contrast for the desired change. As Strathern puts it, "increasing social discourse of the role of 'social' construction in the conjoining of natural and social relationships—of the artificiality of human enterprise—has given a different visibility to natural relationships. They acquire a new priority or autonomy" (Strathern 1992a, 53). Strathern also suggests that this contemporary cultural discourse renders explicit what has long been an implicit assumption within Euro-American ideas about kinship: namely, that individuals (children) "descend," through time, out of a state of nature (their families of origin) into a state that is relatively "cultured."

> Time is seen to flow downward. It thereby contributes to the asymmetry in relations between parents and children, and to the contexts in which parents are regarded as acting more from convention, children more from their capacity for individual choice. Out of the fact and direction of generation, the antitheses between convention and choice

or relationships and individuality acquire a temporal dimension. Convention, like tradition, seems to be antecedent, to "come from" the past, while choice, like invention, seems to lie in the future. In kinship idiom, children are future to the parents' past. (Strathern 1992b, 20–21)

According to this set of ideas, staff members' families of origin hold the key to many problems that staff experience within the therapeutic family, which is, after all, a "constructed" family form designed to move patients into the future developmentally, as independent individuals who are relatively free from their own families of origin. Generationally speaking, staff members' roles as natural mothers, like their roles as therapeutic mothers, are seen to be inherently more free from the constraints of nature that produced staff as daughters and, as historically prior, appear to work against individuation. Thus if staff become overinvolved and enmeshed with patients, their perception is that the problem must be due to unresolved issues from their pasts.

In keeping with this "progressive" logic, a logic that apparently moves people away from familial constraints, appropriate therapeutic mothering is figured as minimal mothering. What holds true for patients' mothers in this regard also holds true for therapeutic mothers. I have argued that ideal mothering for parents is defined primarily in the negative: mothers' seemingly intrusive interest in their daughters' care—which is, at least in part, actively produced in the present through the withholding of information at Walsh and through practices of separation and individuation there—must be tempered. It must be reduced to its perceived "essential core," which includes natural, unconditional love for daughters and an instinctive knowledge of how to care for them. I have described how minimal mothering is produced within the therapeutic family, as well, when female staff and clinicians are compelled to protect patients from the aggressive interventions of male psychiatrists, and to perform this care quietly, cautiously, and behind the scenes.

But what of the perceived essential core of therapeutic mothering? Are therapeutic mothers expected to exhibit natural and instinctive abilities to care for patients in a minimal fashion? What does minimal motherhood look like for staff? A version of unconditional love is indeed expected from nurses and counselors. But unlike patients' natural mothers, staff are called on to express this care *while* they are presiding over medical treatments that, as explained earlier, often seem antithetical to "family values." As a result, minimal mothering within the therapeutic family calls into question the presumed naturalness of ideal mothering today. However, this questioning is limited, because therapeutic mothers are not natural mothers to patients in a "natural" setting. But it is telling, and sometimes disruptive, when minimal mothering is difficult to achieve even for professional (surrogate) mothers.

Staff as Minimal Mothers

Several staff members talked with me about the difficulties they face enforcing unit rules while maintaining caretaking roles with patients. One evening when I was following Cecilia (a milieu counselor) during her shift, she announced wryly that it was time for her to be the "pee police," meaning she had to measure the urine output of the eating-disordered patients. As we went from room to room gathering urine samples, Cecilia said that this aspect of her job gets in the way of connecting with patients emotionally (as we may well imagine). Susan, another milieu counselor, once told me that staff have to learn to "set boundaries appropriately: limits like, at the end of the meal, it's the end of the meal. And it's over. It's over! And, knowing when it's time to give leeway," for example, realizing that it might do more harm than good to pressure a patient to "eat the last lousy Grapenut in her cereal bowl." I asked Susan what strategies she uses to keep herself from becoming too rigid with patients. She said, "I keep in mind, I'm doing the best I can at any given time, and so are they. Remembering they're human beings, they're struggling, this isn't a personal thing. Someone once said to me, if you feel like you're being manipulated, you are. And the key to not being manipulated is having some detachment from the behavior." Susan then talked about how this kind of detachment is difficult for her, because she's "the kind of person who doesn't like to go to the SPCA, because I'll want to take home all the stray kittens. I've talked to my [own] kids about, when they're grown and gone, having my house as a home for . . . kids who don't have a home." Given what Susan calls these pulls toward maternal caretaking, she has to go to some lengths to separate out these feelings from her interactions with patients.

Here we can see that in some ways, staff's "natural" mothering tendencies as they exist in their personal lives *in the present* can also

appear to hamper what is considered appropriate therapeutic detachment. Susan described some of the ways she has handled this problem:

> [When I first started working at Walsh], I used to literally sit in my car
> and imagine letting go of all the kids, not taking them home with me.
> It had to be that visual, concrete kind of exercise to set some bounda-
> ries. . . . Once, we were having this major thing where all the kids were
> pushing [the rules at mealtimes] all the time. And I remembered
> Martha talking to one kid about doing a cartoon visualization to help
> them get out of a particularly difficult parent interaction. What I chose
> to do for myself was just imagine I was a clock, and every five minutes
> I told them the time. And when the time was over, the meal went
> away! And it wasn't personal. It wasn't me setting a limit . . . [I did this]
> because it was getting very frustrating, it was like every goddamn
> meal. And I needed some kind of distraction for myself, so I wouldn't
> get angry, overly rigid, punitive.

Note that in this account, the perceived dangers of personal involvement with patients are the two faces of "overmothering" outlined in
chapter 2 (in constructions of "schizophrenogenic" mothers): the risks
are both caring too much (wanting to take patients home) and becoming punitive. A middle ground is called for; staff are expected to temper the potentially controlling (punitive) effects of treatment—as well
as temptations to engage in seemingly excessive forms of maternal
caretaking—with more minimal forms of care and support. Susan as a
clock is a striking example of minimal caretaking in the therapeutic
family. A former milieu counselor I interviewed described another example of minimal caretaking at Walsh when he talked to me about
the potential for therapeutic intimacy through mundane interactions
and the performance of technical procedures: "As a milieu counselor,
it's not so much what you say, as what you do. How you react physically, how you walk by [patients]. Doing vitals [measuring patients' vital
signs] is a chance to be close and touch in a caring and consistent way.
Vitals could be the best part of a shift. One-to-ones are often misunderstood; they are either [routinized as] part of a checklist, or they're
overly therapeutic. One-to-ones could *be* the vitals. You shouldn't always
do [a formal one-to-one]. A patient is more likely to tell you how their
day is if it's not a planned talk."

According to a number of staff, these minimalist forms of caretaking
are difficult for female staff in particular, because they evoke "natural"

maternal feelings that threaten to disrupt the delicate balance required for caring detachment and detached caring. But given a focus on staff members' families of origin as the root of inappropriate caretaking at Walsh, how can we understand the fact that staff's natural maternal identities in the present are also suspect in this way—that this aspect of staff's personal lives needs to be kept in check as well (along with the effects of their personal histories as daughters)? I suggest that this critical stance toward staff members' contemporary maternal instincts parallels a recognition that treatment protocols themselves can participate in creating some of the difficulties that staff members experience with caretaking on the unit.

Staff were often self-reflexive about a parallel process that develops between themselves and eating-disordered patients through their mutual, finely tuned attention to the details of unit rules, especially regarding body weights, calories, time limits for eating, and the like. Wendy described a kind of overmothering on the unit that is related to this problem:

> These patients invite special treatment. They have legalistic and highly developed strategies. There's a pull for us to do more and more of that with them. Also, there's something about them that you like working with them. You tend to get more and more involved with them. It evokes a caretaking and nurturing investment, a preoccupation. And I think we look on that as something special that we do [on this unit]. There are times I don't think it's entirely healthy. For example, over-developing the treatment process for them. [Eating-disordered patients are] sort of obsessional themselves, and it's hard for us not to obsess about them. . . . they invite more rules, more limits, more investigation, intrusiveness. . . . for certain staff, it meets their own needs. There's a countertransference element.

Countertransference refers to the intrusion of the personal within a professional therapeutic relationship; in this case, staff responding in kind to patients' acting as if staff were parents to them. Here we can see that when it comes to the implementation of specific treatment protocols, maternal feelings in the present are seen as a threat.

In addition, staff members sometimes spoke about the requirements of the treatment program actively producing (as opposed to merely invoking) problematic themes that existed within their families of origin, as well. In my conversation with Susan about her description of herself as a clock—an appropriately minimal therapeutic mother—I asked her if she ever felt pressure to go overboard in her detachment, to be as perfectionistic and detail oriented as patients seem to be. She replied,

> Oh, well, that's my nature. I struggle with that a lot. . . . When I came here, it would have been easy to get into a rigid pattern of "a tea-spoon's a teaspoon, a tablespoon's a tablespoon." I really [had] to find whole different ways to deal with that. In this area, I learned a lot about myself, because I grew up in a—my father's an accountant. I came from a family that was very detail oriented and critical. I really see this a lot in the kids, and I really work very hard not to reflect that back to them. Telling the kids over and over again that I trust them, I believe they'll make the right decisions—and putting it right back on them. Rather than struggling. Because what I know for myself in growing up is that [when detail orientation] becomes the area that you function in, . . . you don't get at who's responsible, the control issue behind it, the belief that [patients] might have in themselves, the fact that [staff] do or don't trust them. I mean, in a lot of [the detail-oriented aspects of the treatment program], the message is, implicitly, that we don't trust. So trying whenever possible to give back a message that we do trust.

Similarly, John, a former milieu counselor, compared the detail orientation of the treatment program to upsetting and alienating experiences he had in the hospital as a child when his mother was very ill; and he explained his aversion to, and detachment from, the technical details of the unit's treatment plans in these terms. For both Susan and John, truly intimate, "maternal" caretaking on the unit occurs almost in spite of unit protocols. In this way, the institutional problems with attaining minimal mothering in the therapeutic family are more visible than are the contexts for the problems that patients' mothers experience trying to achieve this ideal.

And yet it would be an oversimplification to say that staff view certain treatment protocols as getting in the way of (or producing the opposite of) ideal surrogate mothering, as if they believed that in the absence of these protocols they would be ideal substitute parents. If effective and intimate caring seems to occur at Walsh in spite of detail-oriented routines and procedures on the unit, it also seems to occur in spite of certain propensities of staff. Susan said that perfectionistic overmothering, not ideal minimal mothering, is her "nature" (and she implied to me on a number of occasions that she felt she had to fight against this tendency even in her relatively "healthy" role as a mother of procreation in the present); and when Wendy (quoted earlier) said that some staff "meet their own needs" through therapeutic mothering, she implied that some staff's natural abilities to be minimal therapeutic mothers were compromised. In these ways—and like the mothers involved in the treatment program, and patients themselves—staff are seen to have to work against (aspects of) themselves to achieve a required ideal.

Let me sum up a bit by pointing out a twofold irony: staff seem to express inappropriately *personal* involvement with patients when they perform their *jobs* with precision (by attending to the minutiae of patients' protocols), but at the same time, many unit practices appear to dovetail with the seemingly problematic personal lives and histories of staff (along with those of patients). The upshot here is that ideal, minimal maternal caretaking on the unit is enabled neither by treatment protocols nor by staff's natural abilities.[10] Staff were hard-pressed to describe these ideal caretaking roles in any detail, beyond prohibitions against overmothering or inappropriate mothering—these roles are simply posited as a personal and personalizing aspect of psychiatric nursing work. As "personal," and therefore natural (because nonprofessional), minimal mothering on the unit is always potentially dangerous. While certain of its positive aspects can be identified (trust, verbal explicitness), these are largely of mysterious character and origin. But how is it possible that minimal therapeutic mothering at Walsh is seen both as a natural skill and as difficult to achieve, or even describe? Cultural anthropologist Anna Tsing's reflections on the ways in which social power comes to be invested in "nature" are instructive here: "Naturalizing power requires empowering nature. Empowering nature means attributing to nature forms of agency we can understand. Yet 'nature' is also, by definition, that which escapes human attributions." Tsing continues, "nature, like God, is both lawful and mysterious; it requires human efforts to know it, yet always slips away from full knowledge" (Tsing 1995, 114). If people on the treatment team claim to know why staff members' maternal natures lead to overmothering or punitive approaches to patients, they do *not* know how it is that they mother *well*. When I asked Mark, the head psychiatrist on the unit, to explain how the unit was set up to create a positive "family environment," he was quite vague about the matter (even though he said the family metaphor was "very intentional"):

We selected the people very carefully that work here, and you had to get into that kind of a spirit, and if you didn't, then you were axed. And there are several people that came and left, don't forget, that didn't like it. The expectation is—well, you gotta be a little bit on the fuzzy side, and you gotta have sort of good humor. You have to like kids; if you don't like kids, it's not a place for you. . . . it's special. It's very unusual. But there's been many places like that through the country and in the world, and it's just, *what it should be like.* . . . anything that's out there should, does feel like that. For a variety of reasons. . . . there's a special skill that goes into [it], that the staff has.

In general, staff consider themselves insiders to special knowledge about how to interact with patients, knowledge that is impossible to teach. Further, this knowledge is expected to permeate one's being: as one staff member put it to me, even the way you carry yourself when walking down the hall is significant and important. Like minimal mothering for patients' natural mothers, then, valued forms of caretaking on the part of staff cannot be specified, even though staff are expected to manifest them in a number of ways, and constantly. This problem has become all the more apparent with the rise of managed care.

The Sexual Politics of Caretaking under Managed Care

I close this chapter with a discussion of how managed care affects the sexual politics of caretaking on the unit. Recent shifts toward more streamlined and "efficient" treatment practices mean that feminized labor at Walsh is culled out of fewer and fewer resources. Interestingly, many staff speak in glowing terms about a "family style" of treatment from the (recent) past when discussing this topic.

Many people who work on the unit describe changes in health care since the mid-1980s in terms of a shift from a family orientation to a business orientation in the workplace. Prior to these changes, staff were able to spend a lot of time with patients one-on-one and also processing the meaningful details of their work among themselves. Most staff—many of whom had worked on the unit for ten years or more when I interviewed them in the mid-1990s—felt that these aspects of their jobs were the most rewarding and equated them with a "family orientation." Recently, however, staff have been expected to be more "businesslike" and efficient in their approach to treatment. Increasingly, insurance companies are requiring constant and quantifiable measures of patients' progress. At the same time, budget cuts have resulted in staff downsizing. In the mid-1980s, the staff-patient ratio was about one to two, and when I was conducting my fieldwork, it was about one to three. As a result, staff relate to one another in more cursory ways. Also, they now have trouble finding the time to interact with patients one-on-one. However, this kind of caretaking work is necessary for the unit to function as it is set up to function. For example, I have shown that psychiatrists often feel that it is their job to provoke and upset patients; it is then tacitly expected that staff will empathize with and soothe them. But hospital management does not consider this caretaking work to be necessary "business," even though management wants this work to continue as a special, defining feature of the unit.

Charlotte, the nurse manager on the unit, was at the forefront of these changes while I was conducting my fieldwork. On the one hand, Charlotte believed that on a psychiatric unit, "We have a different kind of way than medicine. And I've actually advocated that [in negotiations with hospital management]. That we don't just [distribute] meds. Our medicine is being with the kids. So you can't keep cutting our [staff]. In fact I've been successful; we were the only unit last year that didn't get nurses cut." On the other hand, because "being with the kids" seems to be a vague need, Charlotte also believed that as a general trend, staff cuts and a shift toward a hard-line "business orientation" were inevitable:

> The way I see it, the business portion of it, the way the unit was run beforehand . . . was just like a family. And now we've gone to a business. And you've got to have accountabilities, you have to have policies and procedures, you have to have some organization . . . and [staff] can't spend all day talking about how you feel. . . . Before, there was lo-o-ots of processing. And it's really cut back. And there are times I say, "I know that that's how you feel, and you still have to do this." . . . You can have all the feelings you want, but the train's going in this direction. And either you get to have your feelings and get on it, and feel bad about how bad you feel, you know, and keep going with the train, or you can get mowed over.

As Charlotte implies here, the general feeling among staff is that highly meaningful day-to-day aspects of their work with patients are being increasingly devalued. Many staff nostalgically recall the days when, as one former milieu counselor put it, they "really made a difference, really turned patients' lives around," keeping some patients in the hospital for two, even three, months. With managed care, this kind of "life-changing" work is no longer possible. During an interview, Wendy (a nurse) remarked, "As we become more compressed in the kind of time that we have, you just have to be much more efficient than you used to be. We have much sicker kids, you have to do everything more rapidly, you have to accomplish a lot more in a shorter period of time. Both on a daily basis and on an admission-length basis." And Elaine, a milieu counselor, said, "We used to monitor the [unit] environment; there were discussions, there were studies. Now, there's more of an attitude of, you do what you have to do, and try to have it work for everyone. . . . there's more of a 'take it or leave it' attitude. . . . Everything's tightened up. . . . Also, now, as a rule, when kids first come in, they're unstable. So they're just run through the protocol. It's all been cut down to 'need to know.' What you need to know."

Wendy expressed a strong dislike of these shifts toward "efficient" nursing care, speaking to the effects of these shifts on her own experience of her work:

> I'm more like a computer; they may as well just wheel the computer in [rounds], because it's facts and figures. I don't really have time to think about the process of what's going on with patients. My thoughts and feelings about the process [are] not part of what I'm expected to do. It used to be more that way for staff, and that more staff used to be in rounds; and that was helpful, because one problem is, you're in there in rounds, you're taking notes, you're giving the report . . . then you may get called out, and you have to come back in, and you're scrambling. So there's just no time. Everything in general has been speeded up; there's just no time anymore.

Staff resist many of these changes. For example, during the time I was conducting fieldwork, Charlotte (the nurse manager) and Bob (the medical director) requested changes in the weekend nursing report to make it less anecdotal and more informational. For example, they wanted specific information about patients' weight changes to be included. Many staff I spoke with resented this request for extra work and also resented the quantification of their contribution to rounds. Moreover, several staff members argued that patients' individual therapists should be responsible for keeping track of patients' weight changes.

For a period of time, some staff deliberately wrote disorganized and incomplete weekend reports. Bob commented that staff's resistance on this score showed that they "want it both ways. They want more responsibility, but if you give it to them, they balk." Significantly, I heard almost identical comments about patients who chose not to keep track of their weight gain while they were in the hospital, and who argued that managing such details was the staff's responsibility.

Here we can see that staff, like patients themselves, are expected to take up and to incorporate into their identities the quantifiable aspects of unit protocols that supposedly result in streamlined—or economically and structurally "fit"—trajectories toward "health" for patients. But again, at the same time that staff are asked to accommodate the changes required by managed care, they are, as Lorna (a nurse) once remarked, "still expected to run a milieu." Ironically, it is the psychological benefit afforded, in part, by a supportive therapeutic milieu that is thought to engender a will to health for patients. It seems that the value of family-oriented care on the unit is continually both asserted and undermined; it is both represented as an important tradition and devalued as being out-of-date. In this way, the dimension of time that informs the unit's construction of a contrast between traditional overmothering and healthy, minimal mothering is compressed. Once again, we can see that contemporary discourses of minimal mothering deploy ideas about tradition as both foils *and* resources.

Like the personal histories of staff, nostalgia for unit practices of the past haunt the practices of the present in both positive and negative ways. On the positive side, because the constraints of efficient managed care plans undermine the very family environment of the unit that distinguishes the staff's work as psychiatric, nostalgia for "the old days" is one way to affirm the uniqueness of the unit, and to press for at least a minimal continuation of a so-called family style. As Charlotte argued above, the unit's "medicine" is "being with the kids." Often, references to a lost past are a form of resistance to changes in health care that threaten the unit. As Bob put it once, insurance companies today do not seem to appreciate that "the work we do is mysterious" (as noted earlier, maternal caretaking on the unit is considered one of the most mysterious practices of the treatment program). When discussing staff members' verbal evocations of an ideal unit past, Alan, a milieu counselor, granted these references a timeless quality, suggesting mystery and also collapsing past and present. Claiming that recent changes in unit practices are "overplayed by staff," he suggested that "the unit is the same. It's a wonderful, stable thing. Nurses will say the [changes are] horrible . . . [but] I work on this unit, and it's the same. Anguish is part of the way this place works; it isn't real." For Alan, the "wonderful, stable thing" that never changes is staff's unique caretaking roles, and he understood staff members' complaints to be constitutive of those roles. So Alan claimed that the verbal articulation of a loss here actually indexes a constant presence that is extremely valuable and neutralizes the effects of change. On the other hand, Richard, a nurse, framed the question to which Alan spoke very differently, believing that nostalgia for a family style is negative (and in fact falsifies the past). Richard said, "[These days], treatment for patients is road mapped. On day one, you do this. Day two, et cetera. Before, the program was more generic and individually planned. Now, it's more strategic. . . . Before, there were more dollars available to do intensive [work with patients] one-on-one. Which was therapeutic, but not therapy, though some disagree and say it's therapy. But really there's been no big change in nursing, because nurses [shouldn't] do therapy. . . . Nurses basically hand out meds." Richard also collapses the past and present to an extent, but through a representation of maternal caretaking on the unit as unnecessary, even nonexistent.

In contrast to both Alan and Richard, most caregivers at Walsh believe that the unit's family style of old was once powerful, valuable, and valued, but is obsolete under managed care today. Suzanne, a pediatrician who agreed with Charlotte (the nurse manager) that a family style at Walsh is not appropriate today, talked to me about many staff members' anger with Charlotte for promoting this view:

> Charlotte's been told that she has no empathy, that she is a robot that makes staff do things no matter what. Well, you know, there's some truth to that. . . . I think [in the past] it's been like a family. You know, and she's the bad mom now. There's not a professional kind of thinking here. . . . Not only is she the nurse manager, but she should be the therapist, she should be . . . you know, the "golden tit award" is one of my favorite sayings—you know, that she should always be there, to feed them and nurture them. . . . and that's what it was before. . . . but if you ask me, she's not *supposed* to be the mom. But some people want the warm fuzzies, they want . . . the chicken soup, and can you bring the brownies in.

In criticizing the idea that Charlotte should be a "mom" to staff and promote a "warm, fuzzy" environment on the unit, Suzanne invokes powerful images of "bad" and "overbearing" mothers.

Similarly, Bob (the medical director) argued that the "traditional culture" of the staff was overly anxious and protective of patients, and that staff needed to develop the flexibility to provide more efficient forms of care. But he also argued that staff were responsible for maintaining the milieu as "a sustaining, nurturing place. It's like a home. It's [like] sitting down with each of your kids for an hour talking about everything; now that—maybe you can do that *sometimes*. But fundamentally what [we need is a] nurturant environment, the general caring, the kind of opportunities that you provide for growth. *That's* what the nursing staff should be concerned with maintaining, and brokering. And observing. Clinically. That's what I want them to do." Thus maternal caretaking on the unit is constructed as both good and bad, smothering and necessary, old-fashioned and valued in the present. The need to justify the very existence of psychiatric nursing in an era of managed care makes these contradictions explicit.

At Walsh, the responsibility to sustain feminized caretaking appears to rest with the individual capacities of staff members. Staff are often told by their superiors that they must develop attitudes and cultivate personal energy resources to accept and "own" the changes they are experiencing in their work. As Charlotte put it, staff can either carve out caretaking roles "on the train" of change, or they "can get mowed over." In this way, staff are to expected to realize their (healthy, minimal) maternal "natures" through individual effort. Like patients themselves, then, staff are caught up in a discourse that represents individual effort and willpower as the key to producing feminine nature in an acceptable form. But this discourse overresources the very nature that is the desired object, and ground, of feminized work on the unit. So whereas the goal of minimal therapeutic mothering is naturalized and individualized at Walsh (as are treatment goals for individual patients), it also continues to create controversy and conflict in an ever-changing treatment environment.

Conclusion

In this chapter, I have shown that diverse and sometimes contradictory representations of "natural" mothering are deployed at Walsh in the positioning of female staff. Staff are valued for their "maternal" caretaking skills, but by the same token they often appear unable to separate from patients, an apparent problem that is attributed to obsolete caretaking practices at Walsh or to inappropriate personal involvement. The goal for staff, then—as for patients' natural mothers—is to become minimal mothers (in their roles as surrogate parents).

In chapter 2, I argued that the ideal of minimal mothering for patients' parents emerges as a streamlined version of a perceived maternal excess that is invoked in the treatment process. Within the therapeutic family today, this ideal is thought to be always already achieved; it is *assumed* as a gender-neutral feature of treatment. But discourses of gender equality and therapeutic family unity at Walsh (which coexist with a widely acknowledged, and gendered, hierarchical structure there) paper over the fact that "maternal" caretaking on the unit is produced in treatment as well, and is unstable, in part because it is, in fact, shot through with gendered inequalities. For example, when patients are provoked or become upset in the process of treatment (often via a male clinician), female staff often come to the rescue and soothe them. Staff are expected to perform this role, but are also admonished to keep an emotional distance from patients.

Problems with the sexual politics of the therapeutic family are often displaced onto the imagined problems of natural families (those of staff as well as patients). At the same time, however, it is telling when mental health professionals experience difficulty performing minimal motherhood, and occasionally, the problematic institutional politics of the role are the subject of controversy. These problems are especially apparent in the context of managed care, in which maternal feeling is still required of staff but is culled from fewer and fewer resources.

FOUR

"Typical Patients Are Not 'Borderline' ":
Embedded Constructs of Race,
Ethnicity, and Class

This chapter shows that clinical constructions
of "typical" or "true" anorexia—and of patients who are marked as highly atypical (or
"borderline")—encode discourses of race,
ethnicity, and class that are largely invisible.
Clinicians and staff at Walsh describe as "typical" the vast majority of patients in the eating
disorders program. When we consider that
these patients are relatively privileged (white
and middle-class), it is important to recognize
that many working-class and nonwhite patients are excluded from treatment in a number of ways. My focus here is on the rhetoric
of exclusion that helps to produce the clinical
norms against which certain "atypical" patients are measured.

In both psychological and popular bodies
of literature, anorexia is usually presented as
a predominantly white and middle-class phenomenon. However, since the mid-1980s, an
increasing number of studies have cast doubt
on this epidemiological portrait. In a 1996
review of the literature on the relationship
between eating disorders and socioeconomic
status (SES), psychologists Gard and Freeman write that since 1983, "13 studies have
failed to find a relationship between high

socioeconomic status and eating disorders," including anorexia (2).[1] As for anorexia's prevalence among ethnic minority groups, several scholars now acknowledge that very little research has addressed this question: "In North America, most studies either have comprised ethnically homogenous [i.e., white] samples or have included too few members of ethnic [i.e., nonwhite] groups to permit valid estimations of prevalence rates among ethnic groups" (Striegel-Moore and Smolak 2000, 231). Taken together, most studies of anorexia in the United States that do consider racial and ethnic categories suggest that a majority of anorexics are white, that most nonwhite anorexics are Latina or African American, and that anorexics of any other racial or ethnic identity are practically unheard of.[2] But some researchers have argued that these (tentative) conclusions should not be taken at face value. There are a number of issues to consider here.

Eating-disordered symptoms appear to be increasing, but still appear to be relatively rare, within ethnic minority groups. Many have suggested that members of these groups who struggle with eating disorders are trying to "assimilate" to white middle-class norms of slender femininity and self-control.[3] But this explanation leaves some important issues unexamined. While it seems clear that discourses of assimilation are indeed at work here, we must explore as part of this picture the racialized and classed norms that define eating disorders in dominant popular and clinical narratives. These norms may preclude the recognition of significant eating problems that are "nonstandard" and perhaps more widespread (Gard and Freeman 1996; Root 1990; Striegel-Moore 1994; Striegel-Moore and Smolak 2000; B. Thompson 1992, 1994a, 1994b). Also, "nonstandard" meanings may be assigned to the eating difficulties of economically underprivileged or nonwhite people when apparently identical problems would otherwise be labeled as standard (for white and middle-class people); doctors and mental health professionals sometimes participate in this process because of preconceived ideas about "typical" patients (Dolan 1991; B. Thompson 1994a). (Notably, most studies of eating disorders examine patient populations.) In sum, recent scholarship points to a mutually reinforcing set of ideas and practices—operating in concert with social and regional differences in service accessibility (see Dolan 1991)—that add up to significant class, race, and ethnic "biases" in definitions of eating disorders and in procedures of referral and diagnosis.[4]

At Walsh in the mid-1990s, approximately four-fifths of patients were both middle-class and white. I identified patients' class status through household income when this information was available, and also on the basis of parents' reported professional and community standing. Believing that class status is constituted by a set of dispositions and attitudes as well as an income level, I also took into account patients and parents' aspirations and self-identification with regard to class status (discussed during interviews).[5] Out of the fifty-two patients I followed during my fieldwork, only five were both nonwhite and working-class. Three were nonwhite and middle-class, and two were working-class and white. Of the eight nonwhite patients, four were Chicana, one was Filipina, one was Chinese American, and two were Japanese American.

What can we make of the fact that poorer patients and patients of color are rare at Walsh? I agree with several of the authors cited in the previous paragraphs that it is important to challenge the idea that this rarity reflects a pregiven statistical reality about anorexia's incidence. First, Walsh is located in a fairly wealthy and predominantly white urban area. Second, wealthier patients are more likely to seek treatment for longer periods of time, and therefore to remain in more constant contact with the medical system, in part because of access to more comprehensive insurance coverage (I return to this topic later). At the same time, however, it is important to note that during the time I was conducting fieldwork, one-fifth to one-fourth of eating-disordered patients at Walsh were Medicare patients, and no patient was refused treatment because of a lack of ability to pay (Walsh will absorb costs when necessary).[6] However, it still holds true that wealthier patients are more likely to receive treatment after severe medical consequences are no longer an immediate threat.

These demographic and economic questions, while certainly important, are not the focus of this chapter. As I have suggested, there are also questions to consider about the *constitution* of ideal, or typical, patients in the treatment process and in clinical assessments. This chapter shows how certain psychiatric practices and beliefs help to create a higher number of (recognized) cases of anorexia among white and middle-class young women. Moving beyond the question of "bias" or inclusiveness in defining eating disorders and in procedures of referral and diagnosis, I argue that anorexia's "typical" clinical presentation is written through and against constructions of identity that appear to deviate from this normative picture. Specifically, I suggest that "true" or "typical" anorexia emerges at Walsh, in part, through clinicians' justifications for excluding from full participation in the program those nonwhite and working-class anorexic patients who are seen to possess features of "borderline personality disorder," a stigmatized and stigmatizing psychiatric diagnosis that also indicates an atypical clinical presentation of anorexia.[7] In exploring this issue, I pose the following question: How might the very definitions of illness and health that operate in the treatment of anorexia implicate presumed features of racial, ethnic, or class identities?

Nearly everyone working at Walsh believes that its approach to patients is race and class neutral; explicitly racist and classist articulations of inequality are rare. Note that this chapter does not detail specific race and class relations at Walsh. More often than not, the discourses and dynamics analyzed here involve assumptions about patients' identities that are couched in the generalizing terms of psychological "health" and "illness." It is my aim to unpack these terms in order to show that ideologies and practices of social inclusion and marginalization underpin them; however, these ideologies and practices are almost always hidden within medicalized concepts of selfhood and family dynamics and thereby acquire a particular purchase. I am keen to stress the *embedded* constructs of race, ethnicity, and class that lead both to representations of true anorexia and to (informal) diagnoses of borderline personality disorder (which, in turn, authorize exclusion)—*in spite of* an ideology of inclusiveness at Walsh.

All the patients who were excluded during the time I was conducting fieldwork were labeled "borderline" and were also both nonwhite and working-class, but I should stress that the numbers here are small (there was a total of three such patients). My discussion concentrates on one richly described case study. I make no causal claims about the bases of exclusion: there was not a one-to-one mapping between nonwhite and/or working-class patients referred to Walsh and patients who were labeled borderline, nor were all patients labeled borderline marginalized in the treatment program. My arguments focus on the production of norms for typical patients that are largely unmarked as such but appear more strongly as active constructions when juxtaposed to the racialized and classed othering of excluded patients. At Walsh, this othering links discourses of race and class with ideas about borderline psyches.

I also suggest that the clinical production of "typical" anorexia is not seamless; rather, it is fractured and contradictory. Toward the end of this chapter, I show that marginalized patients are sometimes valued, even romanticized, for the very qualities that clinicians identify in them to help justify their exclusion. At times, typical patients are compared unfavorably to borderline patients. Also, these patients are usually identified as "misfits" because they expose in a disruptive way the unit's requirement that they both comply with and resist treatment protocols, a requirement that exists for all patients, but that "true anorexics" are seen to finesse with greater skill. Disagreements among hospital staff about how to care for these "difficult" patients can point up and disturb culturally dominant representations of subjectivity and health at Walsh. However, in these situations, hegemonic representations of illness, health, and true anorexia usually prevail. The final section of this chapter shows how the constraints of managed care participate in these prevailing definitions of illness and health, at a time when coverage for care is harder to come by for everyone.

A comment about terminology is in order here. For ease of expression, I often use the phrases "anorexics" or "anorexic patient(s)," "eating-disordered patient(s)," and "borderline patient(s)." Note that I do so advisedly, mirroring the talk of most clinicians and staff at Walsh that works to essentialize illness as part of people's identities.

Internalizers Run the Place

To compare representations of "typical" and "misfit" anorexic patients at Walsh, I begin with perceptions of typical patients (again, the vast majority of anorexic patients are seen as typical). How do staff and clinicians view these patients, and how do they describe their impact on the unit as a whole? Recall that the unit admits adolescents with a range of so-called psychosomatic diagnoses. The first issue to note here is that most staff believe that an "eating disorder style" dominates the treatment environment on the unit. As a former milieu counselor put it, "There's a bias towards eating disorders. . . . When you look at the day-to-day or hour-to-hour nursing intervention within the staff, it's mostly geared towards the eating disorders." Many workers at Walsh identify detailed attention to, for example, food and eating on the unit as not only catering to the specific "needs" of anorexic patients but also discriminating against nonanorexic patients. During lunchtime one day, several nonanorexic patients had finished their meals early and were talking and making phone calls in the community room (where meals are eaten). Most of the anorexic patients were upset that their concentration over eating was broken, and for the next several unit community meetings, they argued for the imposition of mealtime rules that would promote a quiet atmosphere. Staff were torn on the issue: many do prefer a quiet and orderly environment during mealtimes, partly because it seems to help anorexic patients to relax, and also because of the delicate balance staff try to maintain between observing these patients at mealtimes and trying not to seem *too* intrusive in so doing (a rowdy atmosphere would highlight staff members' roles as observers). However, a few staff members were upset that problems specific to anorexic patients would set the mood at mealtimes for everyone.

Speaking more generally about anorexic patients' influence on unit style, Susan, a milieu counselor, remarked, "We have a history of a focus on eating disorders. What's unfortunate is, eating-disordered kids have critical and rigid natures, and other kids have a hard time breaking in." Susan was referring to the perception that anorexic patients champion unit rules in ways that make it difficult for nonanorexic patients to experience a sense of power and agency within the orderly therapeutic community. I noticed during my fieldwork that many anorexic patients were quite invested in the unit's policies and procedures, and that this investment often conferred a privileged status in the treatment program, since reward systems at Walsh depend on a commitment to its closely regulated schedule of activities. As Bob (the medical director) once put it to me, "Eating-disordered patients have power [on the unit]. They hold the fort, follow the rules." For example, anorexic patients often "earn" the right to facilitate group meetings (in figurehead roles) through "good behavior." They are also known to challenge other patients for not following the rules, and even to criticize staff for failures to enforce rules. I remember one community meeting in which several anorexic patients were upset that one (nonanorexic) patient was always late for these meetings. They reasoned that because there were consequences for them when they did not finish their calories on a given day, there should also be consequences for chronic lateness. Staff clearly feel that anorexic patients go overboard on these kinds of issues. As Cecilia, a milieu counselor, put it in rounds one day, "The girls are so powerful, they run the place." At the same time, staff find it difficult to challenge or temper a form of power that promotes, even perfects, the unit's standards of behavior for patients.

Taking unit rules so seriously is one of the ways that anorexic patients distinguish themselves as "internalizers." According to clinicians
and staff, internalizers turn problems inward, somatizing or intellectualizing them, and they explore conflict rationally and calmly. They
tend toward "law and order," which explains their commitment to unit
ideals of behavior and orderliness. Importantly, most staff consider
themselves internalizers, as well. However, when anorexic patients *perfect* an internalizing stance toward hospital policies and become preoccupied with the unit's detail orientation in its modes of operation,
some staff are moved to question the appropriateness of a unit style that
has been honed with internalizing anorexics. As discussed in chapter 3,
anorexic patients' relationship to unit rules can throw into relief for
many staff the seemingly unnatural and artificial aspects of treatment,
leading some to question the rigidity of unit protocols.

Staff seem especially willing to question the unit's protocols and
procedures when it comes to following and enforcing the hospital rules
that apply to all patients (as opposed to rules that apply only to anorexic
patients, such as rules about calorie counting). Staff's openness to self-
critique in these cases is probably due to the fact that the rules in
question highlight apparent differences between two different types
of patients at Walsh: internalizers and externalizers. Externalizing patients tend to break rules; they "act out" rather than reason through
problems and conflicts. Acting out refers to any emotional, verbal, or
physical expression that is not rational and calm: yelling, hitting, attention seeking, self-harm, testing, pleading. Externalizing patients are
almost always nonanorexic patients, and significantly, they are often
African American or Chicano boys and are usually working-class. More
often than not, when anorexic patients encourage staff to enforce unit
rules, they have in mind an externalizing patient. Clinicians and staff
generally agree that the unit is not as comfortable for, or successful
with, externalizing patients, so anorexic patients' concern about externalizers' adherence to unit rules highlights a perceived discrimination
against these patients.

Some staff I interviewed acknowledged that this perceived discrimination articulates with discourses of race and class, including their own
racial/ethnic and class identities. When asked directly about the effects
of race and class on propriety at mealtimes, Susan said, "Most staff are
white and middle-class. So it's hard to be introspective: do I impose
white, middle-class values on a white, middle-class [anorexic] popula-

tion? Yes, I probably do. . . . [Then there's the question of effects on other patients. Sometimes I say to myself,] 'Maybe I'm being too rigid here; this [nonanorexic] patient doesn't need to eat like Emily Post.' Yet the eating-disordered population has a particularly difficult time with kids who don't eat like Emily Post." Rhonda, another milieu counselor, spoke to similar themes in much stronger terms: "It makes me really angry sometimes, the way staff will impose their [white, middle-class] views and morals on the acting-out [externalizing] kids. Most of them are blind to it. It's not done in race or class terms, but it can really be racist and elitist. Yes, we need an orderly unit, but some staff take it too far, even blame the kids from broken homes or the black kids or the Chicano kids for not being 'proper.' "

However, Susan's and Rhonda's identification of racialized and classed discourses at work on the unit is rare. Because most staff and clinicians believe strongly that unit practices and ideas are race and class neutral, they usually speak as if, for example, the labels "internalizer" and "externalizer" are merely descriptive of a given patient's psychic constitution. In this way, psychiatric understandings of the self, or the psyche, can paper over the race and class politics of treatment. If externalizers do not have the status on the unit conferred to many internalizers, that is due to their own pathological natures.

Caretakers usually represent in similar terms anorexic patients' perfectionism and their tendency almost to parody unit rules and procedures. In spite of some staff members' broad critiques of Walsh's policies that seem to play into anorexia's hands, and their critiques of perceived discrimination at Walsh (and even of their own participation in these problems), the most common explanation by far of anorexic patients' relative power on the unit is not their privileged location there but rather their need for rigid "boundaries"—their creation of a seemingly powerful, so-called pseudo-self in their efforts to cover up a "fragile" or "damaged" self. As Susan put it earlier, when anorexic patients become obsessed with unit protocols, they are expressing their unhealthy "critical and rigid natures." In addition, the most common explanation for a unit style that seems biased toward anorexic patients is couched in terms of an institutional need for externally imposed—if "artificial"—boundaries for all patients (e.g., rules and required activities), to provide a "safe" context for everyone's psychological development on their paths toward health. Thus clinicians and staff are able to explain away the fact that unit boundaries and anorexic boundaries can dovetail in problematic ways by representing hospital boundaries as health giving (within the artificial constraints of an inpatient environment), and anorexic boundaries as pathological. As one staff member put it, the difference between unit boundaries and anorexic boundaries is that "ours [the unit's] are around safety issues. Theirs are kind of a way to protect and hide. They're both artificially created: out of our need to give boundaries, and their need to deal . . . with problems they can't resolve."

In sum, psychiatric constructions of the self and its boundaries mask the race and class politics of distinctions that are drawn between internalizing and externalizing patients, distinctions that grant anorexic patients certain privileges on the unit. Now I turn to examine more closely the racialized and classed specifications of identity that are embedded in the unit's discourses about selfhood and boundaries. I do so through an analysis of an internalizer/externalizer distinction that is sometimes drawn *within* a given group of anorexic patients. Occasionally, an anorexic patient is considered an externalizer. When this occurs, the institutional, and medically sanctioned, production of anorexia as a white and middle-class phenomenon—while still papered over by psychiatric categories of self, health, and illness—becomes more visible than usual.

Constituting the Border between
Typical and Atypical Anorexic Patients

Because anorexic patients usually hold power on the unit—expressing and embodying unit ideals by internalizing them—it is quite noticeable when an anorexic patient is not an internalizer. In general, externalizing anorexic patients do not appear to respect, or work hard to follow, unit protocols and procedures in the way that internalizers do. Clinicians and staff consider externalizing anorexics to be anomalous in a number of ways. In addition, they find these patients to be such a therapeutic challenge that they often deem them inappropriate candidates for inpatient treatment and even take steps to keep them off the unit.

Sandra, a sixteen-year-old Chicana patient admitted to the unit because of dramatic weight loss in a very short period of time, was quickly identified as an externalizer. Sandra loudly tested, pushed, and challenged staff at every turn; in other words, she rarely internalized unit protocols. One evening at dinnertime, while most anorexic patients were quietly and nervously counting their calories, Sandra and Elsie, the nurse who was observing her, had the following dialogue:

> *Sandra*: I'm not going to finish my calories, Elsie.
> *Elsie*: Well, try.
> *Sandra*: They never do anything to me when I don't.
> *Elsie*: I'll have to call the doctor on call.
> *Sandra*: You guys don't have to tell them *everything!*
> *Elsie*: Yes, I do.
> *Sandra*: I'm just going to eat one of these graham crackers.
> *Elsie*: Good. You can eat that.
> *Sandra*: I can't do it in just three minutes!
> *Elsie*: Yes, you can, eat fast. Chew, chew, chew! [pause]. Try to eat two.
> *Sandra*: Will you give me more time?
> *Elsie*: If you eat really fast.
> *Sandra*: No way.
> *Elsie*: Well, just eat one, then.
> *Sandra*: What did they say about me in [nursing] report?
> *Elsie*: An order for unit restriction.
> *Sandra*: Can I see it?

For staff, this kind of overt testing is not only very uncomfortable—it is also considered a sign of a poor prognosis.

What are the theories of self leading caretakers to believe that externalizing anorexic patients like Sandra are so difficult to treat? The perceived problem with these patients is that they have extremely unstable psychological boundaries; they do not have enough of a "sense of self" even to work to acquire a stable identity. In chapter 1, I show that "identity work" is considered central to therapies for eating-disordered patients. This identity work (initially) requires an ambivalent relationship to certain treatment protocols, those that anorexic patients are not expected to embrace readily (i.e., those that are designed to increase calorie consumption and body weights). Patients are encouraged to negotiate a delicate balance between compliance with, and resistance against, these protocols. A "will to health" for most patients involves a (reluctant) internalizing and "owning" of treatment goals, over time. Significantly, treatment goals lose their status as clinically imposed (and therefore "artificial") rules and regulations, and visibly help to constitute health, the moment they become part of patients' hard-won processes of self-transformation at Walsh. To return to perceived problems with treating anorexic patients like Sandra: as I discuss shortly, while clinicians did understand Sandra's struggles at Walsh in terms of her negotiating compliance and resistance, they coded her actions in this regard as categorically different from those of typical anorexic patients. They read her testing of treatment practices and of staff as an extremely problematic form of resistance, one that points not to a will to health but to a potentially untreatable sense of self.

Sandra's positioning as other at Walsh was manifest in her unavailability for interviews with me. I have been unable to record her own voice here to the extent that I have been able to do so for many patients. Her stays at Walsh were too brief (a total of about fourteen days across two admissions), and she was too often "in crisis" and therefore under a constant, one-on-one surveillance that was not conducive to conversation with me. These conditions reflect the institutional politics of exclusion I analyze here.[8]

Externalizing anorexic patients like Sandra are not usually called "externalizers"; instead, (some) clinicians refer to them as "borderline" (short for "borderline personality disorder"). This term indexes supposedly tenuous boundaries around the self. Clinicians often say that borderlines have "bad boundaries," an idea that has a twofold meaning: it refers both to a weak—even shattered—sense of self and to a resulting tendency to confuse one's own sense of self with that of others (or with "external" specifications of behavior and identity, such as those generated by a peer group). A diagnosis of borderline personality disorder—which is, according to the *Diagnostic and Statistical Manual of Mental Disorders* (American Psychiatric Association 2000), one of ten kinds of personality disorders[9]—has been applied to patients who are thought to be able to function at a high social level (anorexic patients are almost always thought of in these terms) but are nevertheless thought to have a severely disordered sense of self. Clinicians on the unit used the term "borderline" for externalizing anorexic patients in an informal way, not as an official diagnosis (which is ordinarily reserved for adults).[10] As described in the *Diagnostic and Statistical Manual of Mental Disorders, Third Edition Revised* (American Psychiatric Association 1987, 346–47), borderline personality disorder is a "pervasive pattern of instability of self-image, interpersonal relationships, and mood" that includes at least five of the following eight criteria (I paraphrase): frantic efforts to avoid abandonment, unstable relationships, identity disturbance, impulsiveness, suicidal threats, affective instability, emptiness or boredom, and inappropriate anger. The diagnosis has been applied overwhelmingly to women (D. Becker 1997).[11] During the time I was conducting fieldwork there were a total of seven anorexic patients admitted to the unit who were said to have features of borderline personality disorder; five of these patients were nonwhite and/or working-class.

Since the late 1980s, an extensive literature has emerged on the prevalence of personality disorders—including borderline personality— in eating-disordered patients.[12] Interest in this topic is fueled by a wide-spread belief that eating-disordered patients with personality disorders are the most difficult to treat and are at the highest risk for chronicity or death (Johnson 1991; Matsunaga et al. 1998; Skodol et al. 1993). How-ever, the results of studies in this area vary considerably, in part because of ongoing controversy about how to "measure" personality disorders. Many consider suspect the accuracy of borderline diagnoses in particu-lar (Scarso et al. 1992). In fact, several authors have noted with concern that a diagnosis of borderline personality "is often applied to difficult patients without adequate diagnostic evaluation, to justify the failure of a treatment plan" (Reiff and Reiff 1992, 460; Scarso et al. 1992; Fine 1989). This concern would seem to apply at Walsh, given that the label "borderline" was strictly informal and often led to exclusion from the treatment program.

Let us return to characterizations of the borderline self at Walsh. Karen, a psychology intern, remarked in an interview with me that patients like Sandra "have no identity." Another clinician said that these patients "have no 'there' there," meaning "no one's home," there is no "coherent sense of self" at all. As a result, they latch onto various "external" specifications of personhood in an attempt to generate a (false) identity. As clinicians and staff on the unit saw it, anorexia was Sandra's current identity of choice; it was not and could not be her true identity. In a circular kind of reasoning that relies on a thoroughly essentialist notion of the self, Sandra was thought to be incapable of truly identifying as anorexic, because she had no identity as "Sandra." Sandra was said to be "doing" anorexia, not "being anorexic"; in other words, she had no secure sense of "being" that could integrate anorexia into itself.

As a result, Sandra developed a "hostile dependency" on the treat-ment program, expressed through her testing and pushing staff. For most of the treatment team, a summary analysis of Sandra's behavior on the unit is as follows: she was both wanting and rejecting attention.

Instead of working to incorporate the unit's rules and protocols into her identity, as would an internalizing patient, she "took them on," in two senses. She invoked and latched onto rules and protocols in lieu of developing a true identity, and as a cover for her lack of identity (this kind of substitution/cover revealed her "dependency"); and she also challenged and rejected these rules and protocols (revealing her "hostility").

We can now begin to see how the unit's ideal anorexic patient is constructed through and against representations of identities like Sandra's. Internalizing anorexic patients are also said to have a deficient (if not severely disturbed or absent) sense of self, and to become anorexic out of a compensatory need to create a (pseudo) self. In addition, the ideal patient both complies with and resists treatment protocols—just as borderline patients do, in their own ways. Patients like Sandra call *more* explicit attention to the contradictions of treatment practices that are designed to be both aversive and transformative, and they refuse to internalize these contradictions (and they therefore render them more visible). When these similarities between borderline and ideal, or typical, patients are ignored or downplayed—when the borderline patient is instead represented as an other—the borderline identity can then serve as a foil for constructions of ideal patients.

In chapter 1, I show that when "typical" anorexic patients take on and internalize treatment protocols, one common result is a disruption of these protocols, because patients often appropriate them for anorexic aims (e.g., repetitive calorie counting at mealtimes; a reading of one's hospital admission weight as falling just below one's maximum allowable weight). I have argued that this kind of resistance to treatment operates largely unselfconsciously, pointing to the unstable convergence on the unit of contradictory discourses surrounding feminine fitness. A central point in chapter 1 is that "power" and "resistance" in the treatment of anorexia at Walsh do not exist as distinct and separate orders of reality; at its very core, psychiatric power is fractured and unstable. For internalizing patients, resistance to treatment operates squarely within the interstices of this power. In my discussion of externalizing (borderline) patients at Walsh, I am developing this idea further, but in a slightly different way: I suggest that discourses of the self and of resistance for patients like Sandra buttress—and sometimes fracture—ideals of health on the unit in their position as *constitutively outside* of these ideals. I am borrowing here from the rhetorician Judith Butler, who argues that hegemonic instantiations of the body, sex, and race entail "the constitutive force of exclusion, erasure, . . . abjection and its disruptive return within the very terms of discursive legitimacy" (Butler 1993, 8).[13]

With these ideas in mind, let us consider the following question: If Sandra was merely "doing" anorexia because she lacked enough of a sense of self to "be anorexic," what kind of self, exactly, did she lack, according to staff and clinicians at Walsh? What constitutes an internalizing identity? More often than not, this question goes unanswered: typical anorexic selves are simply posited as more stable and more manageable than borderline selves. However, workers at Walsh do at times reveal assumptions about specific features of an internalizing identity label, via negative descriptions of borderline patients. These descriptions are racialized and classed. Although they frequently described Sandra as "lacking an identity" altogether, clinicians and staff sometimes depicted her in the following terms: she was a young Chicana girl who was on welfare and was familiar with an unfortunate "street life." They often remarked that Walsh was certain to be the "best home" that Sandra (and other borderline patients) had ever had—and yet, according to some, this (temporary) home was not suitable for Sandra in part because of her ethnic and class status. Several people mentioned to me, on a number of different occasions, that Sandra was trying in vain to overcome a "gang minority status" by taking on the more prestigious status associated with the treatment program. As one clinician put it: "Sandra wants to be a white, middle-class teenage girl." Note that these assessments were couched as interpretations based on Sandra's behavior on the unit, not on any specific knowledge of Sandra's life outside the hospital or on Sandra's own descriptions of her life. Here (some) caretakers were not only assuming that a white, middle-class status is a desired goal but also implying that Sandra's struggles in treatment were futile *because* of the race and class markers of her identity.

More often, however, clinicians' characterizations of Sandra were couched in terms that were not so explicitly racialized and classed. For example, when Sandra's mode of "doing" anorexia became the focus of conflict among clinicians and staff, disagreements about how best to care for her were articulated through concerns about unit boundaries and resources. One weekend, Sandra ran off the unit for a short time, an act that can be read as quintessentially "borderline" in its dramatic testing of unit boundaries. When she returned, she was placed on an

A-code for a period of time, meaning she was under constant observation by a staff member. During rounds the following Monday, Wendy, a nurse, questioned the treatment team's ability to care for Sandra, since her behavior was, as Wendy put it, so unpredictable and manipulative. Gayle, Sandra's individual therapist, defended Sandra, saying that she was not consciously goading staff. Wendy replied, "My question is, can we keep A-coding her? Other kids need attention, and she's taking away from the care of other patients." Wendy's rhetoric is familiar in justifications for transferring "difficult" patients to another unit (often a locked psychiatric facility). Notably, this rhetoric is often directed toward nonwhite and working-class patients, who are thus accused of undeservedly monopolizing unit resources. Indeed, the discussion in rounds turned toward preparation for Sandra's transfer should this move be deemed necessary. Gayle protested: "What is the mission of this unit? To care for sick kids. So when there's difficulty, you transfer them?" Bob (the psychiatrist running rounds) and several others countered that the question was how *long* Sandra could be A-coded, given the overall difficulty of caring for the patients who were on the unit at that time. However, it was clear that the *type* of difficulty that Sandra represented was considered the least acceptable on the unit, since several patients at that time required a lot of attention, and many patients had been A-coded for prolonged periods in the past without incurring caretakers' protests.

As the discussion in rounds continued, objections to ongoing care for Sandra increasingly referenced her seemingly volitional manipulation of the system. As Ron, a psychiatrist, put it, "She sounds manipulative; she's not in a victim role." Several staff concurred. In an effort to support Sandra, Martha (a psychologist) countered that Sandra was playing *both* the roles of victim and manipulator. Martha was representing Sandra as both similar to, and different from, more typical anorexic patients: Sandra might be manipulating the system, but like more "deserving" patients, she is also a "victim" desperately in need of the structured attention the unit provides. No one agreed, at least not openly, with Martha on this latter point; there was general agreement that Sandra is a manipulator.

It is interesting to consider the ideas about more and less treatable versions of identity that emerge through the contrast of victim/manipulator. As "victims" of anorexia and apparent victims of patients who supposedly monopolize unit resources, more typical anorexic patients are seen to be lacking just what patients like Sandra seem to disrespect and even flaunt. In other words, representations of Sandra as a manipulator highlight the degree to which "deserving" patients' subjectivities are naturalized as such: in contrast to Sandra, the typical patient appears to be inherently open to, and in need of, the unit's orderly boundaries and its health-giving forms of staff care (which Sandra is seen to threaten).

However, a depiction of typical patients as victims is unstable, because it contradicts Walsh's promotion of patients' agency in, and resistance to, the treatment process. This contradiction becomes visible when cases like Sandra's are debated—it was precisely Sandra's expressions of agency and resistance that characterized her as untreatable (for some). But this contradiction is also papered over when borderline patients are stigmatized as volitional manipulators. This stigmatizing of borderline patients draws attention away from the fact that clinicians construct the agency of typical patients in a particular way: ideal patients are seen to be in need of unit practices and protocols (conferring victim status), and yet they must exhibit the will to resist treatment and eventually move beyond it. It is taken for granted that victim status and willfulness should exist in *delicate* balance; a focus on Sandra's resistance as "off the chart" contributes to the unmarked status of typical patients' (delicate) resistances.[14] However, when they stigmatize borderline patients, clinicians and staff can also find themselves naming and specifying in more of its complexity the kind of willpower, or the normalized version of subjectivity, that signifies a will to health in typical patients. When normally unmarked norms are named, they can become sites of conflict.

Characterizations of Sandra as unfit for treatment in her displays of "hostile dependency" sometimes revealed (via contrast) particular norms for willfulness at Walsh. Over lunch one day, I asked Bob to elaborate his approach to borderline patients. Our conversation held Sandra in mind; she was the only borderline patient on the unit at the time, and the limits of her care were being hotly debated. Bob said that borderline patients are different from "typical" anorexic patients, "who we engage in struggle, and who *work* to engage in struggle. Borderlines, on the other hand, their needs really drive them. Versus the [true] anorexics, who are repressed. Borderlines often challenge and disrupt the best-laid plans. The challenge is to limit and nurture them. It may mean not seeing a given patient." Some months later, when Sandra was an outpatient (after a second, brief inpatient admission), Bob devised a special rule for her that is extremely telling: in an inversion of normal procedure, Sandra was told she would be considered for a third inpatient admission only if she showed *improvement* in her weight gain and eating habits (note that if she had been found to be medically unstable, she could have been referred to the emergency room or to a different unit, e.g., a general medical unit). This approach to her care not only effectively ruled out any more admissions to Walsh; it also reflected a belief that the treatment team could not help facilitate for her the will to health that is so central to inpatient work with "typical" patients. Sandra was hopelessly pathological in her inability to "work hard" in treatment: she would manifest this ability on her own or live without it.[15]

So while more "typical" anorexic patients often stir up conflict and disagreement within the treatment team concerning the terms and the timing of admissions, we can see here that borderline patients raise larger questions about the very provision of care. In Bob's assessment, these larger questions arise because of borderline patients' levels of pathology. However, Bob is also suggesting that more "typical" patients are deserving of treatment because they show a willingness to work for it. In other words, Bob is representing this form of work—the ability to incorporate and resist treatment protocols, "to engage in struggle"—both as natural qualities of certain patients and as acts of will that justify treatment. Bob is implying that the will to resist treatment properly is a manifestation of an extant type of psyche. Here a desired form of willfulness for patients is not only the result of a process whereby (typical) patients display health by internalizing treatment protocols that are carefully crafted for this purpose; this form of willfulness is also seen as a *prerequisite* for treatment. This prerequisite is *represented* in terms that are race and class neutral, but a subtext of socially "proper" versus marginalized subjectivities is clear: borderline patients lack self-control (they are "driven by needs"), and they disrupt the system. Typical patients, on the other hand, respect the system and work hard within it.

Bob's account of why borderline patients are excluded from full participation in treatment suggests that even though dominant ideologies of fitness (discussed in chapter 1) are rooted in notions of individual effort that posit fitness and health as potentially available to anyone, they also rely on a prior (racialized and classed) construction of subjectivity that is already "fit" to struggle for fitness. Clinicians' views about Pam—one of the few white and middle-class patients I met at

Walsh who was also considered borderline—are telling in this regard.[16] Unlike borderlines who are nonwhite and working-class, Pam was not excluded from full participation in the treatment process. In fact, she had been allowed multiple admissions over the course of about three years when I met her, in spite of the fact that she was over eighteen years old for most of this time, which could easily have been cited as grounds for refusing her admission to Walsh (she could have been referred to a local eating disorders treatment unit for adults). Like Sandra, Pam was considered very difficult to treat, and she required a lot of individual attention (including A-codes for suicidal gestures), which sometimes threatened the treatment team's willingness to care for her. But no one ever seriously floated the idea of shortening an admission for Pam, or refusing admission when she was not faring well as an outpatient. One or both of these steps are often taken with borderline patients, and it is particularly striking that neither step was ever taken with Pam, given that clinicians at Walsh considered her sense of self to be extremely unstable. Most clinicians and staff described Pam's sense of self as permanently damaged. However, her willingness to work hard in the program and to try to internalize treatment protocols protected her status on the unit, even though she did not always comply with the program. Pam herself described the situation this way: "Maybe to other people it looks like I get away with things. I don't know that this is true . . . [because] I'm there [on the unit] to get better, you know. . . . whereas a lot of people there sometimes—I mean, they're there because their parents put them there, or the hospital put them there, and I really just, I want to be able to stay healthy. . . . so staff trust me, I think, enough now, from having known me for a while, that if I'm going a few calories under one night or a couple nights, it's not something to be made a big deal of." Pam pointed out that staff took a harder line with patients who were not personally motivated to get better.[17] She characterized such patients as "cheaters" and "whiners," and she added, "I'm not a whiner."

In other words, Pam was grateful for her treatment and felt responsibility for it. Note that most clinicians also considered Pam to be thoughtful and articulate, features of internalizing identities. These are the qualities—in addition to her class status and racial identity—that distinguished Pam from Sandra (whom Pam considered a "whiner"). John, the intake coordinator, put it to me this way: unlike Sandra, Pam is "a good borderline." John explained: "[Pam] doesn't treat us as bad guys, and she's organized." Significantly, when John described Pam as "a good borderline," he justified the description by locating her sense of self somewhere in between the selves of borderline and typical patients. John compared Pam's identity to a pie that was missing several pieces, permanently. Therapy could help cover over the gap in Pam's identity, John said, but would never fill it in. "Bad" borderline patients, on the other hand, have no discernible sense of self at all, whereas more typical patients were working with a complete pie, according to John. In these latter cases, therapy could "draw on and work with resources that these [typical] patients already have." Again we see that only certain subjectivities (organized, "resourced," hardworking) are imagined to be always already "fit" for full participation in the treatment program.

Race and Class in Family Therapy Discourse

If clinicians believe that internalizing patients, most of whom are white and middle-class, are equipped with certain "resources" of self (in addition to their financial resources) that are uniquely amenable to the therapeutic resources the unit provides, we can see how patients who do not fit this description, and are not described in these ways, can be represented as draining unit resources and taking resources away from typical patients. However, one could argue that in a number of ways, borderline patients are the ones who have been resourced at Walsh. I have already suggested that dominant clinical constructions of borderline patients' subjectivities and resistances serve as foils for crafting typical patients' selves in treatment. In addition to this, the creation of some contemporary therapies for anorexia have rendered externalizing patients therapeutic resources for anorexic patients in a more literal sense. Popular therapeutic strategies and techniques used with anorexic patients at Walsh and elsewhere first appeared in the 1960s through clinical work with poor, nonwhite clients who were characterized as "acting out," or externalizing, and these strategies and techniques are now believed to be most effective for the seemingly overstructured, inhibited, internalizing, and mostly white patients of the middle class.[18] Salvador Minuchin was the primary architect of these techniques, in both of their incarnations. As I discuss in chapter 2, Minuchin was the central figure in the formation of (structural) family therapy for anorexia in the 1970s (which also shaped, and was shaped by, new ideas in mainstream therapies more generally at the time, especially regarding a purportedly gender-equalizing individualism in the context of "flexible" families). The sharp distinction he drew between the two "types" of families he encountered in his career are in evidence at Walsh today.

During my fieldwork, clinicians and staff at Walsh rarely expected to engage in meaningful therapeutic work with the parents of borderline patients, some of whom declined to take part in therapy and were rarely seen on the unit at all.[19] Although clinicians spoke little about these parents, they routinely referred in a general way to the (presumably) "disorganized" families of borderline patients and compared these families to the "overstructured" and "rigid" families of typical, internalizing patients. Contrasts between orderly/controlled and neglectful/disorganized families have been common to racialized and classed depictions of family life in the United States since the end of World War II.[20] Examining the development of structural family therapy through the work of Minuchin and his colleagues is one way to explore the creation of these contrasts.

Cultural constructions of class and race figure strongly in Minuchin's representations of different kinds of families (see Colapinto 1991). Minuchin and his colleagues began to formulate the structural model in the early 1960s through their work with "disorganized" urban families who were living in "slums," helping them "cope" with their sociocultural circumstances by restructuring family interactions. In the 1970s, when family therapy became more widespread, they began to apply the ideas and approaches developed in this latter context to the *destructuring* of middle-class (including so-called anorexic) families that appeared, instead, "to be too tightly organized and, if anything, excessively stable" (Colapinto 1991, 420).

In the early 1960s, Minuchin was a psychiatrist at the Wiltwyck School for Boys, a correctional facility for juvenile delinquents in New York City. In a highly influential work entitled *Families of the Slums* (1967), Minuchin and his colleagues argue that these boys were externalizers: they "acted out" and operated with an "action/excitement orientation." They did not posses reflexive and "insight-oriented" (internalizing) identities. As we have also seen with interpretations of Sandra's behavior on the unit, "acting out" is understood here as a substitution for a coherent sense of self: "You keep moving and running. And you do things. Because when there's excitement and motion you can finally experience yourself as *somebody"* (Minuchin et al. 1967, 6).

According to Minuchin, an action/excitement orientation ultimately stems from social class positionality, not ethnic or racial categorizations. However, his descriptions of families and family members in *Families of the Slums* often include references to racial and ethnic groupings. Minuchin describes the Wiltwyck boys' family situations in this way:

> Impoverished, disadvantaged, unstable, "hard-core." . . . mostly from minority ethnic backgrounds (Negro and Puerto Rican), and they dwell in the congested, rat-infested ghettos and slums of New York City. . . . Their joblessness, lack of productivity, antisocial behavior, and chronic dependency on various social institutions represent not only an enormous financial drain on the resources of the community-at-large, but also a threat to the feelings of well-being and complacency of the middle-class and the more stable elements of the working class that surround them. (Minuchin et al. 1967, 6)

Here we find a succinct representation of nonwhite, working-class externalizers draining resources in ways that threaten "stable" middle-class people, produced during a time in the United States (after World War II) when quasi-Victorian ideals of family life were enjoying a revival. Minuchin draws on Talcott Parsons's model of the nuclear family that is supposedly functional to socioeconomic stability in describing the families of the Wiltwyck boys as "disorganized." Minuchin's work reveals the racial, ethnic, and class politics of Parsons's ideas. According to Parsons, healthy families are organized by hierarchies of age and gender, with the father assuming an "instrumental" role, and the mother an "expressive" role (Parsons and Bales 1955). Wiltwyck families, in contrast, had no fathers or "stable father figures," and the "rearing and education of children [was] exclusively the mother's province" (Minuchin et al. 1967, 10). For Minuchin and his colleagues, the supposed absence of an "executive role" in the family was a major contributor to the so-called action/excitement orientation and acting out of the Wiltwyck boys.

Minuchin's work was in keeping with dominant social discourses of the time related not only to ideas about fixed gender roles in families but also to the family structure of the urban poor. In particular, "female-headed households" in working-class African American communities were thought to create poverty and threaten social cohesion (these concerns were reflected in the infamous Moynihan report).[21] Let me hasten to add here that Minuchin himself does not *explicitly* promote particular gender roles in families; that he supports "alternative" family structures; and that he has also been quite clear in his writings that poverty results from an uneven social distribution of money, jobs, and community resources.[22] Even so, Minuchin tends to look for Parsonian (i.e., socially "functional") solutions for families in distress; in practice, therefore, his work often reinforces socially dominant beliefs about families and "proper" family organization.[23]

Indeed, a major goal of family therapy for the Wiltwyck boys was the creation of "functional" family structure in the Parsonian sense. To approximate the nuclear family norm of the day, these families seemed to require an increase in structure, limits, and control. To this end, the (male) therapist often assumed the role of surrogate father (especially when fathers themselves could not or would not become more involved with the family). Minuchin describes one case in which family members were explicitly encouraged "to accept one of the therapists as a temporary replacement for the [absent] father" (Minuchin et al. 1967, 136). The therapy in this case was considered a failure because, in the end, the family "still relied on one of the therapists as the only problem-solver and as a parental substitute" (136). This situation echoes that of Sandra and other "borderline" patients at Walsh during my fieldwork: although many clinicians and staff thought of the unit as the best "home" these patients had ever had, patients' resulting "dependency" on unit structure was taken as a marker of their untreatability. Ultimately, Minuchin and his colleagues drew similar conclusions about many of the Wiltwyck families with whom they worked.

The fact that, for externalizing patients, clinicians are imagined as improved parental substitutes in almost every way means that these "disorganized" families appear to be something of a lost cause. Recall that clinicians at Walsh hold very different beliefs about typical patients: here, the natural family is capable of reform, in part because it contains a kernel of love and support for which there is no substitute.[24] Interestingly, in the 1950s and 1960s, before family therapy was practiced widely, opinions about families' treatability did *not* differ in these significant ways, according to their levels of "organization" (in part because family therapy was a fledgling subdiscipline at the time). In chapter 2, I describe a *general* picture of families in the literature at that time as largely fixed and unchangeable. Interventions during that early period in family therapy focused on the individuating of male identities from a feminized family environment, which was taken for granted as the (problematic) context out of which (masculine) selves emerged. In particular, "schizophrenogenic" mothers, and hence the families of patients diagnosed with schizophrenia, were considered untreatable (schizophrenogenic families were a model case for the development of family systems therapies). Schizophrenogenic mothers were said to emasculate their husbands and sons; likewise, the female-headed households of the urban poor were seen to compromise masculine identities in families. Family therapy in both cases was deemed ineffective.

Note that questions of gender here are tied to less-visible questions of class status in both cases, as well. Remember that schizophrenogenic mothers were thought to reject and smother family members simultaneously, a characterization that reflected a new, but uneasy, social vigilance to naturalize women as mothers in the 1950s and 1960s. These concerns reflected (and helped to constitute) shifting ideals of family life, ideals that were geared toward the expanding middle class. For the families of the Wiltwyck boys, Minuchin's focus on absent or unstable fathers as one major cause of family disorganization highlights the strongly gendered character of Parsonian order and control. The focus on absent fathers also, of course, papers over both the structural conditions of poverty and the race and class politics of promoting "proper," and highly differentiated, gender roles in the family.

After Minuchin's work at Wiltwyck, research on the topic of family "dynamics" specifically in the context of poverty has been practically nonexistent in the field of family therapy (Luepnitz 1988). That which does exist focuses on "the mobilization of extended family and social network resources" (Colapinto 1991, 419), highlighting the "strength" of the poor to rely on one another in spite of, and in response to, poverty's disorganizing effects.[25] In contrast, family structures as (decontextualized) feminized "environments"—once thought to be outside of therapeutic reach as well—have become a central focus of therapeutic scrutiny (beginning in the 1970s). As I discuss in previous chapters, change in families, and not just for the masculine identities individuating within them, is now both expected and desired. In sharp contrast to therapists' ideas in the 1950s and 1960s about the fixity of family structure, therapists today imagine that family organization—and particularly a feminized "enmeshment" in families—can be actively manipulated. What usually goes unremarked are the classed and racialized assumptions that these therapeutic goals embody. I have argued that family therapy today can be seen as (purportedly gender-equalizing) training for "flexibility" in families, as increasing numbers of women in particular have taken jobs in the expanding service sector. But more generally, flexibility here is about freeing individuals from undue constraint in families, for the pursuit of a certain kind of success in life—success that is marked by the values of autonomy and upward mobility. The "destructuring" approach to seemingly overstructured family environments in the field of family therapy was clearly developed with white, nuclear, middle-class families in mind, the only families that were impacted strongly by the breakdown of the nuclear family ideal in the 1970s (with the loss of the privileged "family wage").

Shifts in Minuchin's work at this time—accompanying a change in his clientele—are instructive. After he left Wiltwyck in the mid-1960s, Minuchin accepted a post at the Children's Hospital of Philadelphia, where, beginning in the early 1970s, he focused his attention on the largely middle-class and white families of psychosomatic children. Minuchin directly compared these families with those of the boys at Wiltwyck, finding them overstructured, intellectualizing, and inhibited in emotional expression. Whereas his work at Wiltwyck emphasized Parsonian order and control, Minuchin began theorizing instead about the family as "an open sociocultural system in transformation" (Minuchin 1974, 51). If families representing the norm in the 1950s and 1960s were seen as orderly and well controlled, these same families were at risk of becoming rigid and controlling in the 1970s.

Minuchin is explicit about the fact that a number of ideas he developed for therapy with psychosomatic families emerged initially through his work with Wiltwyck families.[26] While he was at Wiltwyck, he had engineered therapeutic strategies that focused on action and doing, and that were not verbal or insight oriented. For example, the technique of "enactment" involves the manipulation of spatial relationships among people in the therapy room. If Minuchin found himself under attack by a family member during a therapy session, he might change seats and sit among the family, point to the empty chair, and describe the feeling of being attacked and left out. According to Minuchin and his coworkers, acting out, or externalizing, behaviors in families requires such a "movement language" in therapy (Minuchin et al. 1967, 247; see also Minuchin and Montalvo 1967). It is striking that Minuchin ultimately deemed these ideas unhelpful for the nonwhite, working-class families that inspired them in his work, but that he later found them useful in sessions with white, middle-class families. At the Children's Hospital of Philadelphia, Minuchin began applying the technique of enactment to internalizing families, thereby challenging their "rigidity" and their apparent overreliance on verbal presentations of emotion (Minuchin and Barcai 1969). For instance, he would induce a revealing emotional and interactive crisis in an "anorexic family" by instructing the parents to ensure that their daughter eat during a lunch session, assuming they would fail but display overt conflict (that was ordinarily repressed) in the process (Minuchin, Rosman, and Baker 1978; Rosman, Minuchin, and Liebman 1977).[27] In this way, work with externalizing families proved to be a kind of laboratory for developing techniques that would help loosen up internalizing families; patients who "act out" provided therapeutic resources for more "repressed" patients.

Minuchin and his colleagues also resource externalizing patients for internalizing ones through a Janus-faced representation of externalizing patients' emotional qualities. According to Minuchin, the positive aspects of these qualities include spontaneity, forthrightness, and social ease. Externalizers have something to teach internalizers, because children and adolescents in poor and "disorganized" families are not overprotected and emotionally withholding, central perceived problems within typical "anorexic families." Minuchin sometimes romanticizes externalizers for forms of emotional expression that anorexic patients and their families appear to be lacking. In discussing the "strengths of the poor and of cultural deprivation" (Minuchin et al. 1967, 28), Minuchin and his colleagues draw from a 1962 text entitled *The Urban Villagers* (Gans 1962) to list the following "strengths": "lack of conformity to middle-class values which might be desirable; capacity for affectionate, loyal, intimate relationships with others; a good sense of humor, playfulness, and gregariousness; lack of self-consciousness; informality in peer relations; . . . ability to handle aggressions directly, as opposed to repressing hostility or experiencing guilt" (Minuchin et al. 1967, 28). However, it is telling that these qualities are often linked with discourses about purportedly "preindustrial" and "community-based" family forms among the poor. The concept of "urban villagers" conjures up an image of preindustrial others surviving in a modern urban context that has passed them by. Accordingly, Minuchin describes the negative aspects of externalizing emotionality in the following ways: a "tendency to concrete thinking" (26), an idea that indexes developmental "backwardness";[28] and "marked use of imitation" (26), a construction that evokes animality and "primitive" behavior (Taussig 1993). Here the white middle-class nuclear family, while it might become rigid, represents a relatively advanced social form. And while externalizing families might be romanticized, they are also judged against the *achieved* flexibility of more privileged individuals and families (especially those with a successful history of family therapy).

Thus, in a number of ways, externalizing families served as both an excessive example and a foil for a new focus in Minuchin's work on rendering psychosomatic families more flexible. Beginning in the 1970s, internalizing but flexible families were clearly marked as ideal families for changing times—ideal, that is, for producing autonomous and individuated family members (Minuchin, Rosman, and Baker 1978). With this slice of family therapy history in mind, I turn again to my fieldwork at Walsh to examine both the romanticization and the exclusion of borderline patients diagnosed with anorexia. We will see many echoes of Minuchin's representations of the internalizer/externalizer distinction, and we will also see some differences in their racialized and classed inflections, given an increasing focus since Minuchin's day on individual identity in therapies for anorexia.

Legacies of Family Therapy Constructs for Borderline Patients

Recall that when I interviewed Bob, the medical director at Walsh, about the difference between typical and borderline anorexic patients, he replied in terms that contrasted two types of selves. He said that typical patients are repressed and work actively to engage in struggles with clinicians around reshaping their identities and bodies. Borderlines, on the other hand, are driven by their needs and often disrupt unit protocols rather than "working" with them. According to Bob, the challenge in treating borderline patients is to "limit and nurture" them, which may mean refusing admission. Notice that the hardworking, typical patient is also constrained, or repressed, an idea that is in keeping with Minuchin's analysis of anorexia in its family context. Similarly, Bob's representation of borderlines as "need driven" fits with Minuchin's characterization of externalizers. However, at Walsh, where family therapy is only one part of treatment, there is a stronger focus on qualities of individual patients than there was in Minuchin's work. As a result, borderlines' unruliness appears not primarily as a feature of externalizing families (as it did for Minuchin) but instead as a feature of individual selves (a secondary theme for Minuchin).

I have argued in this chapter that the gold standard for a healthy self emerges at Walsh (in part) in circular fashion, through the othering of borderline patients. How does this process compare with Minuchin's othering of externalizers? When Sandra (the "disruptive" borderline patient discussed earlier) first became an outpatient, Bob took specific steps to prevent another inpatient admission. He stated in rounds that patients like Sandra "never go through a compliant phase" on the unit, meaning that they do not make good use of the treatment process because they act out and do not internalize treatment protocols. Here is the familiar marking of typical patients, via contrast with borderlines, as (somewhat) complying internalizers. In addition, Bob argued that Sandra should not be allowed back onto the unit precisely because she wanted to be an inpatient so badly: "We can't be the glue for her personality. She absorbs so much. And she keeps other patients from being able to come in." Drew, a pediatrician, agreed: "She's *trying* to get into the hospital"; therefore, he said, admission is not "psychologically indicated."[29] Bob's and Drew's thinking here resonates with Minuchin's conclusion that therapy does not address the major problems externalizers face in their lives, and yet there is also the suggestion that Sandra was willfully manipulating and abusing Walsh's services, which are better suited for others. We have seen Sandra characterized in this way at Walsh before (e.g., representations of her as draining unit resources at other patients' expense), but notice here that a focus on the individual psyche highlights a standard of autonomy for typical patients. To be an appropriate patient—to be in need "psychologically" in a legitimate way—one cannot be "needy"; in other words, appropriate psychological need does not allow for too much dependency (this idea also resonates with Minuchin's work but is emphasized more at Walsh).

A focus on the individual here renders Sandra's family life irrelevant. If treatment is not only unhelpful to patients like Sandra but is also itself threatened by their particular expressions of willfulness, then clinicians do not feel compelled to discuss the benefits of another hospital admission for them as compared to their lives at home (as they often do for typical patients). Indeed, Sandra's home life and her relationship with her parents were not part of the discussion at all. Here the racialized and classed contexts for characterizing both treatable and untreatable selves have become invisible.

Even so, we have seen that certain negative characterizations of Sandra and of patients like her are unmistakably racialized and classed (although they are rarely acknowledged as such). Some of these descriptions re-create or echo Minuchin's negative portrayals of externalizers. For example, clinicians often refer to borderline patients' "primitive ego states." When Sandra alternated between overcompliance with, and resistance against, staff, several clinicians described her as "gamy," an animalistic depiction of her so-called hostile dependency on the unit. This representation of Sandra's behavior is consistent with an image of primitive survival in a setting that supposedly overreaches Sandra's means and aspirations. Finally, during a time when Sandra was an inpatient, a nurse declared in rounds that Sandra was "holding the unit hostage" with her time-consuming, attention-seeking behavior, as if her acts were criminal ones.[30] Minuchin does not describe externalizers in this way, but recall that he does portray externalizing families as "antisocial" "threats" to middle-class (and "stable" working-class) "feelings of well-being and complacency" (Minuchin et al. 1967, 6).

Perceptions of Sandra's supposed negative effects on the unit also resonate with Minuchin's descriptions of externalizing family environments. I have said that borderline patients' families are relatively invisible at Walsh, and along with them, the kinds of explicit discourses about family life among nonwhite and working-class people that we find in Minuchin's early work. There is plenty of talk and concern, however, about "family life" *on the unit* with a borderline patient—talk, that is, about these patients' supposed disruptions of an orderly therapeutic family. It is as if perceived disruption in therapeutic processes has replaced Minuchin's focused concern with supposedly disorganized externalizing families (natural families) outside the clinic. Disagreements at Walsh about how to care for borderline patients like Sandra can lead to "splitting," or warring factions, among caretakers on the unit, a definite challenge to therapeutic family unity (as discussed in chapter 2, to the extent that caretakers view themselves collectively as a substitute family for patients, they prize unity among themselves).

Some caretakers find it particularly disturbing that conflict among clinicians and staff regarding the exclusion of borderline patients can, at times, threaten a unified understanding about the course of treatment for typical patients. At these times, procedures and ideas in place for typical patients no longer seem natural. For example, during the discussion in rounds (cited earlier) about the possibility of Sandra's readmission to the inpatient unit, Sally, a psychologist, offered that Sandra was "feeling discriminated against. Other kids are let onto the unit. Which is, you know. . . ." "Accurate" was the word that Sally left hanging. Bob replied, "She wants to *move in* here. We can't support that. . . . And she's very capable of coming in over and over." In my conversations with clinicians and staff after rounds that day, several people complained that by representing Sandra's chronicity and her ambivalent attachment to the treatment program as unusual, Bob was minimizing the fact that unit staff and clinicians struggle to negotiate these issues with *many* patients on a regular basis. Was Bob implying that these struggles with typical patients were also problematic? And if not, why not? Here Sandra's position as constitutively outside the normative constructions of health and subjectivity at Walsh had become visible, raising questions, for some, about status quo procedures at Walsh. As Gayle, Sandra's individual therapist, had asked incredulously in rounds a few weeks earlier: "What is the mission of this unit?" At the time Gayle posed this question, Sandra was still an inpatient, and some were considering transferring her to a locked facility; now that Sandra was an outpatient "trying" to become an inpatient at Walsh again, Bob was firmly recommending a locked unit for her instead, and as a result, a sense of unease about the unit's mission was heightened for a number of people. Sally, the psychologist who was concerned about discrimination against Sandra, remarked, "There's not enough unity here. And the kids feel it; they're the ones who bubble over. We are helping to create the monster that Sandra is."

However, any questions raised about the normal course of treatment for Sandra, and for other patients at Walsh, were quickly overshadowed by stigmatizing representations of Sandra. The prevailing argument about why borderline patients disrupt the unity of the treatment team is the familiar claim that these patients' "pathologies" are so severe. As one clinician said, in reference to the conflicts surrounding Sandra's care, "Borderlines always do this. They create craziness." It is common to find mental health professionals describing borderline patients as *causing* splitting within groups, and particularly among caretakers, when they vacillate between an idealization of others (reflecting dependency) and a devaluation of others (reflecting hostility). So a number of clinicians agreed with Elsie, a nurse, when she offered that the team's divisiveness about Sandra was a symptom of Sandra's psychopathology: the team was "acting out her stuff."

At the same time, clinicians do not view the perceived effects of borderline patients on therapeutic family unity entirely in a negative light. A number of clinicians and staff told me that in caring for Sandra, the treatment team became "humanized": more like a "natural family," with all its internal diversity and conflict, and less like an impersonal and artificial structure that mirrors the problems of internalizing families. A treatment team negotiating conflict is made up of real people, not just technicians. Recall that staff are enjoined to provide healthy "boundaries" for patients that are coded as white and middle-class, that are seen as "artificially imposed" specifications for creating internalizing identities, and that are, ironically, exaggerated by "typical" anorexic patients. Because they represent a foil for these professionalized protocols, borderline patients can also represent an ambiguously desired freedom from the artificial constraints of treatment, and from the "rigidity" of typical, internalizing patients. So at Walsh, as for Minuchin, externalizing (borderline) patients are sometimes romanticized for qualities that seem to be lacking in anorexic patients—and also in caretakers at Walsh, operating with a detail-oriented unit style.

Bob told me that individual therapy with internalizing patients is more difficult in some ways than is therapy with externalizing patients, because whereas the latter openly provide data with which the therapist can work, such data has to be imputed to inhibited internalizing patients, who are relatively emotionally "empty." So while Bob (and others) would exclude patients like Sandra, he also values their emotional expressiveness in his work as a therapist. I once overheard a related conversation between two staff members about what it was like to work on the unit when there were very few eating-disordered patients:

> *Cecilia*: The milieu is better than the damn eating-disordered kids; you have to pry stuff out of them.
>
> *Alice*: [Mocking eating-disordered patients' typical response to questions about their "high" and "low" points of the day]: "I didn't have a high, didn't have a low. . . ."
>
> *Cecilia*: Your low on Thursday—let me guess. Miniteams? You didn't get something you thought you were entitled to?

Here, seemingly entitled and withholding eating-disordered patients are compared with more expressive patients and are found wanting.[31]

We have seen that typical anorexic patients are thought to hold power on the unit not because of their privileged location there but because of a need for rigid "boundaries" (which can overlap and articulate with treatment protocols in problematic ways)—boundaries that help constitute an overly controlled, inhibited self. Following in Minuchin's footsteps, clinicians at Walsh believe that borderline patients offer lessons here for typical, "rigid" patients and for treatment modalities alike. Borderline patients like Sandra, when they are represented as "other" in a romanticized way, generate an apparent excess of emotional expression that can serve as a rhetorical resource for crafting more tempered, healthy emotions for typical patients.[32]

Are You Fit for Managed Care?

The treatment trajectories of borderline patients that I have described here have offered lessons for typical patients in another way, as well: increasingly, insurance companies have endeavored to limit coverage (and hence the duration of hospital-based care in particular) for *all* patients. Recently, the constraints of managed care have narrowed therapeutic options for the poor especially, but also for eating-disordered patients in general, focusing attention on basic biomedical therapies and even narrowing possibilities within this realm. I close this chapter with a consideration of managed care as one of the conditions of possibility for present-day constructions of anorexia and its treatment. All patients and their families—and especially those who are economically underprivileged—stand constitutively outside most of the supposed benefits of managed care.

Managed care in the treatment of anorexia is streamlined and efficient—or economically "fit"—care for disorders of fitness. Increasingly, inpatient treatments are justified to insurance companies day by day, based on a relatively high level of medical and/or psychiatric danger (such as malnutrition or the potential for self-harm). José, who was in charge of utilization management at Walsh, told me that, in contrast, insurance coverage just twenty years ago was "carte blanche." Under managed care contracts, the average length of a patients' stay on the unit is about three weeks, as opposed to about two months in the late 1970s and early 1980s. As a result, many treatment programs now privilege those who can afford expensive private insurance plans. Recently, however, even these latter plans have curtailed or excluded coverage for eating disorders. As part of what we might call a "thousand points of light" approach to the crisis in health care (borrowing a phrase from former U.S. president George Bush Sr.), the managed care system has required that many families show independent economic "fitness" by paying large portions of their bills out of pocket, or struggling on their own to achieve health and fitness.

Even before the crisis in health care that peaked toward the end of the twentieth century, private health insurance benefits were approximately "twice as available for general health care as for mental health care" (Sharfstein and Beigel 1985, 230). With managed care, "higher deductibles and increased copayments are especially visible for mental illness treatment. This has expanded already widespread discrimination" (232). Many plans that have attempted to provide better coverage have eventually cut benefits to remain competitive. As psychotherapist Susan Wooley (1993) also shows in her compelling critique of managed care in the mental health arena, talk therapies and psychiatric care are particularly vulnerable to devaluation and manipulation in an era of cost containment "because, in the absence of hard signs, diagnosis is softer, and mistreatment or undertreatment harder to prove. Even a suicide following denial of care lacks the persuasive force of a cardiac death in a patient whose disease is easily documented by objective diagnostic tests and can even be evaluated post-mortem. Because the sciences of psychology and psychiatry are less precise, profiteers are emboldened to deny the existence of any knowledge at all and experts— painfully aware of their diminished power and fearful of being shut out—can be made to collude in such a claim" (389).

Health care providers are increasingly pressured to formulate treatment plans strictly on the basis of "medical necessity." But many mental health professionals are characterizing a "medical necessity" approach to anorexia as "penny wise and pound foolish" because patients are admitted at an advanced stage of illness and tend to be discharged quickly, a situation that promotes chronicity. A number of clinicians and advocacy groups have publicized these problems.[33] Part of the difficulty, from many health care providers' points of view, is that managed care companies appear unable or unwilling to acknowledge the overlap of patients' physical and psychological needs (Kaye, Kaplan, and Zucker 1996; Sigman 1996). More and more, poor patients in particular are discharged from Walsh when they are barely medically stable; in other words, their coverage for physical symptoms is limited and their mental health coverage is minimal or nonexistent. Over lunch one day, I sat in on a conversation between Sally, a psychologist, and José from utilization management. Sally said, "It's terrible when decisions are based on insurance. Patients going when they're not ready." José countered, "Then again, we're not a hotel. Patients have choices." Sally replied, "*Wealthier* ones do."

Consider Leslie, a seventeen-year-old working-class white patient with a four-year history of anorexia. At the time I met her, Leslie had adapted to a state of starvation so that she appeared medically stable at very low body weights, according to her pediatrician at Walsh. Leslie's chronic state of starvation was, in part, enabled by her insurance company's requirement that she always be discharged from the hospital program when her vital signs were minimally stable. Shortly after I finished my fieldwork, I learned that on the day after her sixth discharge from the program, Leslie slipped into a coma caused by malnutrition.

A second, more common example from my fieldwork shows that managed care plans can be so restrictive and convoluted that parents are at risk of receiving large medical bills—even for acute care—that would otherwise be covered. Tanya, a fourteen-year-old middle-class Chicana patient who was new to Walsh, was admitted under a medical diagnosis because her vital signs were unstable. Tanya's primary physician (outside of the hospital) was part of a physician group that contracted with a managed care company. But because this company had an exclusive provider for acute medical admissions, her admission to Walsh was not authorized. It turns out that the *authorized* hospital had found Tanya to be medically stable and had sent her to Walsh's outpatient clinic in the hopes of a hospital admission under psychological criteria that could be covered under a special plan. But Tanya was found to be medically unstable, by criteria used at Walsh. The managed care company refused to pay for the admission, and so Tanya's doctor's physician group was stuck with the bill. I asked José why the physician group was held responsible, given that no one at Walsh had contacted them about the specifics of Tanya's admission (a phone call would have cleared things up, and Tanya would have been sent back to the authorized hospital). José said that though such a call is normally made, it is still the physician group's responsibility "to play the managed care game" correctly. When I pressed the issue, José said, "Well, let's not exclude the parents here. We're getting the parents involved, because they should know what their insurance plan covers. Now they're sweating bullets, because *they* may be stuck with the bill."

Some insurance companies exclude altogether even basic medical coverage for anorexia. In a highly problematic twist on the failure to acknowledge anorexia's simultaneously physiological and psychological effects, these insurance companies refuse to cover medical services by defining the "basis" of the problem as (purely) psychological. As José explained to me:

> Eating disorders are hard to cover. The majority of insurance companies feel it's a psychiatric disease causing secondary medical problems. So it should come out of a psych [mental health benefits] carve-out for payment, regardless of the intensity of medical complications. So even if a patient has cardiac trouble, and goes to the intensive care unit, coverage eventually comes out of the psych carve-out, which will exhaust the benefit. So it comes down to educating the insurance companies that it's a *medical* problem. . . . I can't always argue that successfully. . . . The past few years I've been losing more of my cases because they're bringing up more of an argument for . . . an exclusionary clause. [Patients may] have mental health benefits, but they exclude any kind of eating disorder.

Many eating disorder programs have closed in recent years because of a drastic reduction in the number of insurance plans that will cover treatment. By locating the burden of health on individual patients and their families, managed care is "rending the fat" from the mental health care system (Mirin and Sederer 1994, 165). This push for patients' and families' economic self-reliance—and "coping skills" outside of the psychiatric system—is consistent with the contemporary ideologies of fitness that treatments have promoted lately (though few clinicians support the specific effects of managed care). These reforms in health care "are based on the thesis that they will increase efficiency and promote quality while reducing costs; i.e., less is more" (Sharfstein and Beigel 1985, 229)—which means, of course, that more and more families are either left without viable treatment options or are resourced dry. Maude's parents (introduced in chapter 2) were asked to pay Walsh $10,000 up front until their insurance coverage was ironed out. The outcome of such negotiations can rarely be predicted, even with verbally preauthorized coverage. George, the father of a patient who had been in and out of the program for many years, commented during an interview, "When we got our first bill, I told my wife this was a sociological move. The idea is, the insurance companies balk, so you go into a lower SES, and then the eating disorder will be cured! We had thought, 'We have the best insurance, there's no problem, we're covered for everything.' We are still having battles, because our daughter was admitted medically, but the insurance company is saying there's a psychological basis. We had put aside money for college—it was in her name, so we had to use it up. An eating disorder can ruin a family, financially."

Embedded in this discourse of "downward mobility" are the conditions of possibility—relative economic privilege—that allow for (more) extensive treatment at all and for such depleting experiences of financial resourcing. Note also that class status and cultural capital heavily influence the outcomes of any insurance battles that may follow such a denial of coverage: insurance companies "are likely to respond more quickly and favorably to an appeal if the individual is articulate, persistent, and has solid support from employees, politicians, and legal council" (Kaye, Kaplan, and Zucker 1996, 802). Recently, a number of eating disorder advocacy groups have been pushing for systemic insurance reforms that would redress some of these inequalities.[34] There have been some successes: for example, in the past few years, a number of states have passed parity laws (some more effective than others) that require insurance companies to cover treatment for eating disorders, regardless of claims about their basis. But as anyone involved in these struggles can attest, much work remains to be done.

Conclusion

This chapter shows that certain patients—nonwhite, working-class, and also "borderline"—are considered to be always already "unfit" for full participation in the treatment program. The treatment team's approach to these patients points up the fact that the racialized and classed distinctions that fitness confers are not only the *result* of efforts to achieve fitness and health; they are also its *prerequisites*. A new focus on individualism in treatments for anorexia masks these racialized and classed distinctions, which are inherited from several decades of family therapy work in the field that ultimately valorizes white, middle-class, nuclear family forms. Trends in managed care threaten to intensify the exclusion of poorer patients while overresourcing the cash reserves of those

who are more well-to-do. These developments are in keeping with ideologies of independence and self-reliance that condition discourses of
fitness surrounding anorexia.

However, the same patients who are considered untreatable are
also thought to embody (to an excessive degree) certain features of
healthy personhood that are supposedly lacking in "typical" anorexic
patients and their families (features that are also ambiguously desired
within the therapeutic family). In other words, these patients are sometimes romanticized for the very qualities that exclude them from treatment. My analysis in this chapter inverts the idea, often expressed
at Walsh, that borderline patients drain resources away from other
patients. One could argue that externalizing (including borderline) patients are "used" at Walsh in various ways.

Therapeutic work with borderline patients also points up the shifting borderline between psychiatric constructions of nature (in this case,
assessments of psychic health) and of individual willpower. When is a
"deficient sense of self" so severe that the task of forging a will to health
is seen as a lost cause? Under what circumstances can willpower and a
desire for treatment overcome this so-called deficiency of self? I have
suggested that patients who are excluded from treatment are seen as
both (1) similar to more "typical" anorexic patients, and therefore un-
fairly discriminated against when they are pushed out of the treatment
program, and (2) fundamentally different from these typical patients,
enacting an unmanageable and improper form of willpower that reflects their essentially untreatable psyches. Negotiating treatment with
these patients raises questions not only about the race and class politics
of health and illness but also about the role and the location of individual volition in therapies for anorexia. At times, ambiguities here lead to
conflicts within the treatment team about the care of borderline patients on the unit, but rarely in such a way that racialized and classed
constructions of patients are scrutinized.

A Narrative Approach to Anorexia

A critical cultural analysis of mainstream psychiatric treatments for anorexia is a first step toward formulating alternative therapies that render explicit the cultural specificity of illness and health. One such alternative is the "narrative" approach that White and Epston describe in their *Narrative Means to Therapeutic Ends* (1990). Rather than providing a comprehensive summary of my critical analyses in the preceding chapters, I prefer to focus my attention here on this alternative therapeutic approach, because it provides specific suggestions for avoiding or wrestling effectively with some of the problems and dilemmas I have addressed in this book.

Michael White of Adelaide, Australia, and David Epston of Auckland, New Zealand, together developed a "narrative metaphor" for therapeutic practice in the early 1980s. Narrative therapy, a spin-off from "family systems" thinking that ultimately broke away from a systems paradigm,[1] grew out of a critique of psychiatric "objectivity" and is inspired by the idea that therapeutic practices are never culturally neutral, because they help reconfigure persons' lives and relationships in particular social contexts. Narrative therapy is not a mainstream practice in the South Pacific but is fairly well known in New Zealand and in parts of Australia as one way to address a range of seemingly psychological or psychiatric problems—including, for example, anorexia, schizophrenia, family and couples conflict, and domestic violence. This form of therapy began to capture the attention of mental health professionals in the United States and Canada during the 1990s through conferences, mainstream publications, and the establishment of a few therapy centers.[2] Narrative therapy is not very widespread, and to date, there are no published studies or statistics on treatment effectiveness.[3]

A narrative approach works to identify and decenter the truth claims of psychiatric objectivity and the dominant cultural discourses that support these claims. At the same time, narrative therapists do not discount the powerful effects of these dominant discourses or posit a therapeutic space that is wholly "outside" of them. In this way, narrative therapy is based on an understanding about the relationship between power and resistance that is similar to a central theoretical premise of this book: namely, as suggested in the introduction, the potential effectiveness (and, to an extent, the very possibility) of "alternative" discourses lies in their ability to persuasively reconfigure dominant social forms. My own analytic practice in this book amounts to such an alternative reading of mainstream psychiatric discourse. A narrative practice further develops such a reading by engaging clients in therapeutic conversations that highlight, and build new meanings around, the contradictions and ruptures that appear within the powerful problems that affect clients' lives. Before I describe narrative therapies for anorexia, let me briefly summarize my argument about resistance to conventional treatment practices.

By examining the complex ways in which patients and clinicians encode, embody, and unsettle contemporary American ideals of individualism, self-control, feminine "nature," and family life, I have shown that psychiatric practices do not simply reproduce and impose a given set of cultural prescriptions that are conducive to anorexia. Rather, the treatment of anorexia is a contested process in which dominant constructions of feminine identity are both created and disrupted. While focusing on power differentials and disagreements among clinicians, staff, patients, and patients' parents, I have refused an easy "romance of resistance" (Abu-Lughod 1990). Young women and girls who struggle with anorexia both appropriate powerful social norms about feminine autonomy and self-control and challenge these norms by enacting them through illness. Sometimes, patients' resistance on the unit is not intentional and can even result from "conservative" premises—as when patients challenge staff's authority by bringing calculators to mealtimes to make sure staff are exact in recording the number calories that patients consume. At other times, resistance to unit practices (and not only on the part of patients) can have conservative effects—as when female clinicians and staff disagree with an approach to a particular patient and incite a perceived need to reinforce "unity" within the therapeutic family.[4] Thus participants in the treatment program are not interpolated neatly into their places (see Althusser 1971), nor do they ever speak and act "outside" the reach of hegemonic systems. Also, clinicians and staff in the treatment program have varied responses to patients' turning the rules of the treatment program to their own ends. Some are led to question the efficacy of medical monitoring, while others argue that its paradoxical effects can be beneficial. In short, my analysis of conflict and cultural contradictions in the treatment of anorexia points not to heroic forms of resistance, or to totalizing inscriptions of medical power, but to powerful constructions of feminine identities *in the making*.

Narrative therapy is centered on the premise that persons' identities are always "in the making." Drawing from Foucault's idea that, in Western capitalist contexts, illness states are routinely essentialized as fixed qualities that inhere in specific types of identity (e.g., "the anorexic," "the schizophrenic," "the neurotic"), narrative therapists instead talk about illness experiences with patients in such a way that these experiences do *not* appear as coterminous with patients' identities. Therapists work to "externalize" problems that have been experienced as internal to persons, so that the ongoing cultural work involved in the construction of illness and health becomes visible. Borrowing from Edward Bruner's (1986) and Jerome Bruner's (1990) theories about the textual constitution of life events, narrative therapists understand illness as a "problem-saturated story" that is co-constructed with dominant cultural ideas about "proper" selves, ideal bodies, and deviant identities; and they work with clients collaboratively to construct (or "coauthor") new stories about the self, the body, and relationships by drawing on aspects of patients' experiences that do not fit neatly into a given problem story.

Rather than representing health as the opposite of illness, narrative therapists help to create these new stories by building on "subjugated knowledges" that are already a part of patients' lives (Foucault 1980c). A narrative approach rejects the idea that therapists have any access to "objective" knowledge about the problems or "alternative" identities of persons who seek their help. Narrative therapists suggest that while such a claim to "expert knowledge" is often couched as culturally and politically neutral, it has the effect of reinscribing dominant cultural assumptions defining illness and health as qualities that are internal to persons (qualities that can be objectified and discerned by "experts").[5] For many, such a stance is problematic also because it implies that therapists can see "outside" of the cultural narratives and practices that constitute persons' lives and relationships (however, there are some differences of opinion among narrative therapists about the basis of the problem here—many do claim to help clients see "outside" the problems affecting their lives. I discuss this topic later).

In part because of what several narrative therapists call the "pro-anorexic" (i.e., "problem-saturated") effects of mainstream psychiatric treatments for anorexia, these therapists often discuss their own approaches to anorexia when providing case examples of their work as an alternative form of therapy. David Epston, a founder of narrative therapy, has written extensively about anorexia (e.g., Epston 1989, Epston, Morris, and Maisel 1998; Maisel, Epston, and Borden [in press]). In an interview about Foucault's analysis of "self-government" in Western capitalist societies, and its crystallization within psychotherapeutic practices, Michael White (the cofounder of narrative therapy) states: "I have, for a long time, considered anorexia nervosa as the pinnacle of achievement of this system of self-government, this system of modern power. Just consider the practices of self-subjugation that persons with anorexia nervosa are recruited into: the rigorous and meticulous self-surveillance, the various self-punishments of the body for its transgressions, the perpetual self-evaluations and comparisons, the various self-denials, the personal exile, the precise self-documentation, and so on" (M. White 1995, 45).

A first step in a narrative approach to anorexia is to create a separation between "the problem" (anorexia) and clients' identities by engaging clients in "externalizing conversations" about anorexia (White and Epston 1990). (This step appears to romanticize healthy identities as other to anorexia, but I will argue for a different interpretation of externalization hereafter.) Creating a separation between anorexia and clients' subjectivities is important because most clients begin therapy with the experience that they "are" anorexic; that is, "anorexia" is a dominant and totalizing description of their identities as persons.[6] In contrast, externalizing conversations personify "anorexia" as an agent with its own motives and purposes, a linguistic move that allows therapists and clients to speak about anorexia's negative effects without requiring clients to indict themselves for their "anorexic" actions. Put differently, therapists help clients to avoid locating the "cause" of anorexic feelings and behaviors within themselves. Note that a number of different therapies may externalize problems to a degree, but unlike narrative work, many of these retain pathologizing elements.[7]

Excerpts from a first session with Jackie, a fifteen-year-old girl who had been struggling with anorexia for three years at the time of this session, will help illustrate how anorexia is externalized in narrative conversations. The article cited here is written by Victoria Dickerson and Jeff Zimmerman, two prominent narrative practitioners in the United States, who are based in Santa Cruz and Cupertino, California, respectively:

> *Therapist*: So the anorexia affects you in a way that being fat seems like the worst thing in the world?
> *Jackie*: Well, I am really afraid.
> *Therapist*: That's a primary effect of anorexia? . . . it makes you afraid?
> *Jackie*: I don't know. I don't really enjoy eating anymore. It's more like a punishment to me. I don't know. I see others, friends, eat, but . . . I don't really like to.
> *Therapist*: So that's one of the effects of anorexia being around in your life. It has stolen your enjoyment of food. It has turned food into a punishment.
> *Jackie*: Yes. (Zimmerman and Dickerson 1994, 301)

By talking about "anorexia" in this way, the therapist begins to open up a discursive space for other possible versions of Jackie's identity. At one point in their conversation, Jackie and her therapist talk about the "pro-anorexic" effects of Jackie's nine hospitalizations and then explicitly mark a "portion" of Jackie's identity that is opposed to anorexia:

> *Therapist*: I'm interested in other ways anorexia affects you. What effect does it have on your attitude to yourself? Does it affect the way you feel about yourself?

Jackie: Mostly in how I look. All of the time I think how bad I look.

Therapist: What should I call this? A state of constant negative self evaluation?

Jackie: I do feel awful. For a while I just didn't feel good enough to want to do anything. I didn't think I could do the things I used to.

Therapist: So anorexia stole certain activities from you. Like what?

Jackie: I used to play softball and really was good at it. Being in the hospital made it hard and then the doctors said I couldn't play because my weight was too low.

Therapist: So what do you think about that?

Jackie: I don't know. I wish they wouldn't watch me so closely. I don't think it's right. When they take all the things away that I care about, that makes it harder to have any motivation to beat the problem.

Therapist: So anorexia got doctors to monitor you, and they took away things you enjoy. This is in addition to getting you to monitor yourself [Jackie had talked about this earlier in the conversation]. Who has been harsher with you—the doctors or the anorexia in how it gets you to treat yourself?

Jackie: About the same. Maybe the doctors. . . .

Therapist: Who has made you feel worse about how you look—the doctors or the anorexia?

Jackie: Not sure. Both have.

Therapist: Who has been more restrictive—the doctors or the anorexia? That's what I hear from others. Anorexia's worst trick is that it gets others to control your life. *(Jackie looks sad.)* . . . are you tired of this? I know anorexia is difficult to resist, but I wondered how you were feeling about it.

Jackie: A little tired, but I'm not sure I want to be rid of it.

Therapist: What would be your estimate, roughly, of how much of you has separated from anorexia and how much it still influences you?

Jackie: Roughly 25% tired of it.

Therapist: What has gone into that 25%? Like I notice you've been out of the hospital during the summer. Would that be evidence of that 25%? (Zimmerman and Dickerson 1994, 303–4)

The next step in the therapeutic work involves identifying specific aspects of patients' identities and experiences that are "anti-anorexic," and uncovering the conditions of possibility for these "alternative knowledges" in clients' lives. Here is an example of a series of therapeutic questions that point in this direction: "You informed me that you refused to go along with anorexia's 'command,' even though it attempted to blame you for everything. How was it possible at this particular point for you to be so disobedient and defiant of anorexia? How were you able to trust in your own thoughts, ideas, opinions . . . ?" (Epston, Morris, and Maisel 1998, 155).

It would seem that by representing anorexia as a totalizing entity that "recruits" individuals into particular beliefs and activities, and by suggesting that clients' alternative subjectivities are other to anorexia ("anti-anorexic"), narrative therapists participate in formulations of power and resistance that I criticize in this book. When therapists locate alternative forms of personhood "outside" of anorexia's influence, do they posit romantic forms of resistance? Does narrative language reify problems in an unhelpful way, representing clients as their victims? And does narrative work essentialize and individualize alternative (relatively problem-free) subjectivities (and thereby risk supporting a central premise of contemporary discourses of fitness and health—that of the "self-made" person)?

Although narrative therapies do maintain a rhetorical distinction between "problems" and "persons," there is, at the same time, no requirement within narrative theory to posit utopian or "problem-free" subjective experiences (although terms such as "freedom" and "liberation" are sometimes used). As White puts it, helping people who struggle with anorexia to identify and challenge its requirements of self-subjugation is *not* about "freeing them to be truly who they really are, but, in fact, freeing them from the 'real.' . . . [It is important] to resist the great incitement of popular psychology to tyrannize ourselves into a state of 'authenticity,' . . . to refuse 'wholeness,' to protest 'personal growth,' to usurp the various states of 'realness.' To open the possibilities for us to default, and to break from the sort of gymnastics that regulate these states of being, that make all of this possible" (M. White 1995, 48).

In keeping with my argument about patients' resistance to discourses of fitness and health operating within the interstices of these discourses, narrative therapists argue that the very possibility of recognizing "alternative" life stories for clients is due to the fact that they *contradict*—and can be seen in a contrasting, transforming relationship to—dominant, "problem-saturated" specifications for identity. As White writes, "the [problem] stories that persons live by are full of gaps and inconsistencies, and, as well, these stories constantly run up against contradictions" (M. White 1993, 38). He continues: "Thus, when considering the proposition that life is constituted through an ongoing storying and re-storying of experience, we are considering a process of 'indeterminacy within determinacy'—or to what Geertz (1986) concludes to be a 'copying that originates': 'The wrenching question, sour and disabused, that Lionel Trilling somewhere quotes an eighteenth-century aesthetician as asking—"How Comes It that we all start out Originals and end up Copies?"—finds . . . an answer that is surprisingly reassuring: it is the copying that originates' " (38).

In short, problem stories are fractured, and alternative life stories coexist with these problem stories, inhabiting their nooks and crannies. The task of the narrative therapist is to give these alternative stories more space. But this therapeutic work involves an ongoing struggle with the powerful problem stories that affect clients' lives and always work to paper over the potential for alternative readings. So a therapist might, for example, ask the following questions about a client's anti-anorexic step: "Just prior to taking this step, did you nearly turn back? If so, how did you stop yourself from doing so?" (M. White 1993, 41). Similarly, David Epston warns a client who has come a long way in her struggle with the problem: "Fran, beware of anorexia's last ditch stand. If other accounts from those who have liberated themselves is anything to go on, prepare yourself for some desperate moves to undo your anti-anorexia by telling you you aren't good enough for it, it's too good for you, or you are unworthy of anti-anorexia, and the only course you have open to you is anorexia's 'fatal embrace.' "[8] Significantly, Epston often talks with clients about anorexia's "last trick" of trying to convince them that because they are not "perfectly anti-anorexic," they may as well return to anorexia (reported in a training workshop for therapists held in Cupertino, California, 9 February 1994).

By these accounts, narrative therapists do not believe that problems are *ontologically* distinct from persons.[9] However, there is some disagreement about this point among narrative therapists. I have spoken with a few therapists who do believe in such an ontological distinction and also operate with what I would call an essentialist notion of (problem-free) subjectivities (subjectivities that are "outside" the influence of problems), and with a view of problems as reified entities.[10] Johnella Bird (2000), a narrative therapist based in Auckland, New Zealand, has noted that the concepts of "externalizing problems" and "separating from problems" do not adequately capture important nuances of the work, because they can lead to simplistic representations of power and agency. The point of engaging in "externalizing conversations" with clients is to create a discursive space to name, unpack, and detail the relational and ideational contexts of problems so that clients can imagine and experience a sense of active agency, rather than passengerhood or inevitability, in connection with these problems.[11] But for some, the rhetoric of externalizing and separation *can* create an imagined, strict dichotomy between "persons" and "problems" in which problems are totalized as seamlessly bad (e.g., attributed a malevolent agency of their own), and clients are seen either as victims (when influenced by problems) or as heroic resistors (when not).[12]

Now, arguably, certain problems—anorexia included—*can* be totalized in this way *without* compromising (many) therapists' stance that it is impossible to see "outside" the narratives that constitute persons' lives and relationships. I will return to this point shortly. But first let me provide an example of narrative work that does not focus on externalizing a problem per se but rather makes constant use of "externalizing language" more generally. Externalizing language is part of any narrative conversation (including those that externalize problems such as anorexia) but is easier to illustrate with examples that do not take on anorexia.

Bird (2000) writes that the kind of linguistic distancing from the self entailed in externalizing language "is not a separation" from the self. Rather, it "allows for a perception of or emphasis on the relational" (9). In the following excerpt from a first therapy session, Bird is discussing the creation of an environment of respect in therapy (she introduces the excerpt first; I have inserted my own commentary, about the use of externalizing language, in brackets and italics):

> Jack is 23 years old and is involved in counselling as a result of being caught intruding on people's property while looking through windows at women. After 15 minutes of conversation Jack's eyes have not left my chest.
>
> *Johnella*: Jack, I've noticed that since we've been talking together your gaze hasn't shifted from my chest [*not: "you have not stopped looking at my chest"*]. I'm wondering if you have other ways of gazing at women or at men?
>
> *Jack*: You've got to be joking, I don't look at blokes like that.

Johnella: What sort of look would you be using if I was a bloke? *[not: "How would you look at me if . . ." The question uses externalizing language because it references "looks" or "gazes" that anyone can take up, rather than suggesting that Jack is the sole author, or "cause," of his gaze].*

Jack: (Shifts in his chair looking down and to the side, runs his hand through his hair) I dunno.

Johnella: I noticed when I talked about your talking with a bloke, you looked down and to the side. Is that the look you would use with blokes, do you think?

Jack: I dunno, it could be.

Johnella: There are possibly two looks we've discovered. One for women and one for men. I'm wondering if you know any other ways of looking.

Jack: I dunno.

Johnella: If the look you use is down and to the side *[not: "If you look down and to the side"]*, how does that affect listening? *[not: "how do you listen?"]*

Jack: What do you mean?

Johnella: Okay. If you are using the look you find yourself using with women—I don't want you to use that look right now. Just think about it—If you used that look, how would that affect listening?

Jack: I dunno.

Johnella: Would you find yourself listening *[not: "Would you listen"]* to my words or would you be listening to the words in your mind?

Jack: Like what words?

Johnella. I don't know. As you're imagining the look used on women, do you find yourself thinking things?

Jack: Yeah, I do.

Johnella: What do you find yourself thinking?

Jack: I don't want to say.

This is a *beginning* conversation that represents Jack and I negotiating as to whether an environment of respect is possible. (Bird 2000, 122–23)

Rather than naming "the male gaze" (a naming that would "externalize the problem") and discussing the ways in which Jack has been "recruited into" this gaze, the phrasing of Johnella's questions allows Jack to (begin to) experience and fill in the content and meanings of his gazes or possible gazes. Now, it is possible that if the therapy were to continue, a problem such as "a gaze used on women" *would* be externalized (and its histories, contexts, and effects explored in depth); again, this is an initial session, and it often takes some time to name a problem. But Bird emphasizes that it is not always necessary to "name a problem" in narrative work. She focuses on the fact that externalizing language constructs a relational "I," an "I" that is never singular but rather is always known and experienced in relationship with a range of concepts (some of them problematic), people, and practices.

Similarly, Sallyann Roth and David Epston (1998) present a training exercise for therapists designed to illustrate the ways in which people develop *relationships with* problems. They too emphasize that problems are not always singular, and they stress that what is externalized may change in the course of therapy several times. For them, externalizing is not a description of a "reality," nor is it a therapeutic "technique." Rather, it is a "principled language practice" that conveys problems in relational, instead of essentialized, terms (223). They stress that it is a common misunderstanding of narrative work to assume that "it aims to eliminate, conquer, or kill off problems. It does not, although it can seem to have a divide-and-conquer aspect" (212). The exercise they describe is meant to convey a lived experience of people's complex relationships with difficulties in their lives.

At a training workshop I attended in Adelaide, Australia (August 2000), Michael White provided yet another way of thinking about externalizing language. He suggested that alternative (preferred) life stories and identities should also be externalized. White stated, and I paraphrase: "We can't unpack discourses of identity we don't like—locate them in the sociopolitical contexts of lives and relationships, and in the politics of experience—and essentialize, or fail to unpack, the ones we do like, because our favorite ideas are also located in culture and history." White emphasizes that unpacking or situating "alternative" (non-problem-saturated) ideas about the self is not a cynical or undermining move. Rather, as with denaturalizing and unpacking problems, it allows these ideas to be more richly understood, or richly described, which increases the range of possibilities for action and thought in connection with these ideas in one's life. Further, White suggests that if a therapist were simply to help a client internalize alternative ideas, she or he would be recycling humanist discourse in narrative practice, which is meant to deconstruct humanist tenets.

Also, according to White, people's lives are *multistoried*. Therefore, it is not always helpful to conceptually corral a problem or set of problems as "one story" and then write another with clients. Again, alternative stories often inhabit the interstices of "problem" stories, and there are multiple and sometimes contradictory stories and possibilities within any given life story. It is important to envision any externalizing of problems in this conceptual context.[13]

That said, it is difficult not to externalize certain problems in a totalizing way. Problems that *already have* a reified reality, such as anorexia, have manifested themselves in these powerful—often fatal—terms in people's lives. In fact, one could argue that externalizing anorexia turns representations of anorexia that pathologize individuals against themselves, by promising to locate this "thing" called anorexia in a wider field of culture and power. Much of David Epston's work on anorexia and "anti-anorexia" circulates around this particular kind of political practice: the work of therapy is explicitly a subversive activity, a form of resistance, a "counter-practice" (see Epston 1993; Epston, Morris, and Maisel 1998; Maisel, Epston, and Borden [in press]). There is a recognition here that the tenacious, pathologizing *internalizing* of problems in the mental health professions, and in clients' everyday lives, has real effects that must be taken on directly—identified as such and refigured using these same terms. Seen in this light, externalizing anorexia is not a therapeutic "trick" or tactic; rather, it is a self-conscious deployment of the rhetoric, and the lived experience, of objectification.[14]

Note also that no narrative therapist recommends that problems *never* be externalized, even when a given problem does not already have a reified reality at the start of therapy. The externalizing of problems in narrative practice can be understood in the following way: when problems are represented as totalizing entities, therapists are naming and acknowledging their discursive and institutional power (which is usually not visible, at first, to clients). Identified problems often have totalizing *effects* that are devastatingly real; externalizing them means insisting that these effects do not originate inside individual persons. Note that externalizing language, then, is not "mere" rhetoric: problems have lives that are larger than persons. Simultaneously, naming and externalizing problems denaturalizes their power (it does not *dissolve* it, as some radical constructionist approaches might suggest; it *does* convey a belief that problems are unstable, or potentially unstable). Importantly, externalizing problems (when this occurs) is an early step in the work, and a *generative* step. When problems are rhetorically separated from persons, the ways in which they "speak the truth" about persons' identities are marked as *achieved*—or "constructed"—and therefore mutable. Then, the meat of the work is the detailed exploration of exactly what goes into these constructions, and what possibilities are made available when problems are denaturalized and unpacked in this way.[15]

To return now to the details of narrative approaches to anorexia: these approaches name and challenge the seemingly "natural" truths surrounding, for example, gendered specifications for thinness and feminine caretaking roles. Therapists often ask questions such as "Who formed the idea that women and girls should be a certain size?" (reported by David Epston in a training workshop for therapists held in Cupertino, California, 9 February 1994). In a therapeutic letter to a client who had said she felt "invalidated and trivialized by men . . . I feel like they are nice to me or take notice of me only when they want something from me or want me to do something for them," David Epston writes: "Do you think your gender training taught you to give? Do you think it 'fits' with men's gender training to take (from women)?"[16]

Similarly, narrative therapists identify and question dominant assumptions about parents' roles in their children's struggles with anorexia. The following example shows how a narrative approach to anorexia is explicitly opposed to the individualizing ideas and practices that shape anorexia (and also many therapeutic responses to it) by challenging the powerful assumption that adolescents must "separate and individuate" from their parents to achieve health. During a training workshop for therapists (in Cupertino, California, 21 March 1994), Michael White described a meeting with a young woman named Sally and her mother, Joan, in which Sally talked about a recent decision to call an old friend on the phone. Michael asked whether this was a good thing or a bad thing, and after some consideration, Sally said it was what she wanted to do, so it was a good thing. This led to a discussion about Sally's anti-anorexic "wants." After marking his appreciation of the odds against making such a call, given anorexia's specifications for isolation, Michael said he was curious about something; he had a feeling that someone else had played a part in this anti-anorexic move. Sally looked over at Joan and said she hadn't known whether to tell Michael about that. Joan spoke up at this point: "Yes, I did it. I know I shouldn't have. It shows I'm controlling, and it only confirms that I should get out." Michael interjected: "Wait—Sally, you said that this was a positive development." Sally agreed that that was the case. Michael continued: "So, did your mom contribute to your own [anti-anorexic] life, or subtract from it?" Sally said her mother had contributed to her own life, and Michael expressed curiosity about "teamwork" between Sally and her mother. He then interviewed the two of them about the history of this teamwork. After a while, Sally asked, with some astonishment, "Do you mean to say I don't have to do this alone?"

In family work, what is ordinarily construed as parental "overinvolvement" is read as an unsurprising—and therefore potentially less powerful—effect of anorexia, not of parental (especially maternal) "nature." Also, therapists assume anti-anorexic intentions and desires on the part of parents, knowing that parents usually blame themselves for the problem. In one example of an early family meeting, the therapist asks the parents, "Have either of you . . . I don't know where you are about this . . . a lot of parents get sucked into the notion that they're to blame for this. I don't know if you've tortured yourself with this. I hope not. I run into that a lot" (Zimmerman and Dickerson 1994, 310).

In addition to locating anorexia in its cultural context and revising certain taken-for-granted premises of family work, narrative therapists challenge the individualizing effects of anorexia and of mainstream psychotherapeutic practices in other significant ways, as well. As a way to "thicken" (Geertz 1973) the anti-anorexic stories of clients and their families—and to encourage new "performances of meaning" in clients' lives that are based on these "alternative knowledges"—clients are often invited to participate in an "Anti-Anorexia/Anti-Bulimia League." Leagues are collectives of clients and other individuals committed to the documentation and proliferation of anti-anorexic knowledges and experiences (through political action, newsletters, speaking engagements, etc.). New clients have ready access to league archives (which include therapeutic letters and videotapes) and themselves eventually become "consultants" for other clients in this way. The two largest leagues are based in Auckland, New Zealand, and in Vancouver, British Columbia. There are also two small leagues in the United States (in St. Paul, Minnesota, and in Palo Alto, California).[17] League materials and conversations have also recently become part of a "virtual community" (see www.narrativeapproaches.com). These forms of ongoing, collaborative work enact practical subversions of privatized, "expert" (professionalized) accounts of anorexia.

It remains to be seen how well a narrative approach to anorexia can be integrated with the biomedical interventions that are sometimes necessary and are supported by powerful institutional arrangements that (usually) do not privilege a so-called anti-anorexic stance.[18] Martha, the psychologist who often adopts a narrative approach in her work at Walsh, employs a twofold strategy in a hospital setting: she "externalizes" the effects of unit "structure" (protocols, "boundaries," and rules) on patients' hospital experiences, and she advocates short hospital stays.[19] Similarly, Zimmerman and Dickerson (1994) suggest that "if the anorexia is so powerful that the situation is acutely life-threatening, a collaboration could occur between parents and medical doctors to briefly hospitalize for weight gain to remove the acute threat. They (parents, doctors) could say that they won't let the anorexia kill [the person] and keep the weight gain separate from the therapy" (316). However, this advice may seem unworkable for parents who are finding it difficult to cover expenses even for basic medical care, not to mention talk therapy. As discussed in chapter 4, short hospital stays can be dangerous for patients who have stabilized at very low body weights and cannot afford to pay for psychotherapy. Clearly, in a context that encourages shortsighted coverages of care for many patients (based strictly on "medical necessity" for some managed care plans), institutional and economic inequities will constrain any possible anti-anorexic life story.

However, it is conceivable that treatment plans including a narrative approach could be arranged within a managed care system, which *has* allowed a space to question the value and efficacy of a strong reliance on (relatively) long-term hospital-based programs such as Walsh (and note that an investment in a promising talk therapy such as narrative therapy would ultimately cost a good deal less than a primary investment in hospital-based treatments). See Kaye, Kaplan, and Zucker 1996 for case examples of negotiating coverages from an HMO that include a wide range of services—services that were, moreover, offered over a more lengthy period of time than would have otherwise been allowed in the managed care system (these coverages were made possible, however, only after extensive documentation of patients' needs and considerable efforts of persuasion on the part of health care providers). However, simply "adding" narrative therapy, or other types of alternative therapies, to the set of possibilities allowed under managed care will not by itself address the social inequalities that privilege some patients in their efforts to negotiate customized managed care plans.[20] Nor will simply adding narrative therapy to a range of available treatment options—regardless of payment plans in place—help to redefine the meanings, and relative power, of biomedical and behaviorist interventions.

Such redefinitions would be an extremely positive step in the treatment of anorexia. I have suggested in this epilogue that given requisite institutional power, narrative therapists can help their clients refuse the internalization of pro-anorexic specifications of personhood that often circulate in hospital settings. Cultivating a narrative stance toward biomedical discourse could help subvert the resourcing logic that would have clients believe that these professional accounts speak the "truth" about their inner "natures" as persons, and that mobilizing and shaping this truth is the key to health.

Throughout this book, I have referenced the resourcing logic that informs anorexia's conditions of possibility and that surfaces regularly in treatment. Within mainstream psychiatric therapies, stubbornly unfit female bodies are posited, created, and resourced in the pursuit of bodies that are "fit," and that themselves naturalize and justify the pursuit of fitness. Seemingly overinvested maternal desire is produced and then mobilized as a resource for the creation of a more minimal form of family support (the latter rests on an apparently unshakable maternal instinct that just needs its volume turned down); in turn, a feminized family environment is posited and then destructured—that is, reduced to a resource for the creation of individualism within families. The sexual politics of many treatment practices create seemingly overprotective and personal forms of maternal caretaking on the unit that provide material for engineering more minimal and professional forms of psychiatric caretaking, and for crafting (masculinized) assertions of therapeutic family unity. Finally, the treatment of so-called acting-out (borderline) patients and families generates a perceived excess of emotion, and of resistance to treatment, that serve as rhetorical resources for the desired, more tempered, "healthy" expressions of emotion and resistance that clinicians and staff encourage in "typical" patients. In addition, so-called borderline patients are excluded from full participation in treatment and are thus throwaway resources.

All of these ideas and practices are premised on objectifications of "nature," which then serve as resources for the production of "healthy" identities. I have argued in this book that psychiatric objectifications of human nature invigorate, or crystallize, dominant ideals of personhood, codifying the power of these ideals, but also rendering their contradictions explicit. Narrative therapists deploy the rhetoric of objectification in such a way that these contradictions move into the foreground. When anorexia is externalized, the politics of personhood that support it are denaturalized, and therapeutic conversations can then serve as "resources" for "anti-anorexia."

Introduction: In Fitness and in Health

1 Reports on anorexia's incidence range from
0.5 percent to 1 percent (American Psychiatric
Association 1994, 2000). However, estimates
of significant anorexic symptoms range from
5 to 10 percent among adolescent girls and
young women and run even higher on some
college campuses (Boskind-White 2000).
Richard Gordon (2000) provides convincing
evidence that anorexia's increase in incidence
in the 1970s and 1980s is an actual increase in
the number of cases (i.e., the increase cannot
be attributed simply to a greater number of
cases being identified or diagnosed).

Apparently, anorexia has not increased in
incidence since the mid-1980s (whereas the
incidence of bulimia, a binge/purge "disorder," may be increasing). However, anorexia's
incidence appears to be on the rise among
preadolescent girls. For a review of literature
on these trends, see R. Gordon 2000.

2 Chapter 4 examines the institutional production of "typical" (white, middle-class) anorexic patients and explores critically the constructs of race, ethnicity, and class that are
folded into patient profiles. Also, considerations of sociocultural privilege infuse this
book. Note that because the vast majority of
patients diagnosed with anorexia at Walsh are
white and middle-class, I indicate individual
patients' class status and race/ethnicity in

this book only when these differ from the normative picture (or when, as in chapter 4, clinicians' constructions of race, class, and ethnicity are the main focus of my analysis).

3 I address these issues in chapter 1.

4 See Bemis 1978; Bruch 1974, 1978; Kaufman and Heiman 1964; Kog, Vandereycken, and Vertommen 1985; Minuchin, Rosman, and Baker 1978; Selvini-Palazzoli 1974; Sours 1980.

5 Charles Lasègue (1873a), professor of clinical medicine in the Faculty of Medicine of Paris, published "De l'Anorexie Hystérique" in 1873 (an English translation was printed in London in two parts that same year; see Lasègue 1873b, 1873c). Also in 1873, Sir William Gull, physician at Guy's Hospital in London, presented "Anorexia Nervosa (Apepsia Hysterica, Anorexia Hysterica)" to the Clinical Society of London (Gull's report was published in 1874).

6 Considering my arguments in this book about treatments for anorexia participating in its conditions of possibility, it is interesting to consider scholars' claims that treatments for hysteria often reproduced its symptoms. See Charlotte Perkins Gilman's *The Yellow Wall-Paper* (Gilman 1973). See also Ehrenreich and English 1981.

7 Waller, Kaufman, and Deutsch 1940 is the most widely cited, classic psychoanalytic account of anorexia. See also S. Freud 1954; A. Freud 1958.

8 See, for example, Allyton, Haughton, and Osmond 1964; Blinder, Freeman, and Stunkard 1970.

9 Many behavioral approaches today are "cognitive-behavioral" (Andersen, Bowers, and Evans 1997; Garner, Vitousek, and Pike 1997; Sesan 1994). Some treatment approaches today rely exclusively on pharmaceutical management (see Lester 1997), but most clinicians who specialize in eating disorders agree that a multidimensional approach is important (Agras 1987; Andersen, Bowers, and Evans 1997).

10 Chapters 1 and 2 explore the (more implicit) gender politics of these new therapies.

11 Reports on anorexia's mortality rate vary from 5 percent to 20 percent (Boskind-White 2000; Levenkron 2000). Higher estimates usually include cases of death from suicide. The most widely quoted estimate is 10 percent.

12 R. Gordon 2000 describes results from a ten-year follow-up study of seventy-six patients, reported in Eckert et al. 1995. Note that body image disturbance and menstrual dysfunction, cited in the following excerpt, are diagnostic criteria for anorexia (which are discussed later in this introduction): "Only 24 percent (18) of the patients evidenced a comprehensive recovery in all areas of functioning—weight, eating patterns, body image, social adjustment, menstrual function—at follow-up. Another 25 percent

(20) of the subjects were considered to have a 'good' outcome, meaning they had fully recovered their weight and regularly menstruated, although most of these had varying degrees of body image disturbance or disordered eating. A third group, consisting of 32 percent (24) of the subjects, were judged to have an intermediate outcome, meaning they had only partially recovered their weight and evidenced some degree of menstrual disorder and a more severe degree of other problems than the 'good' group. Finally 12 percent of the anorexics had a poor outcome and 7 percent had died" (28).

13 See Goldner, Birmingham, and Smye 1997 for a discussion of this issue as it relates to clinical, ethical, and legal questions about how to address treatment refusal. See also Tiller, Schmidt, and Treasure 1993; Zerbe 1992.

14 See Swartz 1987 for a related argument about professional writing and educational material on the topic of anorexia. See also Hepworth and Griffin 1995.

15 See DiNicola 1990. Eating disorders appear to be increasing in Japan (Pate et al. 1992), Argentina (see http://www.edeo.org/newsdetails/October 19.htm), and Fiji (Bosch 2000).

16 Note that women who emigrate from places where eating disorders are rare to places where they are prevalent have been known to develop eating disorders (Dawkins 1995; DiNicola 1990). See Weiss (1995) for debates about how to theorize this phenomenon.

17 Probyn (1987) argues that anorexia "is an important manifestation of current societal contradictions" (204), but also cautions against an *insistence* that anorexia is a contemporary phenomenon, noting that such an insistence can have the effect of collapsing together the different discourses that constitute anorexia and that may have arisen at different times. Later in this introduction, I discuss analyses of anorexia that locate it at the nexus of several, and sometimes contradictory, discourses.

18 Diagnoses other than anorexia (or bulimia, discussed hereafter) that indicate suitability for admission include, for example, attention deficit and hyperactivity disorder (ADHD), asthma with behavioral problems, and psychoses with an organic component.

19 I question the term "anorexic" as an identity label, because I consider anorexia to be a discursive construct. In this book, when I use the adjective "anorexic" to describe people, I hold in mind a critique of the cultural and clinical discourses that have produced such pathologized identities.

20 During my fieldwork, ages ranged between eleven and twenty.

21 Hepworth and Griffin (1995) wonder if anorexia may be more common among men and boys than is realized, "because of the discursive structure through which anorexia is represented as a typically female condition. This process then contributes to the overwhelming presence of anorexia

amongst women which is reflected in official statistics. Changing social perceptions might allow more males to report, or be diagnosed as having, specific eating disorders" (74). During informal conversation with me, the head psychiatrist at Walsh remarked, "Anorexic girls are really pretty normal. But the boys? They're weird." This comment suggests that boys with eating disorders are stigmatized (and may therefore be less likely than girls to seek help); it also supports the idea that girls struggling with anorexia enact normative aspects of femininity (even though girls in treatment are routinely pathologized). It would be interesting to explore the question of whether boys and men who struggle with eating and food are feminized.

It is clear that the ideals of fitness examined in this book that are constitutive of "disordered eating" have affected both males and females, and that a growing number of men and boys are concerned with their body image; however, I believe we should be wary of any move to represent these impacts as similar or equivalent. In chapter 1, I (briefly) compare cultural discourses of male and female fitness and suggest that, in spite of similarities, these discourses are distinctive and their effects on women and girls are particularly problematic. As far as I am aware, no cultural or clinical analyst disputes the idea that eating disorders appear much more frequently among women and girls.

22 The same is not true of staff. In the mid-1990s, the staff-patient ratio was about one to three. Staff had more time to consult with each other before staff downsizing began in the mid-1980s (see chapter 3).

23 Bulimia is more common than anorexia. The ratio of females to males diagnosed is about ten to one (American Psychiatric Association 2000). The diagnostic criteria for bulimia in the *Third Edition Revised* are "(A) recurrent episodes of binge eating (rapid consumption of a large amount of food in a discrete period of time); (B) a feeling of a lack of control over eating behavior during the eating binges; (C) the person regularly engages in either self-induced vomiting, use of laxatives or diuretics, strict dieting or fasting, or vigorous exercise in order to prevent weight gain [note: these are 'purging' behaviors. Unlike the *DSM-III-R*, the *DSM-IV* and the *DSM-IV-R* distinguish between 'purging' and 'nonpurging' 'types' of bulimia, the purging type involving 'self-induced vomiting or the misuse of laxatives, diuretics, or enemas,' and the nonpurging type involving 'other inappropriate compensatory behaviors, such as fasting or excessive exercise' (American Psychiatric Association 2000, 594)]; (D) a minimum average of two binge eating episodes a week for at least three months; (E) persistent overconcern with body shape and weight" (American Psychiatric Association 1987, 68–69).

24 These discussions are fascinating for what they reveal about the *DSM*'s focus on discrete clinical entities. Both the *DSM-IV* and the *DSM-IV-R*

(American Psychiatric Association 1994, 2000) identify similarities and links between anorexia and bulimia. The *DSM-IV* states that individuals with bulimia "may closely resemble those with Anorexia Nervosa in their fear of gaining weight, in their desire to lose weight, and in the level of dissatisfaction with their bodies" (546–47). The *DSM-IV-R* repeats this wording (591). The authors of both volumes also state that the onset of bulimia, like the onset of anorexia, often occurs in the context of dieting. In addition, the authors of the current *DSM* state that "particularly within the first 5 years of onset, a significant fraction of individuals with the Restricting Type of Anorexia Nervosa develop binge eating, indicating a change to the Binge Eating/Purging subtype. A sustained shift in clinical presentation (e.g., weight gain plus the presence of binge eating and purging) may eventually warrant a change in diagnosis to Bulimia Nervosa" (American Psychiatric Association 2000, 587). Finally, the authors of the *DSM-IV* and the *DSM-IV-R* acknowledge that both anorexia and bulimia are most common, by far, among women and girls, and that they both appear most frequently in the same locations in the world. However, in spite of their citing these close connections between anorexia and bulimia, these latest two *DSM*s insist on distinguishing two essentially different conditions. In contrast, feminist philosopher Susan Bordo (1993c) suggests that anorexia and bulimia (and obesity) are difficult to conceptualize as discrete entities in the context of consumer culture and its accompanying anxieties surrounding bodily control.

25 Clinicians and staff advise patients to remain in the hospital until they have gained enough weight to surpass their "exercise weight" by a few pounds (provided that their insurance plans allow for this treatment strategy). The thinking here is to provide patients with a "buffer" against weight loss after discharge—weight loss that would ordinarily result in patients falling below their "exercise weights."

26 Note that a number of programs in the United States discourage patients from paying too much attention to, or even discussing, calories and body weights (e.g., Andersen, Bowers, and Evans 1997). However, these aspects of treatment remain central organizing features of most hospital programs, whether or not there are attempts to discourage patients from dwelling on them openly.

27 To satisfy insurance companies' regulations for allowing coverage, clinicians are under increasing pressure to document patients' progress in terms of weight gain, in minute detail and on a daily basis. This pressure encourages a focus on behavior modification programs. Chapter 4 covers additional aspects of insurance requirements and constraints.

28 In chapter 3, I analyze Walsh in these terms. These problems with treatment are not as well studied as are problems with behavior modification.

See Wooley and Wooley 1985 on guarding against the "reinforcement of [gendered] cultural prejudices" within a professional team that oversees outpatient programs for the treatment of bulimia (401). Writing about one-on-one psychotherapy, Wooley (1991) also challenges conventional wisdom about countertransference in similar terms. On the topic of decentering the therapist's status as "expert," see the epilogue, as well as Brown 1994; Burck and Daniel 1990; Jones 1990.

29 I address staff members' views on this topic in chapter 3.

30 Clinicians at Walsh are not alone in this stance. Articles in the influential *Handbook of Treatment for Eating Disorders* (Dare and Eisler 1997; Goldner, Birmingham, and Smye 1997) warn against the potential punitive effects of behavior modification and recommend strong therapist/patient/parent alliances to guard against them.

31 A "typical" day on the unit is, of course, an anthropological fiction. There are, however, certain aspects of everyday life on the unit that are heavily regulated and repeated daily (if never in quite the same way).

32 Early on in my research, Bob, the medical director, suggested that I would have to be silent while on the unit and fade into the woodwork as much as possible (fortunately, this approach proved impracticable). At other times, he referred to me as "just a pair of eyes," and as someone who seemed to "sit behind a glass booth." Eventually Bob told me that he was envious of the fact that I could "step back and observe" the workings of the entire treatment program—a role he himself liked to take on—without the additional responsibility of patient care.

33 Several patients also told me that they liked the fact that I "just listened to and tried to understand" them, rather than "analyzing" them (in psychiatric terms). Similarly, many parents said that talking to me was "therapeutic," and "a way to vent." These remarks point to my unusual "outsider" status on the unit (reflecting the insular quality of the treatment program): as one patient put it, I was "a reminder of the outside world" to her.

34 Several staff told me that when I interviewed them, they felt as if they were able to "process" their daily experiences on the unit in a way that was more familiar to them before staff downsizing, and an increase in the number of patients who were acutely medically compromised, had forced them to adopt a more quantitative approach to their work. See also chapter 3.

35 On the near side of the nursing station are several private rooms for therapy sessions, a room where patients are weighed, the clinician/staff charting room, and a storage room.

36 Eckerman (1997) identifies this architectural design as a standard feature of inpatient programs for the treatment of anorexia.

37 It is clear that one purpose of random weights is to show suspicion and create a deterrent. Sometimes, for morning weigh-ins, patients are indeed

concealing such heavy weights on their bodies or "waterloading" to such an extent that an afternoon weight proves to be lower than the morning weight. But as a rule, body weights measured in the afternoon are a good deal higher than morning weights, anyway.

38 However, a diet of 100 percent Ensure is routinely prescribed for eating-disordered patients at the beginning of an admission, regardless of their medical condition. There is an element of behavior modification at work here: Ensure is easier for staff to control, and more difficult for patients to hide or throw away; and if patients begin with Ensure, they can "graduate" to solid food. I say more about the uses of Ensure at Walsh in chapter 2.

39 Many patients combined hospital foods in unusual ways. I did not ask them questions about this issue, because I got the sense that it was an extremely touchy topic for them. I did ask clinicians and staff about it, though. Mark, the head psychiatrist at Walsh, suggested to me that eating-disordered patients want to make eating as unpleasant as possible, either as a form of self-punishment or as a way to ensure that eating is an aversive experience. Ann, the nutritionist, speculated that patients want their food to seem as much *unlike* food as possible. This latter idea resonates with my analysis of hospital food as "medicine," discussed in chapter 2.

40 In chapter 4, I discuss the high cost of treatment (and detail problems that result for poorer patients in particular).

41 I take up this topic in chapter 2 and also explore its articulation with expressions of, and curbs on, individualism at Walsh.

42 Many treatment programs claim a low mortality rate, as does Walsh, but an often unspecified number of patients lose contact with programs over time and are unavailable for follow-up assessments. Also, a program with a reputation for success will tend to attract patients who are very ill and may thus (eventually) achieve "poorer 'success rates' than a program with less expertise" (Lemberg and Cohn 1999, 190).

43 My analysis is quite different from sociologist Erving Goffman's 1961 take on the asylum as a "total institution."

44 See also Berg and Mol's 1998 volume *Differences in Medicine* for an excellent collection of essays showing that "Western medicine" is not a coherent and unified field, and that differentials of power within medicine are part and parcel of its constitution.

45 See Haraway 1997a for a thought-provoking discussion of Scheper-Hughes's work as a "clerk or keeper of the records."

46 Writings on this subject include Fallon and Wonderlich 1997; Schwartz and Cohn 1996; Wooley 1994. Another topic that has generated debate is therapists' ideas about "transference" (or "projection") in their work with anorexic patients (Wooley 1991; Zerbe 1995). I do not take up this topic

directly in any depth (though some readers may recognize it in the pages of this book, analyzed in different terms).

47 These accounts must be produced actively, in part because they work to paper over contradictions.

48 An ethnography of the medical and psychological training that leads to the perspectives and practices of mental-health professionals in this field would be helpful for identifying the different layers of intention and belief these practitioners hold.

49 The cultural theorists here include Littlewood and Lipsedge 1985, 1987; Malson and Ussher 1996; Swartz 1985. The clinicians include Dare and Eisler 1997; R. Gordon 2000.

50 See Bruch 1978; Strober and Humphrey 1987; Vandereycken and Meerman 1984. See also Lague et al. 1993. Much clinical research on anorexia fuels the perception that anorexia is, at root, an acultural problem by investigating links to a range of already established (and pathologizing) categories of disorder. These include obsessive-compulsive disorder and other anxiety disorders, cognitive malfunctions, serotonergic hypothalamic disorders, interpersonal and family problems, depression, and personality disorders (see Lester 1997; Way 1995).

51 Bordo 1993c; Chernin 1981, 1985; Lawrence 1984; Orbach 1985, 1986; Polivy and Herman 1987; Way 1995. See also Garner, Olmsted, and Garfinkel 1983.

52 For examples of the latter, see especially Lawrence 1984 and Orbach 1986 (both authors are therapists). See also MacSween's (1993) insightful analyses of these two works.

53 Way (1995) points out that depictions of anorexia as a " 'disease of the rich and privileged' [were] reinforced in stories about Pat Boone's daughter Cherry Boone O'Neill in 1982, Karen Carpenter's death in 1983, and in rumored innuendoes throughout the 1980s about Princess Diana" (97).

54 See Mimi Nichter 2000 and Way 1995 for a review and discussion of these claims. Note that in her criticism of these claims, Nichter accepts a medical model of eating disorders by distinguishing "true pathology" from "normal" concerns about dieting and fatness.

55 See also Hepworth 1999; Hepworth and Griffin 1995; Turner 1984; Way 1995. Malson and Ussher 1996; Probyn 1987; and Turner 1984 are the authors here who concentrate on contradictions within and between cultural discourses in anorexia's production. For example, Malson and Ussher write about a "romantic discourse" of "traditional heterosexually attractive femininity" that exists alongside a discourse of "Cartesian dualism" that "constitutes the thin/anorexic body as proof of control over an alien, eruptive and threatening body" (277). Turner addresses contradictions within certain (idealized) family structures and within consumption practices and

beliefs in postindustrial contexts. Probyn, in her call to locate anorexia as "an embodied moment of negotiation" at the nexus of several different discourses (202), criticizes Turner for an overly structuralist reading of anorexia that "seems to ignore the ways in which discourses are multiply interwoven" (203).

Bordo (1993c), like Turner, analyzes contemporary imperatives to consume while also controlling consumption, especially feminine consumption. She often writes about anorexia's contradictions not so much in terms of its cultural production as in terms of its paradoxical effects (e.g., control resulting in lack of control, "protest" that operates within the terms that are being protested), or in terms of a contradiction between "older" and "newer" ideals of femininity. I take up a number of these topics in this book.

56 Early work in medical anthropology that focuses on a critical analysis of mind/body dichotomies includes D. Gordon 1988; Kleinman 1988; Martin 1987; Scheper-Hughes and Lock 1987. See Abu-Lughod and Lutz 1990 for an astute analysis of "embodied emotion" that also challenges mind/body dichotomies. M. Lock (1993) notes that Young (1982) and Comaroff (1982) were probably the first anthropologists "to question explicitly why epistemological scrutiny should be suspended for biomedicine" (144–45). Since that time, a number of critical analyses of biomedical categories have appeared. Lock's 1993 article contains an extended reference list on this topic, including more "radical" approaches to deconstructing bodies in medicine that I discuss later in this introduction. For her (and a coauthor's) selective update on this line of research, see Lock and Kaufert 1998.

57 See chapter 1, note 9, in this volume.

58 For examples of feminist appropriations of Foucault's work on the body that focus on the disruptive, or potentially disruptive, effects of gender, see especially Abu-Lughod 1990; Bordo 1993c; Butler 1990, 1993; Martin 1987; Price and Shildrick 1999; Sawicki 1991; Shildrick and Price 1998. While gender is not a significant theme in Foucault's writings, Shildrick and Price (1999) note that it is clear in his work that female bodies in particular are rendered "docile" (useful, manipulable). Feminists have seized on this gendered differential of power in the social construction of bodies that is embedded in Foucault's analyses. McNay (1992) identifies another reason why feminist constructionists who focus on the body have made good use of Foucault: his "insistence on the body as an historically specific entity distinguishes [his] theory from those of other [founding poststructuralist] theorists, such as Derrida, where the body is a metaphorization of the more general philosophical problem of difference . . . this stress on specificity is important because . . . the representation of the more general philosophical issue of difference in the metaphor of the feminine body

allows poststructuralist thinkers to bypass altogether the question of sexual difference as it relates to the experiences of women" (16). However, McNay acknowledges that Foucault himself does not take up the problem of sexual difference, for reasons that can also be subjected to feminist criticism. See also Braidotti 1989, 1991; Grosz 1994; and Butler 1993 regarding Foucault's neglect of the material specificities of "sex" or sexual difference.

59 For an extended discussion of this approach, see Comaroff and Comaroff (1991). Note that some scholars reject the term "resistance" if it is not fully conscious (see Lock and Kaufert 1998). I continue to use the term, in part because patients and therapists do.

60 In a widely cited article, medical anthropologists Nancy Scheper-Hughes and Margaret Lock (1987) argue that biomedicine excludes the "three bodies" that are the individual/phenomenologically "lived" body, the social body, and the body politic. My own analysis is at odds with one possible (and prevalent) reading of Scheper-Hughes and Lock's position here: namely, that these three bodies, in their rhetorical absence from biomedicine, are literally absent from biomedicine.

61 See, for example, Casper 1998; Franklin 1997; Franklin and Ragoné 1998; Haraway 1991c, 1997b.

62 Also more visible and manipulable in this context are cultural narratives about pregnancy.

63 Works that question the assumption that medicalization always produces negative effects include Lock and Kaufert 1998; Riessman 1998.

64 In response to such concerns, Connell (1995) writes of an irreducible "bodily dimension in experience and practice" (51). At the same time, however, he points out that simply reincorporating biological determinism, even as one explanatory "factor" that does not stand alone, is problematic: "If biological determinism is wrong, and social determinism is wrong, then it is unlikely that a combination of the two will be right" (52). Connell goes on to argue that "these two 'levels of analysis' cannot be satisfactorily added," partly because the level of biology is always imagined to be the most "real," and partly because social processes shape our very perceptions of the body, and of what would count as an example of biological determinism. He discusses data from a study on gender identity in the Dominican Republic that some have used as evidence that testosterone determines masculinity and others have used as evidence that social conditioning determines masculinity (48–49).

65 A number of cultural theorists have written about this problem in Foucault's work. Fraser (1989) remarks that because the body, for Foucault, is constituted by dominant discourses in a totalizing manner, it appears as a "transcendental signified" (60); analytically, it is posited outside of these

discourses as the ground for their inscription. One might say that if constructionists undertheorize the body, Foucault *overmaterializes* the effects of power, so that "the body" itself becomes an abstraction. Katherine Hayles (1999) argues that Foucault both undermines and "fetishistically reconstructs" the disembodied gaze of panoptic society "by positing a body constituted through discursive formations and material practices that erase the contextual enactments embodiment always entails" (194). Foucault's bodies thus become "a universalized body worked upon in a uniform way by surveillance techniques and practices" (194). One difficulty here is an overly stabilized representation of power; a multiplicity of social relations are "wholly absorbed into that great non-essentialist Essence, that final Kierkegaardian trace in the Foucault episteme, The Body" (Hall 1988, 51).

66 Cultural anthropologist Stefan Helmreich (1998) writes: "Social constructionism has been a politically powerful tool for contesting naturalizations of inequality. People interested in dismantling structures of domination organized according to categories of gender, race, and sexuality and through economic patterns like capitalism have been eager to show that these categories and patterns are not natural, not biologically given, but are the result of historical and cultural processes. . . . While such critical deconstruction has been useful, it has begged the question of what nature remains when the work of social construction is done" (21–22).

67 For related discussions, see Butler 1993; Haraway 1991c; Strathern 1992a; Tsing 1995. Ironically, constructionist theories of the body are designed to question this kind of nature/culture split. This same analytic split informed a version of feminist social constructionism that was popular in the 1970s and early 1980s. This earlier generation of feminist constructionists adopted a sex/gender distinction, construing gender as a culturally specific elaboration of "natural" biological facts (and thereby forfeiting an analysis of the body itself, leaving "nature" to the "hard" sciences). When contemporary constructionist theorists of the body attempt to erase the category "nature" altogether, one might say that the effect is a return of the repressed. For critical analyses of the sex/gender distinction, see Gatens 1983; Grosz 1994; Haraway 1991b. See Hausman 1995 on the problem of constructionist theories forfeiting the body to biomedical categories of analysis.

68 Phenomenological accounts of embodiment within anthropology include Csordas (1990, 1994) and M. Jackson 1989. For a review of this literature see M. Lock 1993, 137–38. Phenomenologists sometimes suggest that embodiment is "prior" to consciousness, or that the body has analytically discrete physical, psychological, and sociocultural "levels." In contrast, I follow Probyn (1991) in her refusal to conceptualize the body as "a privi-

leged site" or "stable platform" for experience or analysis (111). In fact, it is my aim to explore the cultural production of this particular vision (and experience) of the body.

69 See MacSween (1993) for an insightful critique of Turner on these terms. I thank David Epston for drawing my attention to Turner's position here and to MacSween's challenge.

ONE Crafting Resourceful Bodies
and Achieving Identities

1 As a minor, Sarah had no choice about coming to the clinic, because her parents had consented to her treatment.

2 Writing about treatments for anorexia, Eckerman (1997) discusses a general trend toward "self-maximisation, self-actualisation, self-discovery in psychology and in community services" and adds, "Thus to qualify as a 'normal' person one must torture oneself in relation to strict and constricting criteria (in both mind and body)" (158). Because most patients at Walsh are adolescents, ideas about self-development and identity formation are particularly powerful.

3 In the next section of this chapter, I examine connections among culturally dominant ideas about work, bodily fitness, and anorexia.

4 Young 1982 describes a similar phenomenon in the treatment of so-called post-traumatic stress disorder: resistance to treatment is not only seen as a confirmation of the diagnosis but also appropriated in the treatment process (see also Young 1995). Clinicians treating anorexia go one step further when they *encourage* resistance.

5 See especially Bordo 1993c. See also Chernin 1981, 1985; Orbach 1986; Steiner-Adair 1986.

6 Alan Watts (1970) also describes anorexia as a seemingly endless paradox of control: "The more consciousness is individualized by the success of the will, the more [the body 'outside' of it] seems to be a threat. . . . Every success in control therefore demands a further success" (quoted in Bordo 1993a, 145).

7 I place "willfully" in quotes because the question of agency here is a difficult one. It is important to stress that a person who struggles with anorexia is not the passive victim of a disease entity; this idea has led to power struggles in treatment that can re-create the problem (Bemis 1978; Bruch 1974; Gremillion 1992). However, by "willful" I do not mean to imply a self-conscious deployment of anorexia that entails overt tactics of control and "manipulation." This idea is the mirror image of the victim theory and has had similar effects in treatment.

8 Medical anthropologist Lorna Rhodes pointed out to me that Abu-Lughod's formulation politicizes the treatment team's reading of patients' resistance to treatment as diagnostic of "health" (personal communication, April 1996).

9 Abu-Lughod suggests that we invert Michel Foucault's 1978 assertion that "where there is power, there is resistance" (95) to read, "where there is resistance, there is power," a proposition that is "both less problematic and potentially more fruitful for ethnographic analysis because it enables us to move away from abstract theories of power toward methodological strategies for the study of power in particular situations" (Abu-Lughod 1990, 42). Abu-Lughod points out that Foucault himself has advocated this inversion (see Foucault 1982). Such a move is helpful for avoiding overly generalized representations of resistance, as well.

  See McNay 1991, 1992, for detailed discussions of Foucault's ideas about resistance. Foucault's focus on resistance is apparent in his later work, particularly *The History of Sexuality* (1978). His ideas about resistance in *The History of Sexuality* are complex. Foucault states that resistances are often mobilized in support of the status quo but can sometimes codify strategically to create social change. Although he claims not to conceptualize resistance in reactive terms (96), he also suggests that resistances are defined by an already constituted field of power relations. In addition to the statement "Where there is power, there is resistance" (95), he writes that resistances "play the role of adversary, target, support, or handle in power relations" (95) and are "inscribed in [relations of power] as an irreducible opposite" (96). The problem here, in my view, is *not* Foucault's position that "resistance is never in a position of exteriority in relation to power" (95); on this point I concur. Rather, as I suggest in the introduction, the problem lies in Foucault's representations of power as monolithic (in spite of his representations of power as dispersed and anonymous). For a related discussion, see Lock and Kaufert 1998.

10 Following the Italian socialist Antonio Gramsci, O'Hanlon (1988) writes: "Each form of the hegemonic comes into existence around diversities of interest and potential sites for resistance which fracture and constrain it even as it exerts its conforming power" (222). See also Hall 1986, 1988.

11 An anonymous reviewer of this manuscript suggested to me that the psychiatrist's language here is overtly sexist: girls who are "mousy" at first end up resisting him "tooth and nail."

12 Many patients are very well informed about representations of anorexia in popular culture, and some (like Maude) are quite well versed in psychological theories about the problem, as well. Most maintain an idea that these representations and theories do not capture their own experiences, which,

for them, are unique and widely misunderstood. On the one hand, cultural and clinical discourses about health/fitness, anorexia, and the struggles of adolescence contribute directly to this perception of specialness. On the other hand, such a perception of specialness allows room for patients to challenge and resist mainstream understandings of, and treatments for, anorexia. While some might characterize patients' claims to uniqueness as a form of "denial" or avoidance (of illness), the situation here is clearly more complex than a notion of denial would allow.

13   "Wellness at work" programs have increased since the 1980s, and they focus on worker productivity as well as stress reduction (Roberts and Harris 1989). In an article entitled "CEO Fitness: The Performance Plus," Rippe (1989) suggests that CEOs who "manage stress" through exercise "feel pressure" at work "but have learned to live with it—perhaps even thrive on it. They're what researchers call 'contented hard workers,' not harried, Type-A workaholics" (53).

14   This contemporary, dominant mode of capitalist production and consumption was consolidated in the early 1970s. Advanced capitalism is characterized by "just-in-time," small-batch production aimed at specific market niches that can change rapidly. "Flexible" system production reduces turnover time and is designed to promote increased consumption (Harvey 1989; Mandel 1972). Emily Martin (1994) discusses the ideal of a "flexible body" in this context.

15   Black women in the United States have long been represented as dangerously and inappropriately powerful in their position as other to the ideal white woman. One important thread of these portrayals is the coding of black women as similar to, or even more powerful than, black men. In their analysis of nineteenth-century European evolutionary theories, Haller and Haller (1974) point to the belief that a distinctive difference between the sexes (e.g., purportedly larger male brains on average) indicated an "evolved" society or civilization. Black men and women were thought to be less evolved than white people (and less evolved than a number of "racial" groups) in part because they were thought to be very similar to one another physically. These beliefs justified black women's slave labor (see D. White 1990) and also surfaced more recently in the myth of a black matriarchy in the United States that was thought to emasculate black men and to contribute to, or directly cause, the "breakdown" and impoverishment of many African American families (see A. Davis 1984; hooks 1984).

The othering of black women vis-à-vis the ideal white woman produces contradictory representations of black women. On the one hand, if black women are seen as similar to, or more powerful than, black men, they can be figured as asexual (unfeminine) beings (the black mammy embodies this image). On the other hand, if they are "uncivilized" and therefore relatively animalistic, they can be figured as wildly sexual, in contrast to a more reserved and "proper" (ideal) white female sexuality (Collins 2000; hooks 1997).

I thank Roopali Mukhergee and Radhika Parameswaran for their help with my conceptualizing these particular intersections of race, class, and gender.

16 In her discussion of black, Latina, and white girls' experiences of their bodies and of weight watching, Mimi Nichter (2000) claims that black girls are much less likely than white girls to diet and to be dissatisfied with their bodies (but some would question this conclusion; see chapter 4, note 2, in this volume). Nichter's discussion of "alternative," lived expressions of beauty and embodied selfhood among African American girls offers many interesting insights. However, Nichter comes close to romanticizing African American beauty ideals and practices by representing them as other to those of whites. For example, she suggests that in their refusals to diet, black girls reveal more "authentic" selves than do white girls. Her focus on apparent contrasts between black and white girls is underscored by the fact that she incorporates her data from Latina girls into the category "white" while making a special effort to ferret out "difference" from her black sample.

17 Chapters 2 and 3 show how heteronormative masculinities and femininities are also produced through therapeutic constructions of family (particularly maternal) roles.

18 See chapter 2, notes 31 and 32.

19 In 1985, Americans spent more than $5 billion trying to lose weight (Brumberg 1989). If we include "lite" foods and diet soda in our definition of weight-loss products, more than $30 billion is spent annually (Nichter and Nichter 1991). But dieters consume "a sizeable proportion of foods supposedly avoided while one is on a diet. For example, [a 1985 survey showed that] dieters ate approximately one-fifth of all cookies and ice cream consumed" (Nichter and Nichter 1991, 272). To quote a Lempert Report on the diet foods business: "Don't let all this talk of exercise and dieting fool you. Americans want to have their lo-cal dinner and super premium dessert too. It's part of the workout/pigout syndrome—Americans' bad habit of exercising and eating lite only to end the day with a rich gooey dessert, feeling they have earned it. While sales of diet foods have risen 7.4% last year, sales of chewy candy shot up 17% and the super-premium ice cream industry doubled since 1980" (Lempert Report 1986, 3). Bordo (1993b) writes about bulimia as "a characteristic modern personality construction" in this context (201).

20 One patient I met pinched her arms habitually, hoping that this would help dissolve fat on her body. When she was first admitted to the hospital at close to 0 percent body fat, she told hospital staff she would do anything they asked if they would just give her a knife so that she could slice the fat off her body (as if body fat were an isolable entity). She did not think she would hurt herself in this way; and generally speaking, someone who lives with anorexia does not believe that continued weight loss will hurt them. Fatness as a resource for fitness seems to be ever renewable.

21 Note that "anticonsumption" should not be misconstrued as a mere repression of the desire to eat. For most patients, food refusal engenders hunger. As the psychologist Hilde Bruch noted long ago, "anorexia"—indicating a loss of appetite—is a misnomer; most patients are intensely preoccupied with food and with controlling temptations to eat (Bruch 1978).

22 See Messner and Sabo 1990 for an excellent collection of essays on many of the problems and contradictions entailed in sport and fitness for men.

23 Bordo 1993b, 211.

24 The popular "Hints from Heloise," syndicated in 512 newspapers across the country, offered tips designed to save time and money in housekeeping, which would allow for more extensive and creative attention to "do-it-yourself" projects around the house (Heloise 1967). Similarly, the "Wife-Savers" project that began in Denver in 1964, sponsored by the Denver Area Home Economists in Homemaking Group, "started out on a 'whistle while you work' theme aimed at helping the homemakers in our group to help themselves and each other to gain more time, more poise, and more charm for happier family living" (McMeekin and Reed 1955, 617).

25 From the 1980s TV commercial for the perfume Enjolie.

26 However, as long as she maintained a low pulse, she would have to sign paperwork stating that she was leaving "against medical advice."

27 In an article on the medicalization of chronic pain, Jean E. Jackson (1992) suggests that the (often unhelpful) contradictions and paradoxes that such medicalization produces may at times be helpful to patients. See also Kleinman 1988.

28 Sylvia Yanagisako and Carol Delaney (1995) offer a similar critique of theories of materiality that are implicit in the concept of "naturalizing power," which, they argue, can conjure up a preexisting realm of nature in which power differentials are embedded and appear commonsensical. Anna Tsing (1995) also identifies a tendency of cultural analysts "to write of 'naturalizing' social relations as a synonym for 'justifying' them," which "ignores the cultural specificity of the justification through reference to nature" (114).

TWO Minimal Mothers and Psychiatric
Discourse about the Family

1 A clinician at Walsh tells me that more recently, parents have been encouraged to become more involved in their daughters' treatment (personal communication, March 2002).

2 The 1970s and 1980s saw a proliferation of family therapy models, and many argue that all of them have drawn on systems theory, if in different ways and to different degrees (Guttman 1991; Hoffman 1981). There are three types of family therapy that are widely considered to be at the center of systems thinking: structural family therapy (Minuchin 1974; Minuchin, Rosman, and Baker 1978); strategic family therapy (Haley 1973, 1980; Madanes 1981); and systemic family therapy (Selvini-Palazzoli 1974; Selvini-Palazzoli et al. 1978).

The underlying theory for family systems therapy is cybernetics, which was created in the 1940s during a series of interdisciplinary conferences in New York City sponsored by the Josiah Macy Foundation (and attended by prominent scientists, engineers, mathematicians, and social scientists). Norbert Wiener (1948), a mathematician, coined the term "cybernetics" and was particularly interested in information processing and feedback mechanisms, in both animals and machines (Weiner was a founding figure in the development of computers). Cybernetics was made possible by new communications technologies deployed during World War II, technologies that both signaled and shaped new ideas about human relations, couched in the "scientific" rhetoric of information, communication, and feedback (Heims 1991). Haraway (1989) shows how these ideas found their way into the human sciences, including psychiatry, which began to privilege smooth (nonstressed) and effective communication networking and information exchange among individuals.

Gregory Bateson, an anthropologist who attended a number of the Macy conferences, is widely credited as providing family therapy with an intellectual foundation through his work applying cybernetics to family interactions in the 1950s (though a number of family therapists were developing related approaches at the same time; see Hoffman 1981). Bateson formed a research group (operating out of the Mental Research Institute in Menlo Park, California) to study communication in families, especially families containing a member diagnosed with schizophrenia (discussed later in this chapter with reference to representations of mothers in early formulations of family therapy). This group sought to rewrite Freud's individualistic approach to understanding psychopathology "in terms of information, communication, feedback, and systems" (Heims

1991, 127). For an account of the group's formation and research, see Haley 1976.

3 For a description of the structural model, see Minuchin 1974; for a discussion of this approach to family therapy in the treatment of anorexia, see Minuchin, Rosman, and Baker 1978. The idea of breaking the family system is particularly strong in the structural model because compared to other systems approaches, there is more of an emphasis on shaking families out of their familiar patterns (Guttman 1991). Spatial and organizational metaphors predominate, not only in describing problems but also in formulating solutions, which involve very active and often deliberately disruptive interventions on the part of the therapist (Colapinto 1991; Hoffman 1981). Hoffman (1981) suggests that while his conceptual framework is certainly systemic, Minuchin "leans very little on the cybernetic paradigm.... For the most part his language seems to derive from organization theory and role theory, drawing heavily on spatial metaphors like boundary, mapping, territory, structure, role" (264). I discuss the development of the structural model in chapter 4.

Arguably, any family systems model will compromise the tenets of cybernetics—which include a belief in circular (nonlinear) "causes" of problems—by virtue of the fact that commonsense understandings of family roles, and individualizing notions of pathology, will be present in the therapy room and will have real effects. A therapist adopting a cybernetic approach may "act as if" these ideas about roles and individuals do not hold the key to understanding reciprocal patterns and interactive meaning making in families, but he or she is not likely to name and critically examine these taken-for-granted ideas in the process of therapy. To the extent that a cybernetic approach does not encourage a deconstruction of normative beliefs and practices surrounding hierarchy, roles, and individualism in families, it falls short of its goal to identify (and alter) the workings of family "systems." A detailed examination of this issue is beyond the scope of this book, but let me add here that some have advocated an integration of psychodynamic and family systems approaches (see, for example, Humphrey 1991; Scharff and Scharff 1991). Also, the premises of some systems thinkers are, self-consciously, not radically distinguishable from those of individual therapies in the first place (Guttman 1991; Hoffman 1981, 1985). Still others have incorporated social constructionist and feminist ideas into family systems thinking to deconstruct some of the norms that a cybernetic approach to therapy alone would leave untouched (and would therefore, arguably, reinscribe unknowingly). See Dare and Eisler 1997 for a discussion of feminist family therapies, and also constructionist therapies, that have borrowed from one school of family systems therapy called the Milan systemic approach. Narrative therapy, discussed in the epilogue of this book, derives in part from this latter group of post-Milan thinkers. Narrative therapy works to unpack dominant cultural constructions and normative practices surrounding illness and health, and to identify alternatives operating within and against these constructions and practices. This therapy has ultimately broken away from the systems thinking that is part of its history–its practitioners do not call themselves systems therapists.

4 On the popularity of the structural model in family therapy for anorexia, see Dare and Eisler 1997. Most family therapies for anorexia are eclectic, drawing on a number of different therapy traditions (Andersen, Bowers, and Evans 1997; Vanderlinden and Vandereycken 1991).

5 Consider the "superwoman syndrome" (coined by the popular feminist writer Betty Friedan in 1981) that influences many relatively well-to-do women, and the current popularity of "welfare to work" programs (see Rose 1995 for an insightful discussion of the latter).

6 See DeLair 2000. Cussins 1998b shows how infertility clinics enforce heterosexuality, "unlike sperm banks, which have long been associated with gay and lesbian reproductive rights" (Cussins 1998a, 193).

7 In the 1930s, schizophrenia was treated primarily through convulsive therapies and psychosurgery. See Tomlinson 1990 for a history of treatments for, and concepts about, schizophrenia.

8 Bateson et al. 1956; Lidz et al. 1964; Lidz et al. 1958; Lidz and Lidz 1952. Guttman (1991) notes that the idea that one person is the cause of problems within a family is antithetical to systems theory, which assumes a reciprocal circularity in relations among family members. Bateson and his colleagues later retracted the linear thinking in their early formulations about schizophrenia that led to mother blaming. However, as I discuss later in this chapter, family systems therapies continue to blame mothers today (usually in more subtle ways).

9 See Hare-Mustin 1978 for a discussion of feminist family therapy that holds this slice of history in mind.

10 Bateson's use of "first-order" cybernetics to understand schizophrenia was part of what led to a description of the family as a bounded system of communication among the individuals within it (for Bateson and his colleagues, schizophrenia resulted from communications "jamming"; see Goldenberg and Goldenberg 1991, 63–64). In first-order cybernetics, although information flow is an organizing concept, the "observer," or therapist, is not considered to be part of this flow. Because "observer effects" are not taken into account, the overall structure of the system being observed is thought to remain unaltered. As we have seen, this assumption was

related to therapeutic representations of the family as a given, feminized environment and indexed psychiatry's participation in sociocultural naturalizations of the family at the time.

The changes that occurred in family therapy in the 1970s were informed by a shift to second-order cybernetic theory, in which "the observer and the observed are treated as part of the same system" (Heims 1991, 283). "Homeostatic" family systems have become more "open" systems, allowing for greater degrees of individualism and flexibility.

11 Dare and Eisler (1997) write: "Anorexia nervosa has a special place in the development of family therapy, for it has played an important role in the work of a number of influential figures in family therapy (Minuchin, Selvini-Palazzoli, Stierlin, Whitaker, White, Liebman, etc.). For this reason, anorexia nervosa can be seen as having become a paradigm for the therapy, in much the same way that hysteria served as a paradigm for psychoanalysis and phobias served for behavior therapy" (308).

12 See Hare-Mustin 1978; Hare-Mustin and Marecek 1990; Luepnitz 1988; Perelberg and Miller 1990; Rieker and Carmen 1984; Walters et al. 1988.

13 In the case study material involving Deborah and her parents, Deborah's father states the following when he is trying to persuade Deborah to eat: "If you had a little more flesh on you, I'd beat the shit out of you! . . . I'm going to give you three minutes to eat [this hot dog], and if you don't start, you're going to find it in your ears and your eyes and down your mouth and everywhere else!" (7). And before Minuchin intervenes, the father adds: "Now Deborah, don't put me in a position where I'm going to get violent, goddamn it. . . . Eat that hot dog! God damn you! You son of a bitch! You eat the goddamn hot dog! I told you to eat it!" (8). Minuchin and his colleagues do not comment on the father's verbal assaults (merely his "ineffectiveness," which, they suggest, is exacerbated by Deborah's mother). Luepnitz 1988 presents a critical analysis of Minuchin's focus on changing mothers even when important questions about the scope of fathers' violence remain unexplored.

Note that it is a common move in family systems therapy to attack enmeshment in order to involve a "distancer" in the family. Walters et al. (1988) write:

> [in therapy] there is often an initial and negative focus on relationships perceived as "enmeshed," as well as a courting of the distant male in a positive or placating fashion that leaves the impression that the wife/ mother is to *blame* for a dysfunctional relationship, or she alone is responsible for bringing about change. This bias is treated as a *neutral* principle of good practice, and is reflected in training slogans such as the following:

1. Never pursue a distancer in treatment.
2. Always intervene first with the overfunctioner or the overresponsible one.
3. The enmeshed relationship has to be loosened *before* the distancer can move in.
4. Begin with the one who is most available to change.

Such teaching slogans ignore or deny the fact that terms such as "distancer," "overfunctioner," "enmeshed," and the like almost always refer to specific, predictable genders carrying out socially mandated tasks, and are not neutral terms describing dysfunctional positions. This terminology is linked with the clinical assumption that if only the wife/mother will "back off" or "let go," then the "distancer" will move in, which really does imply that the engaging partner is blocking the distant one, and so is to blame for problems in the family. (21)

14 There is, of course, no such thing as a typical family. My generalizations here cannot capture important differences between any two families.

15 Because of this treatment program's prestigious reputation, a number of patients drove several hours from their homes to be admitted.

16 Cubic centimeter (a liquid measurement).

17 Andersen, Bowers, and Evans (1997) report that in one hospital-based program for the treatment of anorexia, patients are told that the treatment team is "going to ask you to trust us to prescribe your food like medication" (341).

18 Of course, practically speaking, it *was* inevitable that Maude would take Ensure into her body in the hospital: if she had refused to drink it there, she would have been tube-fed (a rare occurrence at Walsh).

19 See also the introduction, note 38. The notion of a "developmental arrest" is linked to the prevalent idea that anorexia results from a deficiency of self (discussed in chapter 1).

It is interesting to note that the concept of reparenting (and of substitute parenting more generally) through hospitalization was first proposed by sociologists in the early 1950s. In an interdisciplinary article that cuts across the fields of sociology, medicine, and psychology, Talcott Parsons and Renée Fox (1952) develop Parsons's pathbreaking concept of the "sick role"—which, according to Parsons, accompanies any illness—by relating it to family and kinship roles in North America. Parsons discusses the idea of the sick role in a chapter of his book *The Social System* (1951), which has generated much commentary and also new research in the sociology of medicine. For a summary discussion of the sick role concept and a list of Parsons's publications on this topic, see Fox 1989.

Parsons and Fox argue that the sick role embodies a "pathological dependency" that reveals problems and vulnerabilities in the urban American nuclear family. In particular, mothers' (necessary) "specialized" burden of emotional caretaking for all family members renders the family an unsuitable environment for nurturing the sick, because this environment only reinforces the dependency that is attached to the sick role (or requires the ministrations of a healthy mother). The sick role must therefore be converted into the patient role. In the hospital, the patient relives his or her dependency: "There are intimate psychodynamic relationships between the processes which occur in the normal system of family interaction, and those which obtain both in the doctor-patient relationship and in such more elaborately differentiated healthcare institutions as the hospital" (Parsons and Fox 1952, 31). For this reason, the sick role can be addressed meaningfully in the hospital: the patient can be reparented because doctor-patient relations are "functionally alternative to those of the family" (31). At the same time, the "impersonal professional character of the hospital" (42) creates the emotional distance required to "cure" the patients' dependency. (According to Parsons and Fox, adult patients are reparented as well, because they regress through illness. This idea appears in so-called symbolic-experiential family therapy, developed by Carl Whitaker in the 1970s. Sometimes used in family therapy for anorexia, symbolic-experiential therapy attempts to reparent children, adolescents, and adults alike "so that all family members are able to achieve a higher level of individuation" [Neal and Herzog 1985, 146]. See also Napier with Carl Whitaker 1978; Neill and Kniskern 1982; Whitaker 1975.)

We have seen that constructions of substitute parenting at Walsh are quite similar. Indeed, Salvador Minuchin, the primary architect of structural family therapy, was greatly influenced by Parsons's writings on "the American family" (see especially Parsons and Bales 1955). (Minuchin adopted Parsons's model of "functional" family roles. A number of feminist psychotherapists have addressed problems with presumed gender roles in family therapies that can be traced to Parsons's influence in the field [see esp. Hare-Mustin 1978; Luepnitz 1988]. I discuss these topics in greater detail in chapter 4). It is striking that this slice of medical sociology from the 1950s has been folded into the common sense of contemporary psychiatric hospital practice. However, at Walsh, visions of maternal caretaking differ from those in Parsons and Fox's model. While mothers are still posited as the primary caretakers in families today, caretaking is no longer imagined as an exclusive or specialized role for mothers. Also, clinicians at Walsh endeavor to rework motherhood, not simply transform hospitalized patients. Parsons and Fox's analysis of the nuclear family in its socioeconomic context, and their discussion of hospital treatment as a form of social control, have dropped out of sight as well.

20 Part of the reason that parental substitution is figured in this way is that the hospital is seen as a "holding environment" for patients, a concept applied to mothers through the work of psychologist D. W. Winnicott. Note that while "therapeutic fathers" (male clinicians discussed in chapter 3) play an important role in treatment, their role is not imagined in terms of paternal reform. See my discussion earlier in this chapter of Minuchin's ideas about maternal versus paternal change.

21 Later in this chapter, I discuss psychological literature on anorexia describing fathers who are achievement and goal oriented in this way, and are thought to encourage approval seeking in their children.

22 On this note, it is interesting to consider the fact that maternal attachments have an ambiguous status within individual psychotherapies as well as family therapies. In addition to the institutionalization of family therapies, the 1970s saw the ascendancy of "ego psychology," in which the self is imagined to develop through relationships and differentiate out of relationships (Greenberg and Mitchell 1983). In rejecting Freudian theories that posit the arrival of the ego—coded male—with the resolution of Oedipal conflict, ego psychologists argue that the self, male and female, emerges out of an interpersonal matrix starting from birth. This idea borrows from object relations theory, which focuses on early attachments with the mother, as opposed to Oedipal conflict with the father. So the founding interpersonal "matrix" of personhood is thought to be a *maternal* encompassment of the self, though this idea is not explicitly stated within ego psychologies, since the focus of these theories is the development of the individual (*through* this early attachment).

23 Martha drew from a therapeutic approach called narrative therapy. I explore this approach to anorexia in the epilogue.

24 I do not mean to suggest that Martha thought Carol was "mean" (by analogy). Martha believed that Maude's experience of hospital "structure" crystallized many different problems and themes in her life; in her conversations with Maude, she never simply equated the effects of structure with the effects of Carol's mothering.

25 Patients were sometimes required to come to the clinic twice a week, on a *temporary* basis, if they were not gaining weight at home; this deterrent was removed if coming to the clinic twice a week was set up as a longer-term arrangement.

26 Patients at Walsh were never strapped to their beds. They were sometimes confined to them. It is true that some patients were not allowed into the bathroom alone—those who were under constant observation because of a risk of self-harm or a dangerous frequency of vomiting.

27 See Bograd 1991 for alternative (nonmainstream) perspectives on fatherhood and fathering in the family therapy literature.

28 In chapter 4, I write about some of the postwar literature that links "weak" or absent fathers to emotional problems in boys, and to teen delinquency.

29 Recall from chapter 1 that contemporary ideologies of fitness are thought to turn "type A workaholics" into healthier and less-stressed "contented hard workers."

30 I would like to thank John Neal for this formulation.

31 Aspects of Bordo 1993a and Orbach 1986 include the idea that anorexia embodies androgyny, though both authors also complicate this view.

32 The idea that fathers should be more feminine for the sake of their daughters also presumes a natural femininity for daughters and construes anorexia as a deviation from it.

33 I owe this formulation in part to Donna Haraway, who writes about a "paradoxical intensification and erosion of gender" within late capitalism (Haraway 1991a, 167). There is a parallel here with the creation of the female body as a stubborn resource for practices of "fitness." In chapter 1, I show how anorexia and its treatment create the female body as a quintessentially consuming body that is therefore rendered an inexhaustible resource for fitness. Similarly, motherhood is imagined as a natural and therefore indestructible form of caretaking that can be continually invoked and whittled down without affecting its essential core.

THREE Hierarchy, Power, and Gender in the "Therapeutic Family"

1 For ease of expression, I no longer place "natural" in quotation marks when describing "natural mothers" or "natural families," but I continue to challenge many of the assumptions that are attached to this term.

2 I heard critical comments about the program's more punitive aspects almost exclusively from female staff and clinicians. To provide one example, during our conversation about the treatment team's "united front," Wendy remarked, "They cannot get away with it from any of us. And you know it's like, when you're in prison, and every single guard will shoot you if you try to run away. I mean it kinda comes down to that because they're so opposed to gaining weight. And it must be horrible for them. It must be like feeling cornered."

3 Steve was not "out" about his sexual orientation with patients and their families.

4 As suggested in chapter 2, "sensitivity" is seen as additive to masculinity; it is not integrated into men's identities in the same way that it is for women. This is particularly true for relatively powerful men on the unit (psychiatrists and pediatricians). However, sensitivity does seem to make male staff less than full "men"; as quoted earlier, they seem to "lack testosterone."

The more ambivalent status of male staff's (as opposed to male doctors') masculinity is probably due to the fact that staff roles are coded as feminine. Even so, male staff are often characterized as "exceptional" men because of the ways they combine masculine and feminine qualities. Lorna, a nurse, suggested during an interview with me that male staff might be faced with a questioning of their gender identity, *and* that they are special individuals because they are both masculine and feminine: "I think we have some really wonderful men counselors that work on our unit [who] are very caretaking. Unusually so. . . . We have some really gentle men *who are also appropriately male*, I mean they get into playing, and they can certainly do—you know they're into the outdoors, playing ball, and all those kinds of things. But they can be very gentle doing vital signs and talking to kids. I think the expectation is that they do that, and I think we have some *exceptional* counselors in that sense."

In contrast, female pediatricians and psychologists are not masculinized at Walsh, nor are they considered exceptional individuals. They have, of course, "moved up" in Walsh's gendered prestige hierarchy. It is possible that for this reason—given the mainstreaming of liberal feminist notions of success in the professional world—any potential questioning or reformulation of gender identity in their cases is muted. However, professional women's presumed roles as maternal caretakers exist in problematic tension (versus "exceptional" combination) with the perceived requirements of their jobs (as I discuss throughout this chapter with reference to female staff in particular, but also with reference to Martha, a prominent psychologist at Walsh).

5 In keeping with the hierarchical structure of professions within the therapeutic family, patients knew all psychiatrists and pediatricians on the unit by their surnames but addressed psychologists, interns, and staff by their first names.

6 Whereas in most cases, the treatment team has some flexibility in their decision making about admissions to the unit, the team is legally required to recommend admission if a clinic patient is extremely physically or psychologically unstable. The team does have the option of sending an unstable patient to a different unit, but Martha is suggesting here that it is unwise to see a patient in outpatient clinic on a regular basis if it is understood that she will not be admitted to Walsh under any circumstances.

7 Lorna said: "So when my daughter was a year and a half, I started back at college part-time, and she was in day care. . . . it was co-op care, so I was there a lot; I was very conscious of taking care of her a lot. . . . it took me three years to finish my degree in psychology."

8 On the whole, however, staff are frustrated with parents who have a hard time handing their children over to the treatment team. After talking about

her new sensitivity toward parents about this issue, Wendy said that she still believed it was important for parents to relinquish the care of their children to the team, and she added: "I guess I still get very frustrated by how long it takes parents to change. I'm really aware of this with the screwier parents on the unit. I'm like, 'c'mon—this kid is getting older, you're losing time. You've done a bad enough job as it is. Let's turn this around, before this child is twenty!' I guess I probably still have some of those punitive, judgmental kind of feelings."

9 While describing dominant understandings of English society in the modern period, Strathern (1992a) writes: "Modernists characterized English society as complex or plural, a product of a long history and much change. The typical was timeless, and tradition or continuity implied homogeneity; change implied innovation, the introduction of foreign elements, heterogeneity, in short, diversity. Hindsight tells us that it was, of course, the sense of continuity which was subject to change, and all that was necessary to transform a tradition was to bring it into the present and give it a contemporary place. . . . It was simply a matter of valuing one's already established values" (7). Strathern's view contrasts with Stacey's (1990) claim (discussed in chapter 2) that the romanticization of "traditional" family forms indicates that the family serves as a kind of restorative, or a reactionary emotional glue, in these unstable and changing times.

10 Staff and patients often note that mealtimes on the unit are hardly training in "natural" or "reality-based" eating. Staff at Walsh seem at a loss to explain how presiding over Walsh's rules and regulations in this case is supportive of patients (though most would argue that it is necessary work for patients' health). Mark, a psychiatrist, said that mealtimes "essentially communicate to [patients] at their level. . . . and at the same time [we] make it safe and predictable, and doable for the nurses, and all that. It's very primitive, if you will. . . . for crying out loud, that's not how people usually function." But in spite of this recognition, it is very difficult to modify rules for eating on the unit. One eighteen-year-old patient named Sue requested in miniteams that she be allowed to have a relaxed meal schedule, "since I'm a responsible adult." Her individual therapist agreed with this plan, to help prepare Sue for independent eating in college. But several members of the treatment team did not think Sue's plan was a good idea, because they predicted that she would use a relaxed schedule to try to avoid eating (ultimately, Sue's request was denied). Sue said she thought such a schedule would put her at ease: "It would make me feel like I'm in control, not others. This is supposed to be training for natural eating—it's not very natural for people to be looking over your shoulder. . . . it feels like there's a start and stop gun."

FOUR "Typical Patients Are Not 'Borderline' ":
Embedded Constructs of Race, Ethnicity, and Class

1 Gard and Freeman (1996) conclude that "the relationship between anorexia nervosa and high socioeconomic status is not proven. Further, there is increasing evidence to suggest that if there is a skewed relationship between bulimia nervosa and socioeconomic status, that it is of a preponderance of cases in low socioeconomic groups" (10). See also R. Gordon 2000. Note that very few studies of this kind have been conducted in the United States. More than half of the studies that Gard and Freeman cite were conducted in Britain (the remainder were based in the United States, save one that was based in Hong Kong).

2 See, for example, Abrams, Allen, and Gray 1993; Dolan 1991; Smart 1999; Zhang and Snowden 1999. Note that methodological differences, and differences in study samples, mean that it is difficult to compare the results of these studies. Note also that some studies suggest contrary results. For example, in their review of the literature on eating disturbances among American minority youth, Crago, Shisslak, and Estes (1996) report that eating disorders appear to be comparably prevalent among "Hispanics" and the white population and appear to occur with less frequency among Asian Americans and with greater frequency among Native Americans (however, specific claims about anorexia's prevalence rates cannot be gleaned from these conclusions, as they do not separate out anorexia from a range of eating problems). In contrast, Cachelin et al. (2000) describe results from a study suggesting that eating-disordered symptoms (including symptoms of anorexia) occur with equal frequency among Hispanic, Asian American, African American, and white women (see also Le Grange, Stone, and Brownell 1998). For discussions of debates and disagreements about the widely held belief that anorexia has a very low prevalence rate among African Americans, see Crago, Shisslak, and Estes 1996 (see also Dawkins 1995; R. Gordon 2000).

3 See Dawkins 1995 and Pate et al. 1992 for discussions of some of this literature. See also my own discussion of this issue in chapter 1.

4 My use of quotation marks around the term "bias" is intended to signal my belief that the concept of bias does not by itself adequately capture the ways in which anorexia is represented, and constituted clinically, as an illness affecting primarily white and middle-class young women.

5 Lamont 1992 and Overby and Dudley 2000 assert that middle-class status is a moral stance, not just an income level. Class status can be seen as a fluid formation that is always defined locally in relation to other classes (Lamphere 2000).

6 Note that some of these Medicare patients have middle-class backgrounds. Chronic illnesses that require long stints of hospitalization often bankrupt households, and Medicare steps in when such families lose insurance coverage. I thank an anonymous reviewer of this manuscript for reminding me of these points.

7 Borderline personality features are considered more common among patients diagnosed with bulimia (Dennis and Sansone 1997).

8 I was able to speak with Sandra one-on-one briefly, on one occasion (and on the fly—i.e., without my tape recorder). Sandra's first admission was suddenly cut short when the medical director arranged to have her transferred to a locked psychiatric unit following a suicidal gesture. Her individual therapist and the medical director agreed that I could speak with her briefly in a therapy room after she and her therapist had met there for an hour. Sandra was quite willing. She responded to almost all of my questions about her stay at Walsh with nervous but enthusiastic questions for me about my study: What would I say about the unit? How long would it take me to write my book? When I asked about her plan for the evening, she became very sad and said, "Well, I guess I'll be packing. I guess they're moving me out of here. I don't know what will happen to me." A nurse arrived at that moment to escort Sandra to her room.

9 These include Paranoid, Schizoid, Schizotypal, Antisocial, Borderline, Histrionic, Narcissistic, Avoidant, Dependent, and Obsessive-Compulsive Personality Disorders. One can also receive a diagnosis of "Personality Disorder Not Otherwise Specified" (American Psychiatric Association 2000, 685). These categories also appear in the *DSM-IV* (American Psychiatric Association 1994) and in the *DSM-III-R* (American Psychiatric Association 1987), although the latter also includes "Passive Aggressive Personality Disorder," which has since disappeared as a diagnostic category.

10 The trouble with diagnosing a personality disorder during adolescence is that identities often shift and change for this age group (see D. Becker 1997 and Stone 1980 on this point). A clinician at Walsh told me, "All adolescents are borderline" (though she added, "You can tell when an adolescent will get the real diagnosis as an adult."). The *DSM-III-R* (American Psychiatric Association 1987) states that a person under the age of eighteen who exhibits features of borderline personality disorder should be diagnosed with an "Identity Disorder" instead, unless "the Personality Disorder criteria are met, the disturbance is pervasive and persistent, and it is unlikely that it will be limited to a developmental stage" (336). Identity Disorder falls under "Disorders Usually First Evident in Infancy, Childhood, or Adolescence" (and is normally diagnosed in late adolescence); its diagnostic features are "severe subjective distress regarding uncertainty

about a variety of issues relating to identity, including three or more of the following: (1) long-term goals, (2) career choice, (3) friendship patterns, (4) sexual orientation and behavior, (5) religious identification, (5) moral value systems, and (6) group loyalties" (90–91).

Interestingly, Identity Disorder does not appear as a diagnostic category in the *DSM-IV* or the *DSM-IV-R*, although the related but minimally specified diagnosis of "Identity Problem" appears under "Other Conditions That May Be a Focus of Clinical Attention." According to the *DSM-IV*, borderline personality disorder can be diagnosed in adolescence only if features of the disorder have been present for at least one year (American Psychiatric Association 1994, 631). This specification also appears in the *DSM-IV-R* (American Psychiatric Association 2000, 687).

11 As far as I am aware, there is no evidence in the literature that a borderline label or diagnosis is attached more frequently to working-class and/or nonwhite groups.

12 See Dennis and Sansone 1997 for a review of this literature.

13 For similar theories that focus on the cultural constitution of racial/ethnic difference and inequality, see Frankenburg 1993; Pratt 1989; Trinh 1989.

14 Attention is drawn away from the constitution of treatable subjectivities on the unit also when debates among clinicians about the care of borderline patients are cast strictly in terms of possible "discrimination" (as is usually the case).

15 My fieldwork ended before I could follow up on Sandra's experiences in the outpatient clinic. Note that with increasing restrictions in recent years on insurance coverage for eating disorders, Sandra's outpatient plan would no longer fly as official policy (personal communication with clinician at Walsh, December 2001).

16 Shelly, a psychology intern, was surprised to discover Pam's SES, given her "borderline" characteristics. Shelly's surprise is notable for understanding practices of exclusion at Walsh, given that borderline characteristics are not class specific according to psychiatric literature on the topic.

17 Pam was definitely an exception—it is not unusual for clinicians and staff at Walsh to implement corrective measures when patients are even slightly under their calorie quotas at the end of the day. Some patients have an order for an "NG backup," meaning that unfinished calories are to be force-fed. As mentioned in the introduction, the threat of tube feeding is usually sufficient for patients to finish their calories on their own. However, patients with so-called borderline features are more likely to "test" staff in this regard and are therefore more likely to be tube-fed. One night during my fieldwork, a middle-class borderline patient was force-fed twenty calories (one-quarter of an apple contains about twenty calories),

precisely because she was apparently testing staff to see how many calories she could "get away with" omitting that day. A number of staff members believed that the measure was unnecessarily punitive.

18 These latter patients may be diagnosed with one of a number of psychosomatic illnesses (e.g., diabetes with psychosomatic complications; psychosomatic asthma).

19 Note that financial considerations do not prevent therapeutic contact with parents; family meetings are offered as part of every patient's inpatient experience, regardless of ability to pay (Walsh picks up costs when it must). Every patient I met at Walsh had at least a few family meetings with at least one parent and a therapist. But parents of borderline patients are less likely to visit their daughters at Walsh or contact clinicians and staff with questions and concerns. Also, clinicians and staff tend to presume that these parents are "out of the picture" with regard to helpful involvement in their daughters' lives.

20 Beginning in the 1970s, orderly/controlled families sometimes became overstructured and rigid in the family therapy literature (I address this topic later).

21 United States Department of Labor 1965.

22 On Minuchin's support of alternative family structures—specifically, families in which the adult couple is a homosexual couple or otherwise not legally married—see Minuchin and Fishman 1981. On the topic of poverty: Minuchin has criticized the entire field of family therapy for limiting itself to the therapy room, and he argues for the importance of reform in juvenile courts, mental hospitals, and welfare departments (Luepnitz 1988; Simon 1984). Minuchin himself has worked to reform large systems of service delivery for the poor (Colapinto 1991).

23 When Minuchin began his work at the Wiltwyck school, he argued that altering the social conditions of poverty would do nothing for these families in the absence of therapy. He set out to alter "the culture of the family," or its "internal affairs" (Minuchin et al. 1967, 5), citing Oscar Lewis's work on the intergenerational and familial "causes" of poverty (O. Lewis 1959, 1961). However, Minuchin did complicate any simplistic picture of poor families within this paradigm, arguing that these families can assume many different forms (they cannot be lumped together into one type; see Hoffman 1981 on this point).

Minuchin later concluded that family therapy is not, in fact, an effective vehicle for addressing the major problems of "disorganized" families: therapy cannot provide the answer to poverty (Malcolm 1978). To the extent that one believes in "familial causes of poverty" (again, this position is reflected in, but does not itself adequately describe, Minuchin's own stance), one is easily left with the impression that poor and disorganized families are not the best candidates for family therapy, as opposed to an understanding that family therapy itself is inflected with discourses of class, race, and ethnicity.

24 I discuss these points in chapter 2.

25 See Aponte 1976. Note that this approach still focuses on qualities that are supposedly internal to poor families. Also, like Stack's 1974 romanticization of "kin networks" as strategic adaptations to poverty in working-class African American communities, it inadvertently valorizes nuclear family structures as "functional" to upward mobility. Based in part on Stack's work, Dizard and Gadlin (1990) have argued (more recently) that kin networking and same-sex companionship among the urban poor are pre-industrial forms of family survival, an idea that reinforces Parsons and Bales's 1955 notion that the middle-class nuclear family is the optimal family structure within capitalist economies.

26 For example, Minuchin developed the concept of "enmeshed" families through his work at Wiltwyck (Minuchin et al. 1967).

27 I cite an example in chapter 2.

28 Jean Piaget (1954), a well-known cognitive psychologist, argued that in "normal" psychological development, "concrete operational thinking" is surpassed by "formal operational thinking" (abstract reasoning) once a person reaches the age of twelve.

29 In spite of strong objections from many clinicians and staff at Walsh, Sandra was admitted a second time a few weeks later. But her second stay was very short (only a few days).

30 Thanks to an anonymous reviewer for this insight.

31 The dichotomies "rigid/unstructured" and "withholding/expressive" are sometimes explicitly racialized at Walsh. In particular, Japanese American "anorexic families," the most common group of nonwhite and internalizing families on the unit, are thought to exaggerate the seemingly rigid qualities of reserve and secrecy. Mark, a psychiatrist and an avid follower of Minuchin, once remarked, "I couldn't function in an Asian family. You sit with them in a family meeting and say, 'Wait a minute, when you said that, she was looking over here.' Then the father looks at the floor and says, 'Well, the weather's nice in Japan this time of year.' I'm just like an elephant. Give me Mediterranean families any day, they're much easier to deal with. They just go: [Mark makes an exploding sound and gestures wildly]." Cultural anthropologist Sylvia Yanagisako pointed out to me that as "model minorities," Japanese Americans are sometimes seen to "overdo it" in their apparent assimilation of white middle-class ideals of personhood (personal communication).

32 With the advent of "flexible" families, cultural difference in family structure and style becomes instructive, a therapeutic resource. Several staff

members talked with me about how their own lives and their nursing practices were "enriched" through contact with "culturally different" patients and their families. On a few occasions, staff alerted me (the resident anthropologist) to the fact that a "culturally interesting" (i.e., nonwhite) patient was about to be admitted to the unit. Writing about therapy with the "new poor," Aponte (1994) refers to the "spirit of love, courage, and hope in those communities" (7), in spite of the fact that the family structure of the poor is "not fully developed" (17).

33 On problems with premature discharge from the hospital, see Kaye, Enright, and Lesser 1988. On the increasing acuity of patients admitted to the hospital, see Litt 1999. For comprehensive discussions about both of these issues, and about additional problems with third-party providers, see Kaye, Kaplan, and Zucker 1996; Silber 1994. See also Sigman 1996. For less-critical accounts of the effects of managed care on the treatment of eating disorders, see Bravender et al. 1999; Kaye, Kaplan, and Zucker 1996.

34 See especially http://www.anad.org, the Web site for the National Association of Anorexia Nervosa and Associated Disorders.

Epilogue: A Narrative Approach to Anorexia

1 See chapter 2, notes 2 and 3.

2 These include the Bay Area Family Therapy Training Associates in Cupertino, California, and the Evanston Family Therapy Center in Evanston, Illinois (near Chicago).

3 Results reported from a small pilot study comparing narrative and non-narrative group therapy for first-time hospital patients diagnosed with anorexia suggest that a narrative approach leads to high levels of participation in treatment, hopefulness about recovery, a sense of separation from anorexic ideas and practices, and reduced shame about the problem (Madigan and Goldner 1999).

4 My ideas here about the ambiguous origins and effects of resistance borrow from Janice Radway (1984), a professor of literature who shows that reader responses to romantic fiction—whether they are, at face value, oppositional to, or reinscribing of, patriarchal values and structures—are always already linked to hegemonic production through chains of signification or resonant practices. She points out that any particular reading can therefore have contradictory and unintended effects. For example, Radway writes that if "women construct and understand [a romance] in a positive manner" (213) that is overtly oppositional to hegemonic interpretations, this same reading can "leave intact the very cultural categories, assumptions, and institutions that prompt the readers' desire to demonstrate re-

peatedly that they are capable and to be told again and again of the worth and power of a romantic heroine" (214). Conversely, a seemingly "passive" consumption may ultimately "change women in unforeseen and unintended ways, although perhaps always within certain limits" (218).

5 See Weingarten 1991 for a critical analysis of therapeutic techniques that reify and internalize "qualities" of personhood.

6 John Neal, a narrative therapist, knows of a young woman named Ann who is struggling with anorexia and refers to herself as "Ann O. Rexic" (personal communication). Estroff (1993) writes about illnesses that are routinely collapsed into patients' identities (she calls them "I am" illnesses, as opposed to "I have" illnesses); notably, her list includes anorexia and schizophrenia (I analyze psychiatric discourses about schizophrenia in chapter 2).

7 For example, the Maudsley model, developed at the Maudsley Hospital in London, externalizes anorexia to an extent but also reproduces aspects of Minuchin's approach to treatment (analyzed critically in this book in chapters 2 and 4). For descriptions of the Maudsley model as it has been recently applied in the United States, see Goode 2002 and Lock et al. 2001.

8 This quote is from a therapeutic letter written by David Epston. This letter is part of the archives of the Anti-Anorexia/Bulimia League of Auckland, New Zealand (see also Epston, Morris, and Maisel 1998). I say more hereafter about therapeutic letters and leagues.

9 In my view, the idea of an ontological distinction between problems and persons grants too much power, too high of a truth status, to the individualizing discourses of psychotherapy by implying the following: if the psyche is not the "cause" of problems, then we should locate problems "outside" of the psyche and thereby "cut the psyche loose" for a different experience/narration. In this formulation, problematic categories are left intact.

10 Accordingly, these therapists tend to represent mainstream mental health professionals as a monolithic block, and as people who reproduce problems' conditions of possibility in uniformly top-down ways. At a number of narrative conferences and workshops I have attended, a good deal of debate and differences of opinion have circulated around these points.

See note 13 for a discussion of a related issue: narrative therapy with persons, such as men who abuse, who occupy a position of power (relatively speaking) with respect to problems. In contrast to mainstream mental health professionals' experiences of their work, such persons are, of course, experiencing the kind of pain and difficulty in their lives that would lead them to therapy, either on their own accord or through the actions of authority figures.

11 Michael White discussed the problem of "passengerhood" in problem-saturated stories about people's lives during a training workshop I attended (in Adelaide, Australia, February 2001).

12 In some narrative therapy conversations, problems are occasionally collapsed into a monolithic concept of "culture" or "institutions" that, taken together, are said to "recruit" individuals into negative life experiences and negative conclusions about themselves. The idea that people are recruited or "hailed" by powerful discourses was first articulated by the French Marxist Louis Althusser (1971), who was Foucault's teacher. Compared to Foucault, Althusser held a fairly top-down understanding of the operation of power in social life. Katherine Hayles (1999) and Stuart Hall (1985) have argued that Foucault's writings about micropractices of power have not sufficiently reworked more top-down analyses of power and have simultaneously produced a vision of subjectivities that are not adequately linked to the complex contexts of their production. These tensions appear in narrative work. At times, narrative practitioners appear to construe Foucault's ideas about power as anonymous and dispersed to mean that when analyzing power, agency should be displaced from individuals to "culture" or "institutions," quite a structuralist reading of Foucault. The reverse of this coin is to wax toward an "anything goes" understanding of preferred identity construction. Extreme versions of these positions would suggest, respectively, that power is monolithic in its operations, or absent altogether.

13 A more simplistic understanding of "externalizing problems"—one that suggests, for example, that persons are victims of problems—is obviously inadequate when the person in therapy occupies a position of power with respect to the problem (for example, men in therapy who abuse; see Jenkins 1990). Nuanced narrative work in this kind of situation first emphasizes the devastating effects of the client's actions on others, to an extent that might not occur with clients who have not been in a position of power (relatively speaking) with respect to a problem. Then the problem is explored in its wider context, so that the client can begin to separate his or her actions, and "training" in the life of the problem, from a narrative about his or her "nature" (see M. White 1993).

14 On this topic, Michael White (1993) has noted that in *Homo Academicus*, Bourdieu (1988) contrasts the history of "domesticating the exotic" in the discipline of anthropology with the study of one's own world in its most familiar aspects. For Bourdieu, anthropological work "at home" requires an initial critical step of "exoticizing the domestic"—breaking with a given "relation of intimacy with modes of life and thought which remain opaque . . . because they are too familiar" (Bourdieu 1988, xi–xii). White suggests that to exoticize the domestic, we must first make it seem alien and extraordinary. One way to do this in narrative therapy is to "objectify,"

or externalize problems—or, in the case of anorexia (for example), objectify problems *differently.*

15 Note also that externalizing problems often works very well with children. For example, in the event of indiscriminate soiling (encopresis), the problem might be named "Sneaky-Poo," and the therapist and young client might discuss the ways in which Sneaky-Poo is "messing up" the client's life, and then discuss ways of "outsmarting" Sneaky-Poo (see M. White 1989).

16 From the archives of the Anti-Anorexia/Bulimia League of Auckland, New Zealand (discussed hereafter). Narrative therapists use written material in ways that subvert the objectifying power of medical charts. For example, therapists often write their notes into letters that they then send to clients, as a way to document the emergence of alternative knowledges. Some consult with clients about note taking and share what they are writing on the spot. In addition, clients are sometimes invited to take notes themselves during a session.

17 Narrative work can operate beyond the standard margins of therapy in a number of ways: for example, it can engage an analysis and critique of state responses to male violence (which often assume persons' "violent natures"). Johnella Bird (2000) remarks on the "contradictory structure" of narrative work (133), which sometimes deconstructs therapy itself by challenging not only presumed categories of self but also institutional structures that support these categories, including those that privilege the "therapy space" and the "therapy hour" when effective interventions would entail community responses, as well. Bird points out that this deconstruction of therapy occurs within the context of therapy; that is, people approach therapists because they "believe their psychological pain is a problem of the self, and that the self can be changed in therapy" (133). Bird recommends that therapists "expose and explore" the contradictory structure of therapy "both inside and outside of the therapeutic relationship. This may mean establishing discussion groups, action groups, newsletters, etc. In these ways the individual's experience of their experience is explored in a community. Collective experience challenges the pathologizing of individuals, while drawing attention to the group who benefits from the prevailing discourses" (133).

Community work and community activism via narrative practices might take the form of "definitional ceremonies," or group articulations and enactments of identity (M. White 1995, 2000). In developing the idea for such ceremonies, White borrows from cultural anthropologist Barbara Meyerhoff's ethnographic work in the 1970s with an elderly Jewish community in Venice, California. This community became consciously involved in a collective identity project in the face of discrimination and invisibility in Venice (Meyerhoff 1980, 1982, 1986). Definitional ceremonies can also be incorporated into more standard therapy work through the use of "reflecting teams" or "outsider witness groups" to help articulate and authenticate clients' alternative narratives. White emphasizes that these semipublic events are not cheerleading experiences: rather, they are a self(group)-consciously unfolding production of intersubjective meaning through tellings, retellings, and reflections about tellings. Participants are asked not to proclaim meaning but to situate their reflections and reactions in the contexts of their own lives, experiences, ideas, and so on. Participants also detail the thinking behind the ideas they express—the therapist is interviewed about his or her own thinking, as well. These ceremonies highlight *practices* of meaning making.

18 Methodist Hospital in Minneapolis and St. Paul's Hospital in Vancouver, British Columbia, have been attempting such an integration for some years now.

19 See my discussion of Martha's work in chapter 2.

20 For example, Kaye, Kaplan, and Zucker's (1996) promotion of day treatment as an effective and relatively inexpensive form of care does not apply to borderline patients (see chapter 4 for a discussion of the borderline label as it is used at Walsh). These authors state that day treatment is not recommended for patients who "act out"—those with "underlying character disturbance" (e.g., borderline personality disorder). The argument is that these patients' unstable moods would not allow fruitful participation in intensive group psychotherapy, a central component of many day treatment programs. Kaye, Kaplan, and Zucker suggest that such patients may need the structured containment of an inpatient unit. But one of the advantages of day treatment they discuss in this article is the reduction of costs attributable to the high staff-to-patient ratios required in inpatient settings for acting-out patients in particular. With these kinds of ideas at work, how are "acting-out" patients to receive affordable care?

BIBLIOGRAPHY

Abrams, Kay K., La Rue Allen, and James J. Gray. 1993. "Disordered Eating Attitudes and Behaviors, Psychological Adjustment, and Ethnic Identity: A Comparison of Black and White Female College Students." *International Journal of Eating Disorders* 14 (1): 49–57.

Abu-Lughod, Lila. 1990. "The Romance of Resistance: Tracing Transformations of Power through Bedouin Women." *American Ethnologist* 17 (1): 43–55.

Abu-Lughod, Lila, and Catherine A. Lutz. 1990. "Introduction: Emotion, Discourse, and the Politics of Everyday Life." In *Language and the Politics of Emotion,* ed. Catherine Lutz and Lila Abu-Lughod, 1–23. Cambridge: Cambridge University Press.

Agras, W. Stewart. 1987. *Eating Disorders: Management of Obesity, Bulimia, and Anorexia Nervosa.* Elmsford: Pergamon Press.

Alexander, Linda. 1981. "The Double-Bind between Dialysis Patients and Their Health Practitioners." In *The Relevance of Social Science for Medicine,* ed. Leon Eisenberg and Arthur Kleinman, 307–29. Boston: Dordrecht.

Allyton, T., E. Haughton, and H. Osmond. 1964. "Chronic Anorexia: A Behavior Problem." *Canadian Psychiatric Association Journal* 9 (April): 147–54.

Althusser, Louis. 1971. "Ideology and Ideological

State Apparatuses." In *Lenin and Philosophy and Other Essays*, trans. Ben Brewster, 127–86. London: New Left.

American Psychiatric Association. 1987. *Diagnostic and Statistical Manual of Mental Disorders: DSM-III-R.* 3d ed., rev. Washington, D.C.: American Psychiatric Association.

——. 1994. *Diagnostic and Statistical Manual of Mental Disorders: DSM-IV.* 4th ed. Washington, D.C.: American Psychiatric Association.

——. 2000. *Diagnostic and Statistical Manual of Mental Disorders: DSM-IV-R.* 4th ed., rev. Washington, D.C.: American Psychiatric Association.

Andersen, Arnold E., Wayne Bowers, and Kay Evans. 1997. "Inpatient Treatment of Anorexia Nervosa." In *Handbook of Treatment for Eating Disorders*, ed. David M. Garner and Paul E. Garfinkel, 2d ed., 327–48. New York: Guilford Press.

Aponte, Harry J. 1976. "Underorganization and the Poor Family." In *Family Therapy: Theory and Practice*, ed. Philip J. Guerin Jr., 432–48. New York: Gardner Press.

——. 1994. *Bread and Spirit: Therapy with the New Poor.* New York: W. W. Norton.

Armstrong, David. 1983. *Political Anatomy of the Body.* Cambridge: Cambridge University Press.

——. 1987. "Theoretical Tensions in Biopsychosocial Medicine." *Social Science and Medicine* 25 (11): 1213–18.

Barrett, Robert J. 1996. *The Psychiatric Team and the Social Definition of Schizophrenia: An Anthropological Study of Person and Illness.* Cambridge: Cambridge University Press.

Barton, Walter E., and Edwin M. Davidson. 1961. "Psychotherapy and Family Care." In *Current Psychiatric Therapies*, vol. 1, ed. Jules H. Masserman, 204–9. New York: Grune and Stratton.

Bateson, Gregory, Don D. Jackson, Jay Haley, and John Weakland. 1956. "Toward a Theory of Schizophrenia." *Behavioral Science* 1 (4): 251–90.

Becker, Anne E. 1995. *Body, Self, and Society: The View from Fiji.* Philadelphia: University of Pennsylvania Press.

Becker, Dana. 1997. *Through the Looking Glass: Women and Borderline Personality Disorder.* Boulder, Colo.: Westview Press.

Bell, Rudolf M. 1985. *Holy Anorexia.* Chicago: University of Chicago Press.

Bemis, Kelly M. 1978. "Current Approaches to the Etiology and Treatment of Anorexia Nervosa." *Psychological Bulletin* 85 (3): 593–617.

Bemporad, Jules R., et al. 1992. "A Psychoanalytic Study of Eating Disorders: I. A Developmental Profile of 67 Index Cases." *Journal of the American Academy of Psychoanalysis* 20 (4): 509–31.

Berg, Marc, and Annemarie Mol, eds. 1998. *Differences in Medicine: Unraveling Practices, Techniques, and Bodies.* Durham: Duke University Press.

Bird, Johnella. 2000. *The Heart's Narrative: Therapy and Navigating Life's Contra-dictions.* Auckland: Edge Press.

Blinder, Barton J., Daniel M. A. Freeman, and Albert Stunkard. 1970. "Behavior Therapy of Anorexia Nervosa: Effectiveness of Activity as a Reinforcer of Weight Gain." *American Journal of Psychiatry* 126 (8): 1093–98.

Bogle, Donald. 1973. *Toms, Coons, Mulattoes, Mammies, and Bucks: An Interpretive History of Blacks in American Films.* New York: Viking Press.

Bograd, Michele, ed. 1991. *Feminist Approaches for Men in Family Therapy.* New York: Harrington Park Press.

Bordo, Susan R. 1993a. "Anorexia Nervosa: Psychopathology as the Crystallization of Culture." In *Unbearable Weight: Feminism, Western Culture, and the Body,* 139–64. Berkeley: University of California Press.

——. 1993b. "Reading the Slender Body." In *Unbearable Weight: Feminism, Western Culture, and the Body,* 185–212. Berkeley: University of California Press.

——. 1993c. *Unbearable Weight: Feminism, Western Culture, and the Body.* Berkeley: University of California Press.

——. 1993d. "Whose Body Is This? Feminism, Medicine, and the Conceptualization of Eating Disorders." In *Unbearable Weight: Feminism, Western Culture, and the Body,* 45–69. Berkeley: University of California Press.

Bosch, Xavier. 2000. "Fat Is Out in Fiji." *Journal of the American Medical Association* 283 (11): 1409.

Boskind-Lodahl, Marlene. 1976. "Cinderella's Stepsisters: A Feminist Perspective on Anorexia Nervosa and Bulimia." *Signs: Journal of Women in Culture and Society* 2 (1): 120–46.

Boskind-White, Marlene. 2000. *Bulimia/Anorexia: The Binge/Purge Cycle and Self-Starvation.* New York: W. W. Norton.

Bourdieu, Pierre. 1977. *Outline of a Theory of Practice.* Trans. Richard Nice. Cambridge: Cambridge University Press.

——. 1984. *Distinction: A Social Critique of the Judgement of Taste.* Trans. Richard Nice. Cambridge: Harvard University Press.

——. 1988. *Homo Academicus.* Trans. Peter Collier. Stanford: Stanford University Press.

——. 1990. *The Logic of Practice.* Trans. Richard Nice. Cambridge: Cambridge University Press.

Braidotti, Rosi. 1989. "The Politics of Ontological Difference." In *Between Feminism and Psychoanalysis,* ed. Theresa Brennen, 89–105. London: Routledge.

——. 1991. *Patterns of Dissonance: A Study of Women in Contemporary Philosophy.* Cambridge: Polity Press.

Bravender, Terrill, et al. 1999. "Is There an Increased Clinical Severity of Patients with Eating Disorders under Managed Care?" *Journal of Adolescent Health* 24 (6): 422–26.

Breazeale, Kenon. 1994. "In Spite of Women: *Esquire* Magazine and the Construction of the Male Consumer." *Signs: Journal of Women in Culture and Society* 20 (1): 1–22.

Brody, Howard. 1992. *The Healer's Power.* New Haven: Yale University Press.

Brown, Laura S. 1994. *Subversive Dialogues: Theory in Feminist Therapy.* New York: Basic Books.

Bruch, Hilde. 1974. "Perils of Behavior Modification in the Treatment of Anorexia Nervosa." *Journal of the American Medical Association* 230 (10): 1419–22.

——. 1978. *The Golden Cage: The Enigma of Anorexia Nervosa.* Cambridge: Harvard University Press.

——. 1982. "Anorexia Nervosa: Therapy and Theory." *American Journal of Psychiatry* 139 (12): 1531–38.

Brumberg, Joan Jacobs. 1989. *Fasting Girls: The History of Anorexia Nervosa.* Cambridge: Harvard University Press.

Bruner, Edward M. 1986. "Ethnography as Narrative." In *The Anthropology of Experience,* ed. Victor W. Turner and Edward M. Bruner, 139–55. Urbana: University of Illinois Press.

Bruner, Jerome. 1990. *Acts of Meaning.* Cambridge: Harvard University Press.

Burck, Charlotte, and Gwyn Daniel. 1990. "Feminism and Strategic Therapy: Contradiction or Complementarity?" In *Gender and Power in Families,* ed. Rosine Jozef Perelberg and Ann C. Miller, 82–103. London: Tavistock/ Routledge.

Butler, Judith. 1990. *Gender Trouble: Feminism and the Subversion of Identity.* New York: Routledge.

——. 1993. *Bodies That Matter: On the Discursive Limits of "Sex."* New York: Routledge.

Bynum, Caroline Walker. 1987. *Holy Feast and Holy Fast: The Religious Significance of Food to Medieval Women.* Berkeley: University of California Press.

Cachelin, Fary M., et al. 2000. "Disordered Eating, Acculturation, and Treatment-Seeking in a Community Sample of Hispanic, Asian, Black, and White Women." *Psychology of Women Quarterly* 24 (3): 244–53.

Casper, Monica J. 1998. *The Making of the Unborn Patient: A Social Anatomy of Fetal Surgery.* New Brunswick: Rutgers University Press.

Chernin, Kim. 1981. *The Obsession: Reflections on the Tyranny of Slenderness.* New York: Harper and Row.

——. 1985. *The Hungry Self: Women, Eating, and Identity.* New York: Harper and Row.

Colapinto, Jorge. 1991. "Structural Family Therapy." In *Handbook of Family Therapy,* vol. 2, ed. Alan S. Gurman and David P. Kriskern, 417–43. New York: Brunner/Mazel.

Collins, Patricia Hill. 2000. *Black Feminist Thought: Knowledge, Consciousness, and the Politics of Empowerment.* New York: Routledge.

Comaroff, Jean. 1981. "Healing and Cultural Transformation: The Tswana of Southern Africa." *Social Science and Medicine: Part B, Medical Anthropology* 15B (3): 367–78.

———. 1982. "Medicine: Symbol and Ideology." In *The Problem of Medical Knowledge,* ed. Peter Wright and Andrew Treacher, 49–68. Edinburgh: Edinburgh University Press.

Comaroff, Jean, and John Comaroff. 1991. *Of Revelation and Revolution: Christianity, Colonialism, and Consciousness in South Africa.* Vol. 1. Chicago: University of Chicago Press.

Comaroff, Jean, and Peter Maguire. 1981. "Ambiguity and the Search for Meaning: Childhood Leukaemia in the Modern Clinical Context." *Social Science and Medicine: Part B, Medical Anthropology* 15B (2): 115–23.

Connell, R. W. 1995. *Masculinities.* Berkeley: University of California Press.

Crago, Marjorie, Catherine M. Shisslak, and Linda S. Estes. 1996. "Eating Disturbances among American Minority Groups: A Review." *International Journal of Eating Disorders* 19 (3): 239–48.

Crawford, Robert. 1985. "A Cultural Account of 'Health': Self-Control, Release, and the Social Body." In *Issues in the Political Economy of Health Care,* ed. John B. McKinlay, 60–103. New York: Tavistock.

Crisp, Arthur H. 1996. *Anorexia Nervosa: The Wish to Change: Self-Help and Discovery: The Thirty Steps.* 2d ed. Hore: Psychology Press.

Csordas, Thomas. 1990. "Embodiment as a Paradigm for Anthropology." *Ethos* 18 (1): 5–47.

———, ed. 1994. *Embodiment and Experience: The Existential Ground of Culture and the Self.* Cambridge: Cambridge University Press.

Cussins, Charis M. 1998a. "Ontological Choreography: Agency for Women Patients in an Infertility Clinic." In *Differences in Medicine: Unraveling Practices, Techniques, and Bodies,* ed. Marc Berg and Annemarie Mol, 166–201. Durham: Duke University Press.

———. 1998b. "Producing Reproduction: Techniques of Normalization and Naturalization in Infertility Clinics." In *Reproducing Reproduction,* ed. Sarah Franklin and Helena Ragoné, 66–101. Philadelphia: University of Pennsylvania Press.

Dare, Christopher, and Ivan Eisler. 1997. "Family Therapy for Anorexia Nervosa." In *Handbook of Treatment for Eating Disorders,* ed. David M. Garner and Paul E. Garfinkel, 2d ed., 307–24. New York: Guilford Press.

Davis, Angela. 1984. *Women, Culture, and Politics.* New York: Random House.

Davis, Mike. 1984. "The Political Economy of Late-Imperial America." *New Left Review* 143: 6–38.

Dawkins, Karon. 1995. "The Interaction of Ethnicity, Sociocultural Factors, and Gender in Clinical Psychopharmacology." *Psychopharmacology Bulletin* 32 (2): 283–89.

DeLair, Catherine. 2000. "Ethical, Moral, Economic, and Legal Barriers to Assisted Reproductive Technologies Employed by Gay Men and Lesbian Women." *DePaul Journal of Health Care Law* 4: 147–92.

Dennis, Amy Baker, and Randy A. Sansone. 1997. "Treatment of Patients with Personality Disorders." In *Handbook of Treatment for Eating Disorders*, ed. David M. Garner and Paul E. Garfinkel, 2d ed., 437–49. New York: Guilford Press.

DiNicola, Vincenzo F. 1990. "Anorexia Multiforme: Self-Starvation in Historical and Cultural Context," Parts 1 and 2. *Transcultural Psychiatric Research Review* 27 (3): 165–96; 27 (4): 245–86.

Dizard, Jan E., and Howard Gadlin. 1990. *The Minimal Family*. Amherst: University of Massachusetts Press.

Dolan, Bridget. 1991. "Cross-Cultural Aspects of Anorexia Nervosa and Bulimia: A Review." *International Journal of Eating Disorders* 10 (1): 67–78.

Eckerman, Liz. 1997. "Foucault, Embodiment, and Gendered Subjectivities: The Case of Voluntary Self-Starvation." In *Foucault, Health, and Medicine*, ed. Alan Petersen and Robin Bunton, 151–69. London: Routledge.

Eckert, Elke D., K. A. Halmi, P. Marchi, W. Grove, and R. Crosby. 1995. "Ten-Year Follow-Up of Anorexia Nervosa: Clinical Course and Outcome." *Psychological Medicine* 25 (1): 143–56.

Ehrenreich, Barbara. 1983. *The Hearts of Men: American Dreams and the Flight from Commitment*. New York: Anchor Books.

Ehrenreich, Barbara, and Dierdre English. 1981. "The Sexual Politics of Sickness." In *The Sociology of Health and Illness*, ed. Peter Conrad and Rochelle Kern, 327–49. New York: St. Martin's Press.

Ellis-Ordway, Nancy. 1999. "How to Find Treatment for an Eating Disorder." In *Eating Disorders: A Reference Sourcebook*, ed. Raymond Lemberg with Leigh Cohn, 189–92. Phoenix: Oryx Press.

Epston, David. 1989. *Collected Papers*. Adelaide: Dulwich Centre Publications.

——. 1993. "Internalizing Discourses versus Externalizing Discourses." In *Therapeutic Conversations*, ed. Stephen Gilligan and Reese E. Price, 161–77. New York: Norton.

Epston, David, Fran Morris, and Rick Maisel. 1998. "A Narrative Approach to So-Called Anorexia/Bulimia." In *"Catching Up" with David Epston: A Collection of Practice-Based Papers Published between 1991 and 1996*, 149–74. Adelaide: Dulwich Centre Publications.

Estroff, Sue E. 1993. "Identity, Disability, and Schizophrenia: The Problem of Chronicity." In *Knowledge, Power, and Practice: The Anthropology of Medicine and Everyday Life*, ed. Shirley Lindenbaum and Margaret Lock, 247–86. Berkeley: University of California Press.

Ewen, Stuart. 1988. *All Consuming Images: The Politics of Style in Contemporary Culture*. New York: Basic Books.

Fallon, Patricia, and Stephen A. Wonderlich. 1997. "Sexual Abuse and Other Forms of Trauma." In *Handbook of Psychotherapy for Anorexia Nervosa and Bulimia*, ed. David M. Garner and Paul E. Garfinkel, 394–414. New York: Guilford.

Faludi, Susan. 1991. *Backlash: The Undeclared War against American Women*. New York: Crown.

Fine, Rueben. 1989. *Current and Historical Perspectives on the Borderline Patient*. New York: Brunner/Mazel.

Foucault, Michel. 1975. *The Birth of the Clinic: An Archaeology of Medical Perception*. Trans. Alan M. Sheridan Smith. New York: Vintage Books.

———. 1978. *The History of Sexuality, Volume 1: An Introduction*. Trans. Robert Hurley. New York: Vintage Books.

———. 1979. *Discipline and Punish: The Birth of the Prison*. Trans. Alan Sheridan. New York: Vintage Books.

———. 1980a. "Body/Power." In *Power/Knowledge: Selected Interviews and Other Writings 1972–1977*, ed. Colin Gordon, trans. Colin Gordon, Leo Marshall, John Mepham, and Kate Soper, 55–62. New York: Pantheon Books.

———. 1980b. "The Eye of Power." In *Power/Knowledge: Selected Interviews and Other Writings 1972–1977*, ed. Colin Gordon, trans. Colin Gordon, Leo Marshall, John Mepham, and Kate Soper, 146–65. New York: Pantheon Books.

———. 1980c. "Two Lectures." In *Power/Knowledge: Selected Interviews and Other Writings 1972–1977*, ed. Colin Gordon, trans. Colin Gordon, Leo Marshall, John Mepham, and Kate Soper, 78–108. New York: Pantheon Books.

———. 1982. "The Subject and Power." In *Michel Foucault: Beyond Structuralism and Hermeneutics*, ed. Hubert Dreyfus and Paul Rabinow, 208–26. Chicago: University of Chicago Press.

Fox, Renée. 1989. *The Sociology of Medicine: A Participant Observer's View*. Englewood Cliffs: Prentice Hall.

Frankenberg, Ruth. 1993. *White Women, Race Matters: The Social Construction of Whiteness*. Minneapolis: University of Minnesota Press.

Franklin, Sarah. 1997. *Embodied Progress: A Cultural Account of Assisted Conception*. London: Routledge.

———. 1998. "Making Miracles: Scientific Progress and the Facts of Life." In *Reproducing Reproduction*, ed. Sarah Franklin and Helena Ragoné, 102–17. Philadelphia: University of Pennsylvania Press.

Franklin, Sarah, and Helena Ragoné, eds. 1998. *Reproducing Reproduction*. Philadelphia: University of Pennsylvania Press.

Fraser, Nancy. 1989. "Foucault's Body Language: A Posthumanist Political Rhetoric?" In *Unruly Practices: Power, Discourse, and Gender in Contemporary Social Theory*, 55–66. Minneapolis: University of Minnesota Press.

Freud, Anna. 1958. "Adolescence." *Psychoanalytic Study of the Child* 13: 255–78.

Freud, Sigmund. 1954. *The Origins of Psycho-analysis: Letters to Wilhelm Fliess, Drafts and Notes: 1887–1902*, ed. Marie Bonaparte, Anna Freud, and Ernst Kris, trans. Eric Mosbacher and James Strachey. New York: Basic Books.

Friedan, Betty. 1981. *The Second Stage*. New York: Summit.

Fromm-Reichman, Frieda. 1948. "Notes on the Development of Treatment of Schizophrenics by Psychoanalytic Psychotherapy." *Psychiatry* 11 (3): 263–73.

Gans, Herbert J. 1962. *The Urban Villagers*. New York: Free Press of Glencoe.

Gard, Maisie C. E., and Chris P. Freeman. 1996. "The Dismantling of a Myth: A Review of Eating Disorders and Socioeconomic Status." *International Journal of Eating Disorders* 20 (1): 1–12.

Garner, David M., Kelly M. Vitousek, and Kathleen M. Pike. 1997. "Cognitive-Behavioral Therapy for Anorexia Nervosa." In *Handbook of Treatment for Eating Disorders*, ed. David M. Garner and Paul E. Garfinkel, 2d ed., 94–144. New York: Guilford Press.

Garner, David M., and Paul E. Garfinkel. 1997. *Handbook of Treatment for Eating Disorders*. 2d ed. New York: Guilford Press.

Garner, David M., Marion P. Olmsted, and Paul Garfinkel. 1983. "Does Anorexia Nervosa Occur on a Continuum? Subgroups of Weight-Preoccupied Women and Their Relationship to Anorexia Nervosa." *International Journal of Eating Disorders* 2 (4): 11–20.

Gatens, Moira. 1983. "A Critique of the Sex/Gender Distinction." In *Beyond Marxism? Interventions after Marx*, ed. Judith A. Allen and Paul Patton, 143–62. Sydney: Intervention.

Geertz, Clifford. 1986. "Making Experiences, Authoring Selves." In *The Anthropology of Experience*, ed. Victor W. Turner and Edward M. Bruner, 373–80. Urbana: University of Illinois Press.

——. 1973. "Thick Description: Toward an Interpretive Theory of Culture." In *The Interpretation of Cultures, Selected Essays*, 3–30. New York: Basic Books.

Gelman, David. 1990. "Fixing the 'Between': Therapists Are Pushed to Examine the Roles of Men and Women in the Family." *Newsweek*, 2 July, 42–43.

Gilligan, Carol. 1982. *In A Different Voice: Psychological Theory and Women's Development*. Cambridge: Harvard University Press.

Gilman, Charlotte Perkins. 1973. *The Yellow Wall-Paper*. New York: Feminist Press.

Gluckman, Max. 1963. *Order and Rebellion in Tribal Africa*. New York: Free Press of Glencoe.

Goffman, Erving. 1961. *Asylums: Essays on the Social Situation of Mental Patients and Other Inmates.* New York: Doubleday.

Goldenberg, Irene, and Herbert Goldenberg. 1991. *Family Therapy: An Overview.* 3d ed. Pacific Grove: Brooks/Cole.

Goldner, Elliot, C. Laird Birmingham, and Victoria Smye. 1997. "Addressing Treatment Refusal in Anorexia Nervosa: Clinical, Ethical, and Legal Considerations." In *Handbook of Treatment for Eating Disorders,* ed. David M. Garner and Paul E. Garfinkel, 2d ed., 450–61. New York: Guilford.

Good, Byron J. 1977. "The Heart of What's the Matter: The Semantics of Illness in Iran." *Culture, Medicine, and Psychiatry* 1 (1): 25–58.

———. 1994. *Medicine, Rationality, and Experience: An Anthropological Perspective.* Cambridge: Cambridge University Press.

Good, Byron J., and Mary-Jo DelVecchio Good. 1993. "'Learning Medicine': The Constructing of Medical Knowledge at Harvard Medical School." In *Knowledge, Power, and Practice: The Anthropology of Medicine and Everyday Life,* ed. Shirley Lindenbaum and Margaret Lock, 81–107. Berkeley: University of California Press.

Goode, Erica. 2002. "Anorexia Strategy: Family as Doctor." *New York Times,* 11 June.

Gordon, Christopher C., Eugene Beresin, and David B. Herzog. 1989. "The Parents' Relationship and the Child's Illness in Anorexia Nervosa." *Journal of the American Academy of Psychoanalysis* 17 (1): 29–42.

Gordon, Deborah R. 1988. "Tenacious Assumptions in Western Medicine." In *Biomedicine Examined,* ed. Margaret Lock and Deborah Gordon, 19–56. Boston: Kluwer Academic Publishers.

Gordon, Richard A. 2000. *Eating Disorders: Anatomy of a Social Epidemic.* 2d ed. Malden, Mass.: Blackwell.

Gramsci, Antonio. 1971. *Selections from the Prison Notebooks of Antonio Gramsci,* ed. and trans. Quintin Hoare and Geoffrey N. Smith. New York: International Publishers.

Greenberg, Jay R., and Stephen A. Mitchell. 1983. *Object Relations in Psychoanalytic Theory.* Cambridge: Harvard University Press.

Gremillion, Helen. 1992. "Psychiatry as Social Ordering: Anorexia Nervosa, A Paradigm." *Social Science and Medicine* 35 (1): 57–71.

Grosz, Elizabeth. 1994. *Volatile Bodies: Toward a Corporeal Feminism.* Bloomington: Indiana University Press.

Guidano, Vittorio F., and Giovanni Liotti. 1983. *Cognitive Processes and Emotional Disorders.* New York: Guilford Press.

Gull, William W. 1874. "Anorexia Nervosa (Apepsia Hysterica, Anorexia Hysterica)." *Transactions of the Clinical Society of London* 7: 22–28.

Guttman, Herta A. 1991. "Systems Theory, Cybernetics, and Epistemology." In

Handbook of Family Therapy, vol. 2, ed. Alan S. Gurman and David P. Kriskern, 41–62. New York: Brunner/Mazel.

Haley, Jay. 1959. "The Family of the Schizophrenic: A Model System." *Journal of Nervous and Mental Disease* 129 (1): 357–74.

———. 1973. *Uncommon Therapy: The Psychiatric Techniques of Milton Erickson*. New York: Norton.

———. 1976. "Development of a Theory: A History of a Research Project." In *Double Bind: The Foundation of the Communicational Approach to the Family*, ed. Carlos E. Sluzki and Donald C. Ransom, 59–104. New York: Grune and Stratton.

———. 1980. *Leaving Home*. New York: McGraw-Hill.

Hall, Stuart. 1985. "Signification, Representation, Ideology: Althusser and the Post-structuralist Debates." *Critical Studies in Mass Communication* 2 (2): 91–114.

———. 1986. "Gramsci's Relevance for the Study of Race and Ethnicity." *Journal of Communication Inquiry* 10 (2): 5–27.

———. 1988. "The Toad in the Garden: Thatcherism among the Theorists." In *Marxism and the Interpretation of Culture*, ed. Cary Nelson and Lawrence Grossberg. Urbana: University of Illinois Press.

Haller, John S., and Robin M. Haller. 1974. *The Physician and Sexuality in Victorian America*. New York: W. W. Norton.

Halmi, Katherine A., Pauline Powers, and Sheila Cunningham. 1975. "Treatment of Anorexia Nervosa with Behaviour Modification: Effectiveness of Formula Feeding and Isolation." *Archives of General Psychiatry* 32 (1): 93–96.

Haraway, Donna. 1989. *Primate Visions: Gender, Race, and Nature in the World of Modern Science*. New York: Routledge.

———. 1991a. "A Cyborg Manifesto: Science, Technology, and Socialist Feminism in the Late Twentieth Century." In *Simians, Cyborgs, and Women: The Reinvention of Nature*, 149–81. New York: Routledge.

———. 1991b. " 'Gender' for a Marxist Dictionary: The Sexual Politics of a Word." In *Simians, Cyborgs, and Women: The Reinvention of Nature*, 127–48. New York: Routledge.

———. 1991c. *Simians, Cyborgs, and Women: The Reinvention of Nature*. New York: Routledge.

———. 1991d. "Situated Knowledges: The Science Question in Feminism and the Privilege of Partial Perspective." In *Simians, Cyborgs, and Women: The Reinvention of Nature*, 183–201. New York: Routledge.

———. 1997a. "Fetus: The Virtual Speculum in the New World Order." In *Modest_Witness@Second_Millennium.FemaleMan© _Meets _OncoMouse™: Feminism and Technoscience*, 173–212. New York: Routledge.

———. 1997b. *Modest_Witness@Second_Millennium.FemaleMan©_Meets_ Oncomouse™: Feminism and Technoscience.* New York: Routledge.

Hare-Mustin, Rachel. 1978. "A Feminist Approach to Family Therapy." *Family Process* 17 (2): 181–94.

Hare-Mustin, Rachel, and Jeanne Marecek. 1990. *Making a Difference: Psychology and the Construction of Gender.* New Haven: Yale University Press.

Harvey, David. 1989. *The Condition of Postmodernity: An Inquiry into the Origins of Cultural Change.* Oxford: Basil Blackwell.

Hausman, Bernice L. 1995. *Changing Sex: Transsexualism, Technology, and the Idea of Gender.* Durham, N.C.: Duke University Press.

Hayles, Katherine N. 1999. *How We Became Posthuman: Virtual Bodies in Cybernetics, Literature, and Informatics.* Chicago: University of Chicago Press.

Hebdige, Dick. 1988. *Subculture: The Meaning of Style.* London: Routledge.

Heims, Steve J. 1991. *The Cybernetics Group.* Cambridge: MIT Press.

Helmreich, Stefan. 1998. *Silicon Second Nature: Culturing Artificial Life in a Digital World.* Berkeley: University of California Press.

Heloise. 1967. *Heloise All around the House.* New York: Pocket Books.

Hepworth, Julie. 1999. *The Social Construction of Anorexia Nervosa.* London: Sage.

Hepworth, Julie, and Christine Griffin. 1995. "Conflicting Opinions? 'Anorexia Nervosa,' Medicine, and Feminism." In *Feminism and Discourse: Psychological Perspectives,* ed. Sue Wilkinson and Celia Kitzinger, 68–85. London: Sage.

Herzog, Wolfgang, Dieter Schellberg, and Hans-Christian Deter. 1997. "First Recovery in Anorexia Nervosa Patients in the Long-Term Course: A Discrete-Time Survival Analysis." *Journal of Consulting and Clinical Psychology* 65 (1): 169–77.

Hoffman, Lynn. 1981. *Foundations of Family Therapy: A Conceptual Framework for Systems Change.* New York: Basic Books.

———. 1985. "Beyond Power and Control: Toward a 'Second Order' Family Systems Therapy." *Family Systems Medicine* 3(4): 381–96.

hooks, bell. 1984. "The Myth of Black Matriarchy." In *Feminist Frameworks: Alternative Theoretical Accounts of the Relations between Women and Men,* ed. Alison M. Jaggar and Paula S. Rothenberg, 369–74. New York: McGraw-Hill.

———. 1997. "Selling Hot Pussy: Representations of Black Female Sexuality in the Cultural Marketplace." In *Writing on the Body: Female Embodiment and Feminist Theory,* ed. Katie Conboy, Nadia Medina, and Sarah Stanbury, 113–28. New York: Columbia University Press.

Hsu, L. K. George. 1983. "The Aetiology of Anorexia Nervosa." *Psychological Medicine* 13 (2): 231–38.

Humphrey, Laura Lynn. 1991. "Object Relations and the Family System: An Integrative Approach to Understanding and Treating Eating Disorders." In *Psychodynamic Treatment of Anorexia Nervosa and Bulimia,* ed. Craig L. Johnson, 321–53. New York: Guilford.

Jackson, Don De Avila. 1968. "Family Therapy in the Family of the Schizophrenic." In *Therapy, Communication, and Change,* ed. Don De Avila Jackson, 204–21. Palo Alto: Science and Behavior Books.

Jackson, Jean E. 1992. " 'After a While, No One Believes You': Real and Unreal Pain." In *Pain as Human Experience: An Anthropological Perspective,* ed. Mary-Jo DelVecchio Good et al., 138–68. Berkeley: University of California Press.

Jackson, Michael. 1989. *Paths towards a Clearing: Radical Empiricism and Ethnographic Inquiry.* Bloomington: Indiana University Press.

Jenkins, Alan. 1990. *Invitations to Responsibility: The Therapeutic Engagement of Men Who Are Violent and Abusive.* Adelaide: Dulwich Centre Publications.

Johnson, Craig L. 1991. "Treatment of Eating-Disordered Patients with Borderline and False-Self/Narcissistic Disorders." In *Psychodynamic Treatment of Anorexia Nervosa and Bulimia,* ed. Craig L. Johnson, 165–93. New York: Guilford Press.

Jones, Elsa. 1990. "Feminism and Family Therapy: Can Mixed Marriages Work?" In *Gender and Power in Families,* ed. Rosine Jozef Perelberg and Ann C. Miller, 63–81. London: Tavistock/Routledge.

Jordanova, Ludmilla. 1989. *Sexual Visions: Images of Gender in Science and Medicine between the Eighteenth and Twentieth Centuries.* Madison: University of Wisconsin Press.

Kaufman, Moses Ralph, and Marcel Heiman. [1874] 1964. *The Evolution of Psychosomatic Concepts: Anorexia Nervosa, a Paradigm.* New York: International Universities Press.

Kaye, Walter H., Allan S. Kaplan, and Murray L. Zucker. 1996. "Treating Eating-Disorder Patients in a Managed Care Environment: Contemporary American Issues and a Canadian Response." *Psychiatric Clinics of North America* 19 (4): 793–810.

Kaye, Walter H., Amy Baker Enright, and Susan Lesser. 1988. "Characteristics of Eating Disorders Programs and Common Problems with Third-Party Providers." *International Journal of Eating Disorders* 7 (4): 573–79.

Keller, Evelyn Fox. 1985. *Reflections on Gender and Science.* New Haven: Yale University Press.

Kleinman, Arthur. 1986. *Social Origins of Distress and Disease: Depression, Neurasthenia, and Pain in Modern China.* New Haven: Yale University Press.

———. 1988. *Rethinking Psychiatry: From Cultural Category to Personal Experience.* New York: Free Press.

Kog, Elly, Walter Vandereycken, and Hans Vertommen. 1985. "The Psychosomatic Family Model: A Critical Analysis of Family Interaction Concepts." *Journal of Family Therapy* 7(1): 31–44.

Kroker, Arthur, and Marilouise Kroker. 1987. "Theses on the Disappearing Body in the Hyper-modern Condition." In *Body Invaders: Panic Sex in America*, ed. Arthur Kroker and Marilouise Kroker, 20–34. New York: St. Martin's Press.

Lague, Louise, Allison Lynn, Lois Armstrong, Gabrielle Saven, and Laura Sanderson Healy. 1993. "How Thin Is Too Thin?" *People Magazine*, 20 September, 74–80.

Lamont, Michèle. 1992. *Money, Morals, and Manners: The Culture of the French and American Upper-Middle Class*. Chicago: University of Chicago Press.

Lamphere, Louise. 2000. "Let's Set the Agenda." In *Anthropology and Middle Class Working Families: A Research Agenda*, ed. Mary Margaret Overby and Kathryn Marie Dudley, 82–85. Arlington: American Anthropological Association.

Lasch, Christopher. 1977. *Haven in a Heartless World: The Family Besieged*. New York: Basic Books.

Lasègue, Charles. 1873a. "De l'Anorexie Hystérique." *Archives Générales de Médicine* 1: 384–403.

——. 1873b. "On Hysterical Anorexia." *Medical Times and Gazette* 2 (6 September): 265–66.

——. 1873c. "On Hysterical Anorexia." *Medical Times and Gazette* 2 (27 September): 367–69.

Lawrence, Marilyn. 1979. "Anorexia Nervosa: The Control Paradox." *Women's Studies International Quarterly* 2 (1): 93–101.

——. 1984. *The Anorexic Experience*. London: Women's Press.

Le Grange, Daniel, Arthur A. Stone, and Kelly D. Brownell. 1998. "Eating Disturbances in White and Minority Female Dieters." *International Journal of Eating Disorders* 24 (4): 395–403.

Lemberg, Raymond, with Leigh Cohn, eds. 1999. *Eating Disorders: A Reference Sourcebook*. Phoenix: Oryx Press.

Lempert Report. 1986. "More Men Counting Calories—Lo Cal Market Faltering." *Lempert Report* 31 (December): 3.

Leonard, Linda Schierse. 1982. *The Wounded Woman: Healing the Father-Daughter Relationship*. Athens: Swallow Press.

Lester, Rebecca J. 1997. "The (Dis)embodied Self in Anorexia Nervosa." *Social Science and Medicine* 44 (4): 479–89.

Levendusky, Philip G., and Catherine P. Dooley. 1985. "An Inpatient Model for the Treatment of Anorexia Nervosa." In *Theory and Treatment of Anorexia Nervosa and Bulimia: Biomedical, Sociocultural, and Psychological Perspectives*, ed. Steven Wiley Emmett, 211–33. New York: Brunner/Mazel.

Levenkron, Steven. 2000. *Anatomy of Anorexia*. New York: W. W. Norton.

Lewis, Ioan M. 1971. *Ecstatic Religion: A Study of Shamanism and Spirit Posses-sion.* Baltimore: Penguin Books.

Lewis, Oscar. 1959. *Five Families: Mexican Case Studies in the Culture of Poverty.* New York: New American Library.

———. 1961. *The Children of Sanchez.* New York: Random House.

Lidz, Ruth Williams, and Theodore Lidz. 1952. "Therapeutic Considerations Arising from the Intense Symbiotic Needs of Schizophrenic Patients." In *Psychotherapy with Schizophrenics,* ed. Eugene B. Brody and Fredrick C. Redlich, 168–78. New York: International Universities Press.

Lidz, Theodore, Alice Cornelison, Dorothy Terry, and Stephen Fleck. 1958. "Intrafamilial Environment of the Schizophrenic Patient: VI. The Trans-mission of Irrationality." *AMA Archives of Neurology and Psychiatry* 79 (3): 305–16.

Lidz, Theodore, Alice R. Cornelison, Margaret T. Singer, Sarah Schafer, and Stephen Fleck. 1964. "The Mothers of Schizophrenic Patients." In *Schizo-phrenia and the Family,* ed. Theodore Lidz, Stephen Fleck, and Alice R. Cornelison, with the collaboration of Yrjo O. Alanen et al., 290–335. New York: International Universities Press.

Litt, Iris F. 1999. "Managed Care and Adolescents with Eating Disorders." *Journal of Adolescent Health* 24 (6): 373.

Littlewood, Roland, and Maurice Lipsedge. 1985. "Culture-Bound Syndromes." In *Recent Advances in Clinical Psychiatry,* vol. 5, ed. Kenneth Granville-Grossman, 105–42. Edinburgh: Churchhill Livingstone.

———. 1987. "The Butterfly and the Serpent: Culture, Psychopathology and Bio-medicine." *Culture, Medicine, and Psychiatry* 11 (3): 289–335.

Lock, James, Daniel Le Grange, Stewart Agras, and Christopher Dare. 2001. *Treatment Manual for Anorexia Nervosa: A Family-Based Approach.* New York: Guilford.

Lock, Margaret. 1993. "Cultivating the Body: Anthropology and Epistemologies of Bodily Practice and Knowledge." *Annual Review of Anthropology* 22: 133–55.

Lock, Margaret, and Patricia A. Kaufert. 1998. Introduction to *Pragmatic Women and Body Politics,* ed. Margaret Lock and Patricia A. Kaufert, 1–27. Cambridge: Cambridge University Press.

Luepnitz, Deborah Anna. 1988. *The Family Interpreted: Feminist Theory in Clini-cal Practice.* New York: Basic.

MacSween, Morag. 1993. *Anorexic Bodies: A Feminist and Sociocultural Perspec-tive on Anorexia Nervosa.* London: Routledge.

Madanes, Chloe. 1981. *Strategic Family Therapy.* San Francisco: Jossey-Bass.

Madigan, Stephen P., and Elliot M. Goldner. 1999. "Undermining Anorexia through Narrative Therapy." In *Eating Disorders: A Reference Sourcebook,* ed. Raymond Lemberg with Leigh Cohn, 138–46. Phoenix: Oryx Press.

Maisel, Rick, David Epston, and Alissa Borden. In press. *Biting the Hand That Starves: A Handbook of Resistance to Anorexia and Bulimia.* New York: W. W. Norton.

Malcolm, Janet. 1978. "A Reporter at Large: The One-Way Mirror." *New Yorker,* 15 May, 39–114.

Malson, Helen. 1991. "Hidden A-Genders: The Place of Multiplicity and Gender in Theorizations of Anorexia Nervosa." *BPS Psychology of Women Section Newsletter* (winter): 31–42.

Malson, Helen, and Jane M. Ussher. 1996. "Body Poly-texts: Discourses of the Anorexic Body." *Journal of Community and Applied Social Psychology* 6 (4): 267–80.

Mandel, Ernest. 1972. *Late Capitalism.* London: Verso.

Martin, Emily. 1987. *The Woman in the Body: A Cultural Analysis of Reproduction.* Boston: Beacon Press.

——. 1994. *Flexible Bodies: Tracking Immunity in American Culture from the Days of Polio to the Age of AIDS.* Boston: Beacon Press.

Matsunaga, Hisato, Nobuo Kiriike, Toshihiko Nagata, and Sakae Yamagami. 1998. "Personality Disorders in Patients with Eating Disorders in Japan." *International Journal of Eating Disorders* 23 (4): 399–408.

McFarlane, William R. 1983. *Family Therapy in Schizophrenia.* New York: Guilford Press.

McMeekin, Lois S., and Nellie Reed. 1955. " 'Wife-Savers' Project Sponsored by Denver Homemakers." *Journal of Home Economics* 47 (8): 617–18.

McNay, Lois. 1991. "The Foucaultian Body and the Exclusion of Experience." *Hypatia* 6 (3): 125–39.

——. 1992. *Foucault and Feminism: Power, Gender, and the Self.* Boston: Northeastern University Press.

Mehler, Philip S., and Arnold E. Andersen, eds. 1999. *Eating Disorders: A Guide to Medical Care and Complications.* Baltimore: Johns Hopkins University.

Merchant, Carolyn. 1989. *The Death of Nature: Women, Ecology, and the Scientific Revolution.* San Francisco: Harper.

Messner, Michael A., and Donald F. Sabo, eds. 1990. *Sport, Men, and the Gender Order.* Champaign: Human Kinetics Books.

Meyerhoff, Barbara. 1980. *Number Our Days.* New York: Simon and Schuster.

——. 1982. "Life History among the Elderly: Performance, Visibility, and Remembering." In *A Crack in the Mirror: Reflexive Perspectives in Anthropology,* ed. Jay Ruby, 99–117. Philadelphia: University of Pennsylvania Press.

——. 1986. "Life Not Death in Venice: Its Second Life." In *The Anthropology of Experience,* ed. Victor Turner and Edward M. Bruner, 261–86. Chicago: University of Illinois Press.

Miller, Jean Baker. 1976. *Toward a New Psychology of Women.* Boston: Beacon Press.

Minuchin, Salvador. 1974. *Families and Family Therapy*. Cambridge: Harvard University Press.

Minuchin, Salvador, and Avner Barcai. 1969. "Therapeutically Induced Family Crisis." In *Science and Psychoanalysis*, vol. 14, *Childhood and Adolescence*, ed. Jules H. Masserman, 199–205. New York: Grune and Stratton.

Minuchin, Salvador, and H. Charles Fishman. 1981. *Family Therapy Techniques*. Cambridge: Harvard University Press.

Minuchin, Salvador, and Braulio Montalvo. 1967. "Techniques for Working with Disorganized Low Socioeconomic Families." *American Journal of Orthopsychiatry* 37 (5): 880–87.

Minuchin, Salvador, Braulio Montalvo, Bernard G. Guerney Jr., Bernice L. Rosman, and Florence Schumer. 1967. *Families of the Slums: An Exploration of Their Structure and Treatment*. New York: Basic Books.

Minuchin, Salvador, Bernice L. Rosman, and Lester Baker. 1978. *Psychosomatic Families: Anorexia Nervosa in Context*. Cambridge: Harvard University Press.

Mirin, Steven M., and Lloyd I. Sereder. 1994. "Mental Health Care: Current Realities, Future Directions." *Psychiatric Quarterly* 65 (3): 161–75.

Modleski, Tania. 1997. "Cinema and the Dark Continent: Race and Gender in Popular Film." In *Writing on the Body: Female Embodiment and Feminist Theory*, ed. Katie Conboy, Nadia Medina, and Sarah Stanbury, 208–28. New York: Columbia University Press.

Napier, Augustus Y., with Carl A. Whitaker. 1978. *The Family Crucible*. New York: Harper and Row.

Neal, John, and David Herzog. 1985. "Family Dynamics and Treatment of Anorexia Nervosa and Bulimia." *Pediatrician* 12 (2–3): 139–47.

Neal, John, and Alan J. Slobodnik. 1991. "Reclaiming Men's Experience in Couples Therapy." In *Feminist Approaches for Men in Family Therapy*, ed. Michele Louise Bograd, 101–22. New York: Harrington Park Press.

Neill, John. 1990. "Whatever Became of the Schizophrenogenic Mother?" *American Journal of Psychotherapy* 43 (4): 499–505.

Neill, John R., and David P. Kniskern. 1982. *From Psyche to System: The Evolving Therapy of Carl Whitaker*. New York: Guilford.

Nichter, Mark. 1998. "The Mission within the Madness: Self-Initiated Medicalization as Expression of Agency." In *Pragmatic Women and Body Politics*, ed. Margaret Lock and Patricia A. Kaufert, 327–53. Cambridge: Cambridge University Press.

Nichter, Mark, and Mimi Nichter. 1991. "Hype and Weight." *Medical Anthropology* 13 (3): 249–84.

Nichter, Mimi. 2000. *Fat Talk: What Girls and Their Parents Say about Dieting*. Cambridge: Harvard University Press.

Obeyesekere, Gananath. 1985. "Depression, Buddhism, and the Work of Culture in Sri Lanka." In *Culture and Depression: Studies in the Anthropology and Cross-Cultural Psychiatry of Affect and Disorder,* ed. Arthur Kleinman and Byron Good, 134–52. Berkeley: University of California Press.

Ogden, Annegret S. 1986. *The Great American Housewife.* Westport, Conn.: Greenwood Press.

O'Hanlon, Rosalind. 1988. "Recovering the Subject: Subaltern Studies and Histories of Resistance in Colonial South Asia." *Modern Asian Studies* 22 (1): 189–224.

Orbach, Susie. 1985. "Visibility/Invisibility: Social Considerations in Anorexia Nervosa—a Feminist Perspective." In *Theory and Treatment of Anorexia Nervosa and Bulimia: Biomedical, Sociocultural, and Psychological Perspectives,* ed. Steven Wiley Emmett, 127–38. New York: Brunner/Mazel.

——. 1986. *Hunger Strike: The Anorectic's Struggle as a Metaphor for Our Age.* New York: W. W. Norton.

Overby, Mary Margaret, and Kathryn Marie Dudley. 2000. Introduction to *Anthropology and Middle Class Working Families: A Research Agenda,* ed. Mary Margaret Overby and Kathryn Marie Dudley, 1–33. Arlington: American Anthropological Association.

Palazzoli, Mara Selvini. 1974. *Self-Starvation: From Individual to Family Therapy in the Treatment of Anorexia Nervosa.* New York: Jason Aronson.

Parsons, Talcott. 1951. *The Social System.* Glencoe: Free Press.

Parsons, Talcott, and Robert F. Bales, in collaboration with James Olds et al. 1955. *Family, Socialization, and Interaction Process.* Glencoe: Free Press.

Parsons, Talcott, and Renée Fox. 1952. "Illness, Therapy, and the Modern Urban American Family." *Journal of Social Issues* 8 (4): 31–44.

Pate, Jennifer E., et al. 1992. "Cross-Cultural Patterns in Eating Disorders: A Review." *Journal of the Academy of Child and Adolescent Psychiatry* 31 (5): 802–9.

Perelberg, Rosine Jozef, and Ann C. Miller. 1990. *Gender and Power in Families.* London: Tavistock/Routledge.

Piaget, Jean. 1954. *The Construction of Reality in the Child.* New York: Basic Books.

Polivy, Janet, and C. Peter Herman. 1987. "Diagnosis and Treatment of Normal Eating." *Journal of Consulting and Clinical Psychology* 55 (5): 635–44.

Pratt, Minnie Bruce. 1984. "Identity: Skin Blood Heart." In *Yours in Struggle: Three Feminist Perspectives on Anti-Semitism and Racism,* ed. Elly Bulkin, Minnie Bruce Pratt, and Barbara Smith, 11–63. New York: Long Haul Press.

Price, Janet, and Margrit Shildrick, ed. 1999. *Feminist Theory and the Body: A Reader.* New York: Routledge.

Probyn, Elspeth. 1987. "The Anorexic Body." In *Body Invaders: Panic Sex in America,* ed. Arthur Kroker and Marilouise Kroker, 201–11. New York: St. Martin's.

——. 1991. "This Body Which Is Not One: Technologizing an Embodied Self." *Hypatia* 6 (3): 111–24.

Radway, Janice A. 1984. *Reading the Romance: Women, Patriarchy, and Popular Literature.* Chapel Hill: University of North Carolina Press.

Rapp, Rayna. 1999. *Testing Women, Testing the Fetus: The Social Impact of Amniocentesis in America.* New York: Routledge.

Reichard, Suzanne, and Carl Tillman. 1950. "Patterns of Parent-Child Relationships in Schizophrenia." *Psychiatry* 13 (2): 247–57.

Reiff, Dan W., and Kathleen Kim Lampson Reiff. 1992. *Eating Disorders: Nutrition Therapy in the Recovery Process.* Gaithersburg, Md.: Aspen.

Rhodes, Lorna A. 1991. *Emptying Beds: The Work of an Emergency Psychiatric Unit.* Berkeley: University of California Press.

Rieker, Patricia Perry, and Elaine Hilberman Carmen. 1984. *The Gender Gap in Psychotherapy: Social Realities and Psychological Processes.* New York: Plenum.

Riessman, Catherine Kohler. 1998. "Women and Medicalization: A New Perspective." In *The Politics of Women's Bodies: Sexuality and Behavior,* ed. Rose Weitz, 46–63. New York: Oxford University Press.

Rippe, James M. 1989. "CEO Fitness: The Performance Plus." *Psychology Today,* May, 50–53.

Roberts, Marjory, and T. George Harris. 1989. "Wellness at Work: How Corporations Help Employees Fight Stress and Stay Healthy." *Psychology Today,* May, 54–58.

Root, Maria P. P. 1990. "Disordered Eating in Women of Color." *Sex Roles* 22 (7–8): 525–36.

Rose, Nancy E. 1995. *Workfare or Fair Work: Women, Welfare, and Government Work Programs.* New Brunswick, N.J.: Rutgers University Press.

Rosman, Bernice L., Salvador Minuchin, and Ronald Liebman. 1977. "Treating Anorexia by the Family Lunch Session." In *Therapies for Children: A Handbook of Effective Treatments for Problem Behavior,* ed. Charles E. Scaefer and Howard L. Millman, 166–69. San Francisco: Jossey-Bass.

Rostain, Anthony. 1986. "Deciding to Forgo Life-Sustaining Treatment in the Intensive Care Nursery: A Sociologic Account." *Perspectives in Biology and Medicine* 30 (1): 120–21.

Roth, D. 1986. "Treatment of the Hospitalized Eating Disordered Patient." *Occupational Therapy in Mental Health* 6 (1): 67–87.

Roth, Sallyann, and David Epston. 1998. "Consulting the Problem about the Problematic Relationship: An Exercise for Experiencing a Relationship with an Externalized Problem." In *"Catching Up" with David Epston: A Collection of Practice-Based Papers Published between 1991 and 1996,* 209–26. Adelaide: Dulwich Centre Publications. First published in Michael F. Hoyt, ed., *Constructive Therapies,* vol. 2 (New York: Guilford Press, 1996).

Sawicki, Jana. 1991. *Disciplining Foucault: Feminism, Power, and the Body.* New York: Routledge.

Scarso, G., S. Fassino, D. Munno, S. Laguzzi, and P. Fila. 1992. "Borderline Pathology: Follow-Up Study, Preliminary Report" (in Italian). *Minerva Psichiatrica* 33 (1): 1–10.

Scharff, David E., and Jill Savege Scharff. 1991. *Object Relations Family Therapy.* Northvale: Jason Aronson.

Scheper-Hughes, Nancy. 1990. "Three Propositions for a Critically Applied Medical Anthropology." *Social Science and Medicine* 30 (2): 189–97.

——. 1992. *Death without Weeping: The Violence of Everyday Life in Brazil.* Berkeley: University of California Press.

Scheper-Hughes, Nancy, and Margaret M. Lock. 1987. "The Mindful Body: A Prolegomenon to Future Work in Medical Anthropology." *Medical Anthropology Quarterly* 1 (1): 6–41.

——. 1991. "The Message in the Bottle: Illness and the Micropolitics of Resistance." *Journal of Psychohistory* 18 (4): 409–32.

Schneider, David M. [1968] 1980. *American Kinship: A Cultural Account.* Chicago: University of Chicago Press.

Schwartz, Hillel. 1986. *Never Satisfied: A Cultural History of Diet, Fantasies, and Fat.* New York: Anchor Books.

Schwartz, Mark F., and Leigh Cohn, eds. 1996. *Sexual Abuse and Eating Disorders.* Bristol, Pa.: Brunner/Mazel.

Schweder, Richard A. 1991. *Thinking Through Cultures: Expeditions in Cultural Psychology.* Cambridge: Harvard University Press.

Selvini-Palazzoli, Mara. 1974. *Self-Starvation: From the Intrapsychic to the Transpersonal Approach.* London: Chaucer.

Selvini-Palazzoli, Mara, L. Boscolo, G. Cecchin, and G. Prata. 1978. *Paradox and Counter-paradox: A New Model in the Therapy of the Family in Schizophrenic Transaction.* Trans. Elisabeth V. Burt. New York: Jason Aronson.

Sesan, Robin. 1994. "Feminist Inpatient Treatment for Eating Disorders: An Oxymoron?" In *Feminist Perspectives on Eating Disorders,* ed. Patricia Fallon, Melanie A. Katzman, and Susan C. Wooley, 251–71. New York: Guilford Press.

Sharfstein, Steven S., and Allan Beigel. 1985. "Epilogue: Less Is More? Today's Economics and Its Challenge to Psychiatry." In *The New Economics and Psychiatric Care,* ed. Steven Samuel Sharfstein and Allan Beigel, 229–40. Washington, D.C.: American Psychiatric Press.

Shildrick, Margrit, and Janet Price. 1998. *Vital Signs: Feminist Reconfigurations of the Bio/logical Body.* Edinburgh: Edinburgh University Press.

——. 1999. "Openings on the Body: A Critical Introduction." In *Feminist Theory and the Body: A Reader,* ed. Janet Price and Margrit Shildrick, 1–14. New York: Routledge.

Sigman, Garry. 1996. "How Has the Care of Eating Disorder Patients Been Altered and Upset by Payment and Insurance Issues? Let Me Count the Ways." *Journal of Adolescent Health* 19 (5): 317–18.

Silber, Tomas J. 1994. "Eating Disorders and Health Insurance." *Archives of Pediatric Adolescent Medicine* 148 (8): 785–88.

Simon, Richard. 1984. "Stranger in a Strange Land: An Interview with Salvador Minuchin." *Family Therapy Networker* 6 (6): 21–31, 66–68.

Skodol, Andrew E., John M. Oldham, Steven E. Hyler, David H. Kellman, et al. 1993. "Comorbidity of DSM-III-R Eating Disorders and Personality Disorders." *International Journal of Eating Disorders* 14 (4): 403–16.

Smart, Rebekah S. 1999. "Role of Ethnicity, Body Dissatisfaction, and Stressful Life Events in Disordered Eating among Asian-American, Chicana/Latina, and European American College Females (Eating Disorders)." Ph.D. diss., University of Southern California.

Sours, John A. 1980. *Starving to Death in a Sea of Objects: The Anorexia Nervosa Syndrome.* New York: Jason Aronson.

Stacey, Judith. 1990. *Brave New Families: Stories of Domestic Upheaval in Late Twentieth Century America.* New York: Basic Books.

Stack, Carol. 1974. *All Our Kin: Strategies for Survival in a Black Community.* New York: Harper and Row.

Steiner-Adair, Catherine. 1986. "The Body Politic: Normal Female Development and the Development of Eating Disorders." *Journal of the American Academy of Psychoanalysis* 14 (1): 94–114.

Stone, Michael H. 1980. *The Borderline Syndromes: Constitution, Personality, and Adaptation.* New York: McGraw-Hill.

Strathern, Marilyn. 1992a. *After Nature: English Kinship in the Late Twentieth Century.* Cambridge: Cambridge University Press.

——. 1992b. *Reproducing the Future: Anthropology, Kinship, and the New Reproductive Technologies.* New York: Routledge.

Striegel-Moore, Ruth H. 1994. "A Feminist Agenda for Psychological Research on Eating Disorders." In *Feminist Perspectives on Eating Disorders,* ed. Patricia Fallon, Melanie A. Katzman, and Susan C. Wooley, 438–54. New York: Guilford.

Striegel-Moore, Ruth, and Linda Smolak. 2000. "The Influence of Ethnicity on Eating Disorders in Women." In *Handbook of Gender, Culture, and Health,* ed. Richard M. Eisler and Michel Hersen, 227–53. Mahwah: Lawrence Erlbaum Associates.

Strober, Michael, and Laura Lynn Humphrey. 1987. "Familial Contributions to the Etiology and Course of Anorexia Nervosa and Bulimia." *Journal of Consulting and Clinical Psychology* 55 (5): 654–59.

Sullivan, Patrick F., Cynthia M. Bulik, Jennifer L. Fear, and Alison Pickering.

1998. "Outcome of Anorexia Nervosa: A Case-Control Study." *American Journal of Psychiatry* 155 (7): 939–46.

Swartz, Lesley. 1985. "Anorexia Nervosa as a Culture-Bound Syndrome." *Social Science and Medicine* 20 (7): 725–30.

———. 1987. "Illness Negotiation: The Case of Eating Disorders." *Social Science and Medicine* 24 (7): 613–18.

Taussig, Michael. 1980. "Reification and the Consciousness of the Patient." *Social Science and Medicine: Part B, Medical Anthropology* 14B (1): 3–13.

———. 1993. *Mimesis and Alterity: A Particular History of the Senses.* New York: Routledge.

Thompson, Becky W. 1992. " 'A Way outa No Way': Eating Problems among African-American, Latina, and White Women." *Gender and Society* 6 (4): 546–61.

———. 1994a. "Food, Bodies, and Growing Up Female: Childhood Lessons about Culture, Race, and Class." In *Feminist Perspectives on Eating Disorders,* ed. Patricia Fallon, Melanie A. Katzman, and Susan C. Wooley, 355–78. New York: Guilford.

———. 1994b. *A Hunger So Wide and So Deep: American Women Speak Out on Eating Problems.* Minneapolis: University of Minnesota Press.

Thompson, Linda, and Alexis J. Walker. 1989. "Gender in Families: Women and Men in Marriage, Work, and Parenthood." *Journal of Marriage and the Family* 51 (4): 845–71.

Tiller, Jane, Ulrike Schmidt, and Janet Treasure. 1993. "Compulsory Treatment for Anorexia Nervosa: Compassion or Coercion?" *British Journal of Psychiatry* 162 (May): 679–80.

Tomlinson, Wallace K. 1990. "Schizophrenia: The History of an Illness." *Psychiatric Medicine* 8 (1): 1–19.

Trinh T. Minh-ha. 1989. *Woman, Native, Other: Writing Postcoloniality and Feminism.* Bloomington: Indiana University Press.

Tsing, Anna Lowenhaupt. 1995. "Empowering Nature, or Some Gleanings in Bee Culture." In *Naturalizing Power: Essays in Feminist Cultural Analysis,* ed. Sylvia Yanagisako and Carol Delaney, 113–43. New York: Routledge.

Turner, Bryan. 1984. *The Body and Society.* New York: Basil Blackwell.

———. 1992. *Regulating Bodies: Essays in Medical Sociology.* London: Routledge.

United States Department of Labor. 1965. *The Negro Family: The Case for National Action* [the "Moynihan Report"]. Office of Policy Planning and Research.

Vandereycken, Walter, and Rolf Meerman. 1984. "Anorexia Nervosa: Is Prevention Possible?" *International Journal of Psychiatry in Medicine* 14 (3): 191–205.

Vanderlinden, J., and Walter Vandereycken. 1991. "Guidelines for the Family

Therapeutic Approach to Eating Disorders." *Psychotherapy and Psychosomatics* 56 (1–2): 36–42.

Veblen, Thorstein. [1899] 1934. *The Theory of the Leisure Class: An Economic Study of Institutions.* New York: Modern Library.

Waller, John V., Ralph M. Kaufman, and Felix Deutsch. 1940. "Anorexia Nervosa: A Psychosomatic Entity." *Psychosomatic Medicine* 2 (1): 3–16.

Walters, Marianne, Betty Carter, Peggy Papp, and Olga Silverstein. 1988. *The Invisible Web: Gender Patterns in Family Relationships.* New York: Guilford.

Watts, Alan. 1970. *Nature, Man, and Woman.* New York: Vintage.

Way, Karen. 1995. "Never Too Rich . . . or Too Thin: The Role of Stigma in the Social Construction of Anorexia Nervosa." In *Eating Agendas: Food and Nutrition as Social Problems,* ed. Donna Maurer and Jeffrey Sobal, 91–113. New York: Aldine de Gruyter.

Weingarten, Kathy. 1991. "Discourses of Intimacy." *Family Process* 30 (3): 285–305.

Weiss, Mitchell G. 1995. "Eating Disorders and Disordered Eating in Different Cultures." *Psychiatric Clinics of North America* 18 (3): 537–53.

Whitaker, Carl. A. 1975. "Psychotherapy of the Absurd." *Family Process* 14 (1): 1–16.

White, Deborah Gray. 1990. "Female Slaves: Sex Roles and Status in the Antebellum Plantation South." In *Unequal Sisters: A Multicultural Reader in U.S. Women's History,* ed. Ellen Carol DuBois and Vicki L. Ruiz, 22–33. New York: Routledge.

White, Michael. 1989. "The Externalizing of the Problem and the Re-authoring of Lives and Relationships." In *Selected Papers,* 5–28. Adelaide, Australia: Dulwich Centre Publications.

——. 1992. "Men's Culture, the Men's Movement, and the Constitution of Men's Lives." *Dulwich Centre Newsletter* 3–4: 33–53. Adelaide: Dulwich Centre Publications.

——. 1993. "Deconstruction and Therapy." In *Therapeutic Conversations,* ed. Stephen G. Gilligan and Reese Price, 22–61. New York: W. W. Norton. First published in the *Dulwich Centre Newsletter* 3 (1991): 21–40.

——. 1995. "The Politics of Therapy." In *Re-authoring Lives: Interviews and Essays,* 41–59. Adelaide: Dulwich Centre Publications.

——. 2000. "Reflecting Team-Work as Definitional Ceremony Revisited." In *Reflections on Narrative Practice,* 59–85. Adelaide: Dulwich Centre Publications.

White, Michael, and David Epston. 1990. *Narrative Means to Therapeutic Ends.* New York: W. W. Norton.

Wiener, Norbert. 1948. *Cybernetics, or Control and Communication in the Animal and the Machine.* New York: Wiley.

Williams, Raymond. 1977. *Marxism and Literature.* Oxford: Oxford University Press.

Winnicott, D. W. 1965. *The Maturational Processes and the Facilitating Environment: Studies in the Theory of Emotional Development.* New York: International Universities Press.

Wooley, Susan C. 1980. "Eating Disorders: Obesity and Anorexia." In *Women and Psychotherapy: An Assessment of Research and Practice,* ed. Annette M. Brodsky and Rachel T. Hare-Mustin, 135–58. New York: Guilford.

———. 1991. "Uses of Countertransference in the Treatment of Eating Disorders: A Gender Perspective." In *Psychodynamic Treatment of Anorexia Nervosa and Bulimia,* ed. Craig L. Johnson, 245–94. New York: Guilford.

———. 1993. "Managed Care and Mental Health: The Silencing of a Profession." *International Journal of Eating Disorders* 14 (4): 387–401.

———. 1994. "Sexual Abuse and Eating Disorders: The Concealed Debate." In *Feminist Perspectives on Eating Disorders,* ed. Patricia Fallon, Melanie A. Katzman, and Susan C. Wooley, 171–211. New York: Guilford.

Wooley, Susan C., and O. Wayne Wooley. 1985. "Intensive Outpatient and Residential Treatment for Bulimia." In *Handbook of Psychotherapy for Anorexia Nervosa and Bulimia,* ed. David M. Garner and Paul E. Garfinkel, 391–430. New York: Guilford.

Yanagisako, Sylvia, and Carol Delaney. 1995. "Naturalizing Power." In *Naturalizing Power: Essays in Feminist Cultural Analysis,* ed. Sylvia Yanagisako and Carol Delaney, 1–22. New York: Routledge.

Young, Allan. 1982. "The Anthropologies of Illness and Sickness." *Annual Review of Anthropology* 11: 257–85.

———. 1995. *The Harmony of Illusions: Inventing Post-traumatic Stress Disorder.* Princeton: Princeton University Press.

Zerbe, Kathryn J. 1992. "Eating Disorders in the 1990s: Clinical Challenges and Treatment Implications." *Bulletin of the Menninger Clinic* 56 (2): 167–87.

———. 1995. "Integrating Feminist and Psychodynamic Principles in the Treatment of an Eating Disorder Patient." *Bulletin of the Menninger Clinic* 59 (spring): 160–66.

Zhang, Amy Y., and Lonnie R. Snowden. 1999. "Ethnic Characteristics of Mental Disorders in Five U.S. Communities." *Cultural Diversity and Ethnic Minority Psychology* 5 (2): 134–46.

Zimmerman, Jeffrey L., and Victoria C. Dickerson. 1994. "Tales of the Body Thief: Externalizing and Deconstructing Eating Problems." In *Constructive Therapies,* ed. Michael F. Hoyt, 295–318. New York: Guilford Publications.

Helen Gremillion is an assistant professor and the
Peg Zeglin Brand Chair of the Department of Gender
Studies at Indiana University, Bloomington.

Library of Congress Cataloging-in-Publication Data
Gremillion, Helen.
Feeding anorexia : gender and power at a treatment
center / Helen Gremillion.
p. cm. — (Body, commodity, text)
Includes bibliographical references and index.
ISBN 0-8223-3133-0 (cloth : alk. paper)
ISBN 0-8223-3120-9 (pbk. : alk. paper)
1. Anorexia nervosa—Social aspects.   I. Title.
II. Series.
RC552.A5 G746 2003
362.2′5—dc21   2002155155